CLUSTERF@#K

VOLUME ONE

Story Jon Parrish
Pencils/Inks Diego Toro
Colors Kote Carvajal
Letters Nic J. Shaw
Script Edits Steven Forbes

ALTERNA COMICS
ALTERNACOMICS.COM

PETER SIMETI
PRESIDENT AND PUBLISHER

FUBAR PRESS
FUBARPRESS.COM

JEFF McCOMSEY
PRESIDENT AND PUBLISHER

JEFF McCLELLAND
STORY EDITOR

CLUSTERF@#K
9781934985496
2016 FIRST PRINTING
Published by Alterna Comics, Inc.
Alterna Comics and its logos are ™ and © 2007-2016 Alterna Comics, Inc. All Rights Reserved.
CLUSTERF@#K and all related characters are ™ and © 2016 Jon Parrish. All Rights Reserved.
The story presented in this publication is fictional.
Any similarities to events or persons living or dead is purely coincidental.
With the exception of artwork used for review purposes, no portion of this publication
may be reproduced by any means without the expressed written consent of the copyright holder.
PRINTED IN TAIWAN BY KRAKENPRINT.

Jon
To my family and friends for humoring
me when I said I wanted to write comics.
And to the Clusterf@#k team because
without you, I'd still just have nothing
but a bunch of scripts.

Diego
My friends Jon and Kote.
Thanks to them, it was fun to do each
page. To Claudio and Julio, thanks for
the help! To my great friends, my
"vecinos", and my GF Gaby :)

Kote
To Daniela, Thanks for your love.

Nic
For Hayley, and my Mother.
Thank-you.

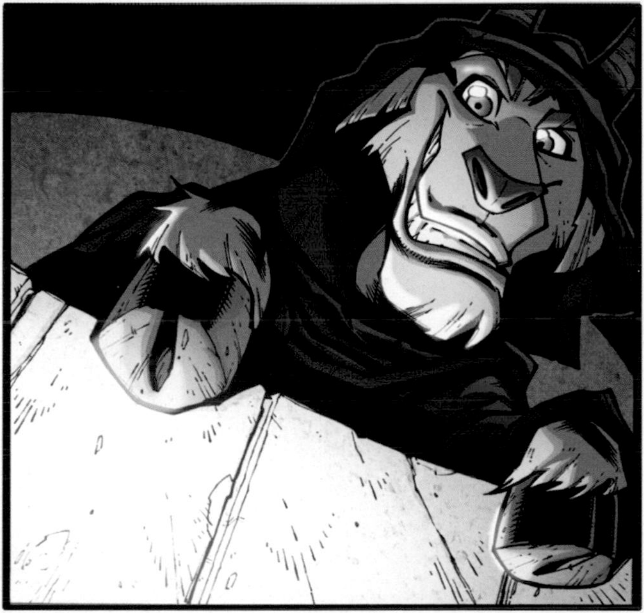

CHAPTER ONE

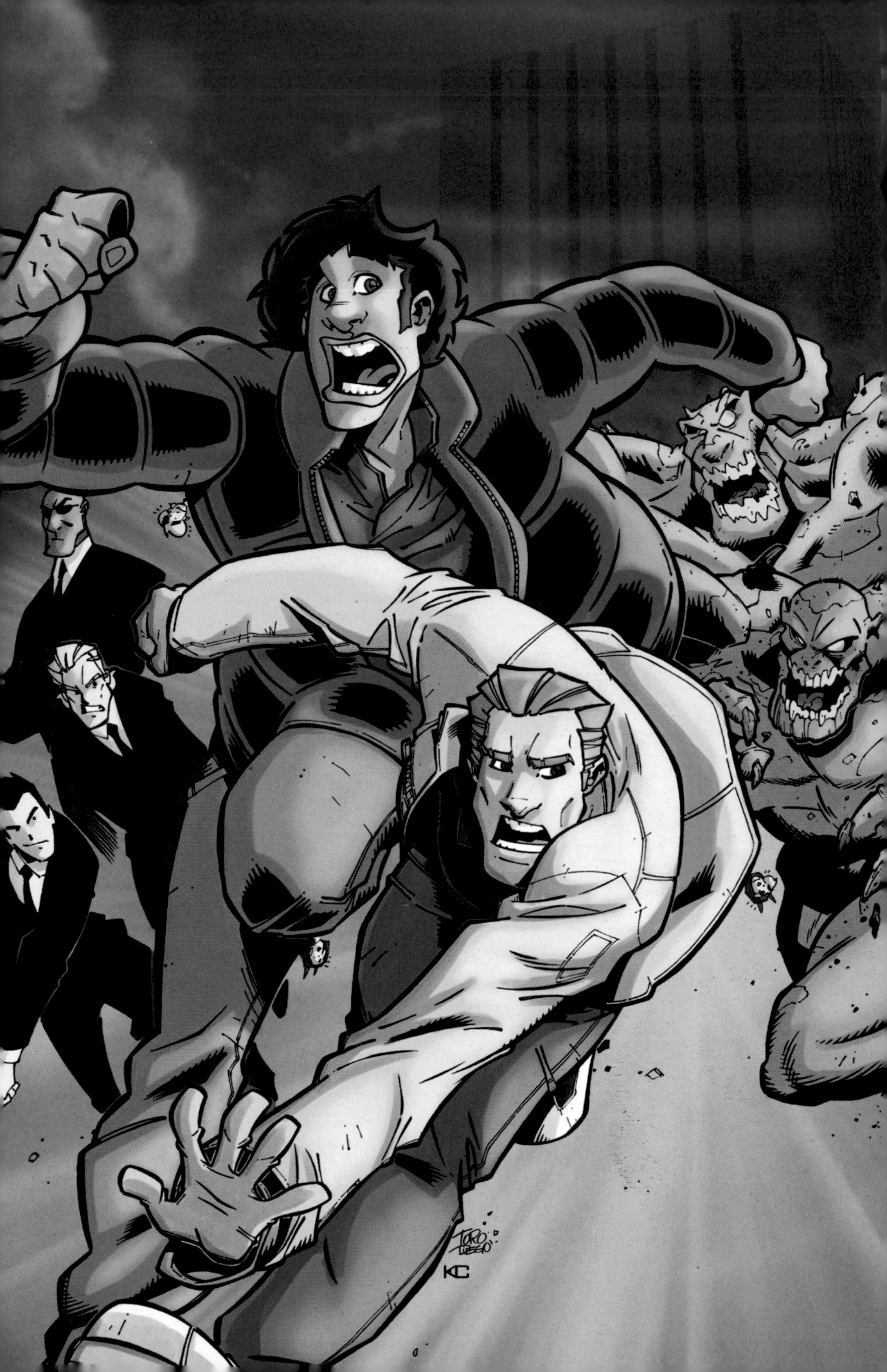

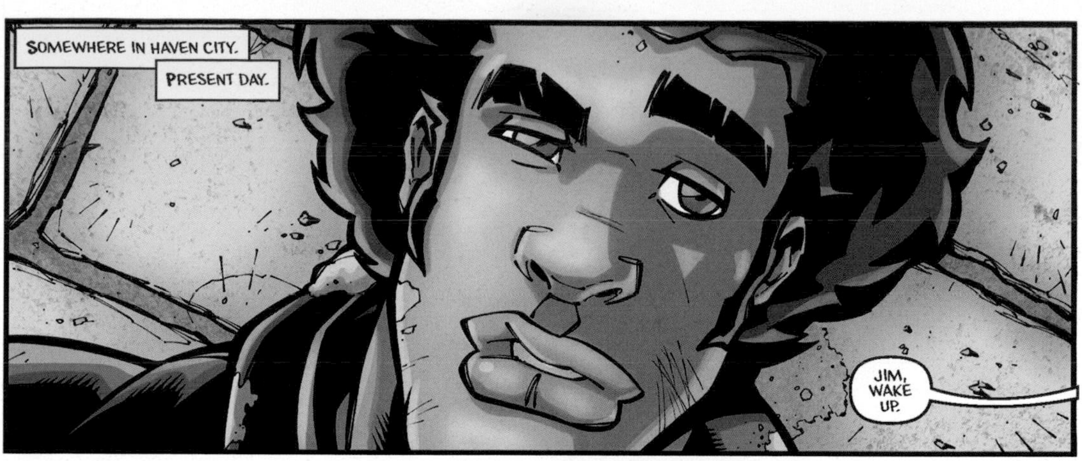
SOMEWHERE IN HAVEN CITY.
PRESENT DAY.
JIM, WAKE UP.

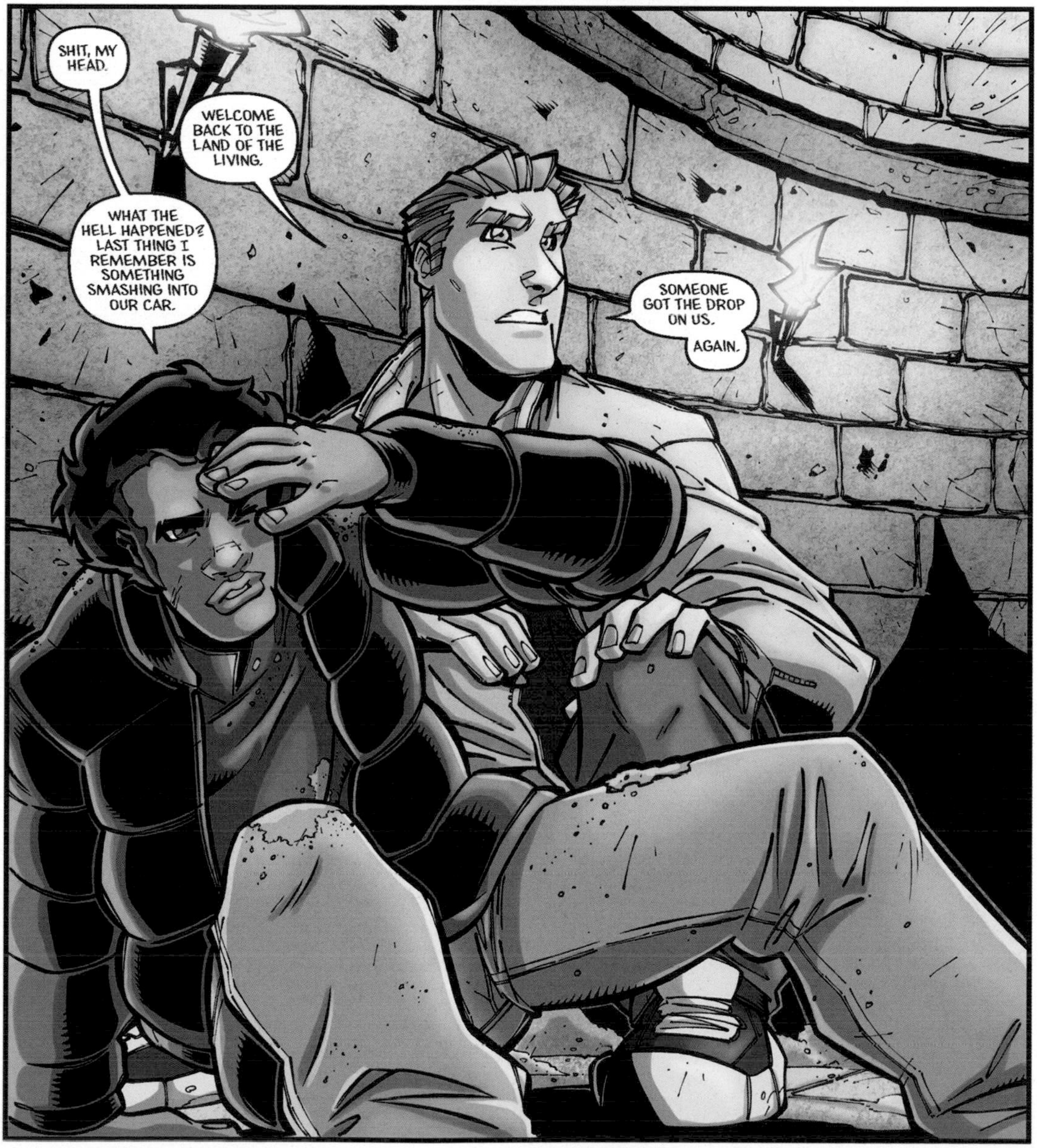
SHIT, MY HEAD.
WELCOME BACK TO THE LAND OF THE LIVING.
WHAT THE HELL HAPPENED? LAST THING I REMEMBER IS SOMETHING SMASHING INTO OUR CAR.
SOMEONE GOT THE DROP ON US.
AGAIN.

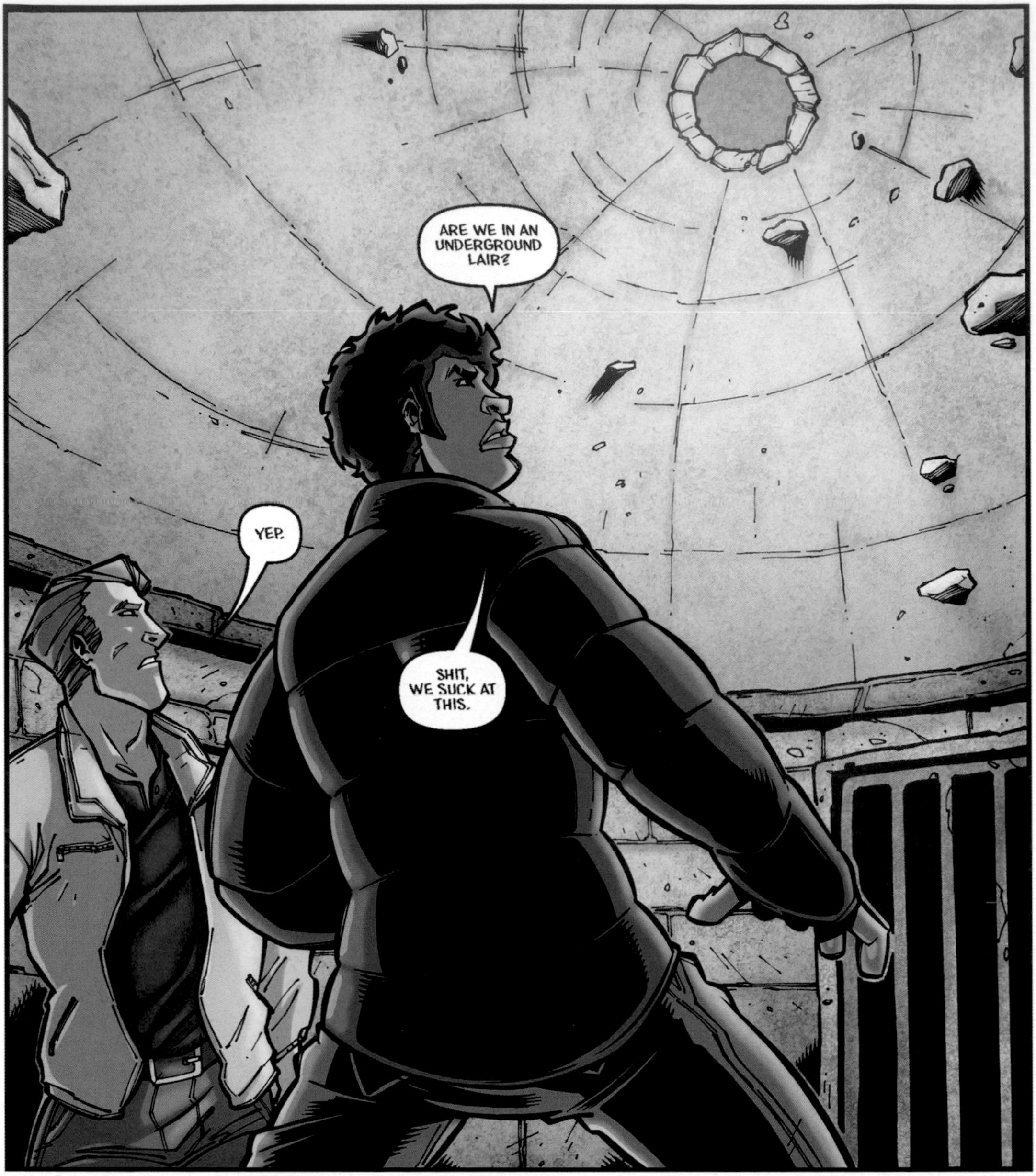
ARE WE IN AN UNDERGROUND LAIR?
YEP.
SHIT, WE SUCK AT THIS.

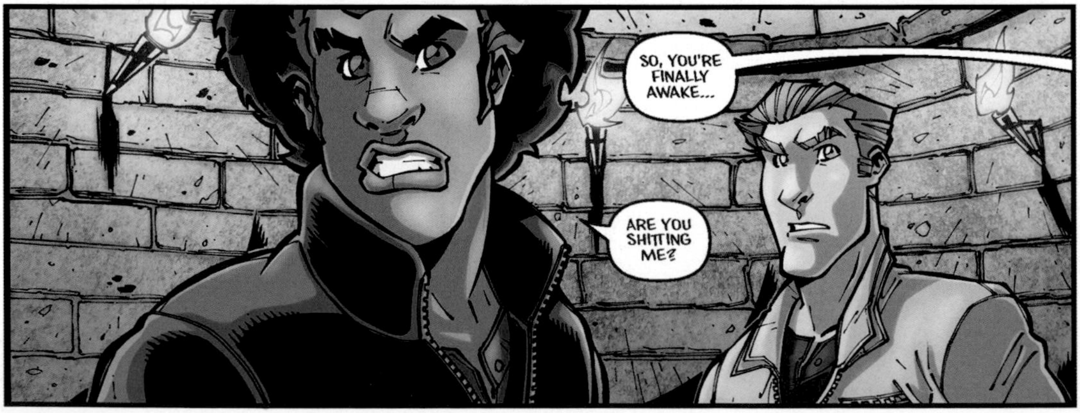
SO, YOU'RE FINALLY AWAKE...
ARE YOU SHITTING ME?

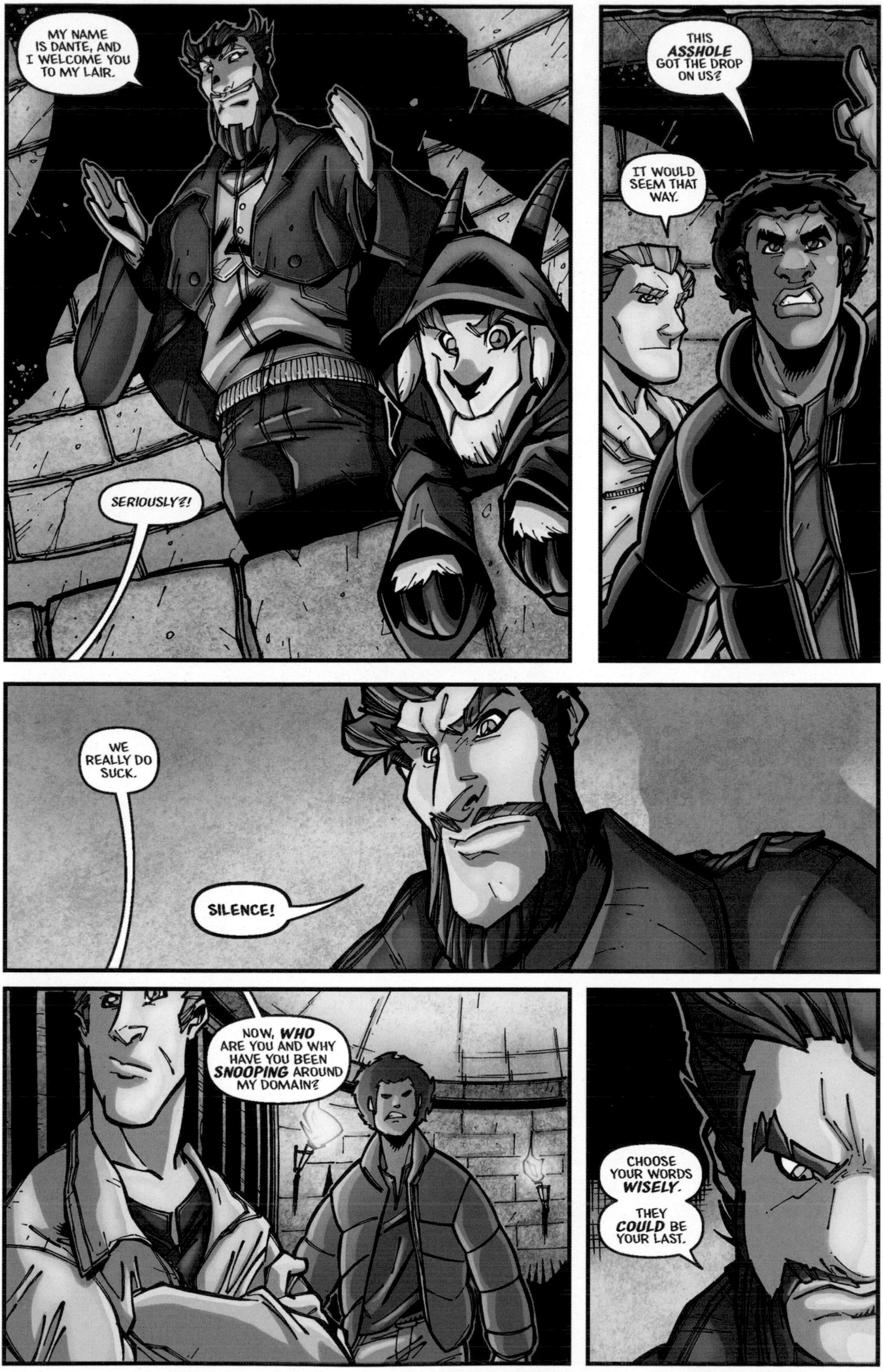
MY NAME IS DANTE, AND I WELCOME YOU TO MY LAIR.
SERIOUSLY?!
THIS ASSHOLE GOT THE DROP ON US?
IT WOULD SEEM THAT WAY.
WE REALLY DO SUCK.
SILENCE!
NOW, WHO ARE YOU AND WHY HAVE YOU BEEN SNOOPING AROUND MY DOMAIN?
CHOOSE YOUR WORDS WISELY.
THEY COULD BE YOUR LAST.

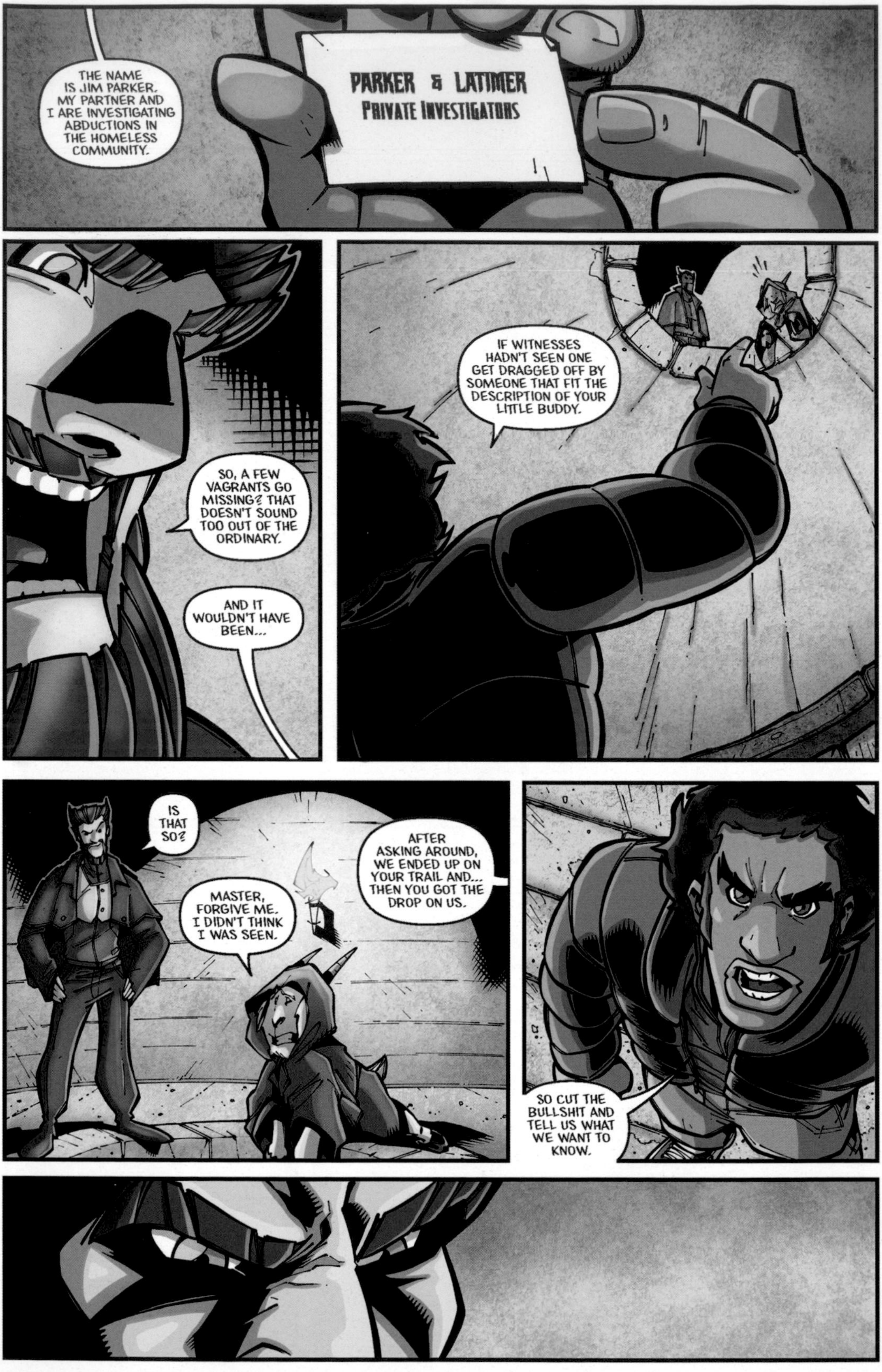
THE NAME IS JIM PARKER. MY PARTNER AND I ARE INVESTIGATING ABDUCTIONS IN THE HOMELESS COMMUNITY.
PARKER & LATIMER
PRIVATE INVESTIGATORS
SO, A FEW VAGRANTS GO MISSING? THAT DOESN'T SOUND TOO OUT OF THE ORDINARY.
AND IT WOULDN'T HAVE BEEN...
IF WITNESSES HADN'T SEEN ONE GET DRAGGED OFF BY SOMEONE THAT FIT THE DESCRIPTION OF YOUR LITTLE BUDDY.
IS THAT SO?
MASTER, FORGIVE ME. I DIDN'T THINK I WAS SEEN.
AFTER ASKING AROUND, WE ENDED UP ON YOUR TRAIL AND... THEN YOU GOT THE DROP ON US.
SO CUT THE BULLSHIT AND TELL US WHAT WE WANT TO KNOW.

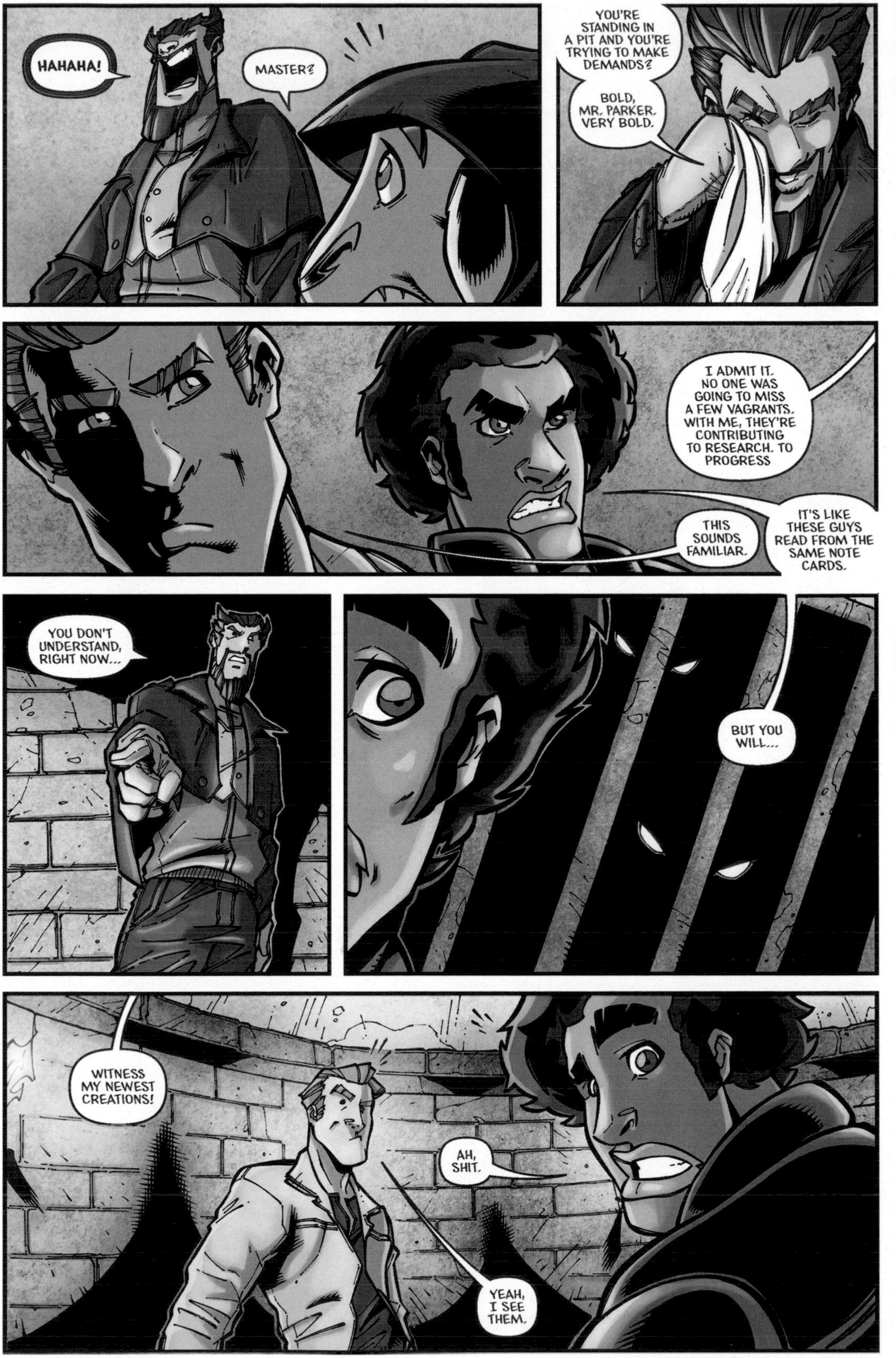
HAHAHA!
MASTER?
YOU'RE STANDING IN A PIT AND YOU'RE TRYING TO MAKE DEMANDS?
BOLD, MR. PARKER, VERY BOLD.
I ADMIT IT. NO ONE WAS GOING TO MISS A FEW VAGRANTS. WITH ME, THEY'RE CONTRIBUTING TO RESEARCH. TO PROGRESS
THIS SOUNDS FAMILIAR.
IT'S LIKE THESE GUYS READ FROM THE SAME NOTE CARDS.
YOU DON'T UNDERSTAND, RIGHT NOW...
BUT YOU WILL...
WITNESS MY NEWEST CREATIONS!
AH, SHIT.
YEAH, I SEE THEM.

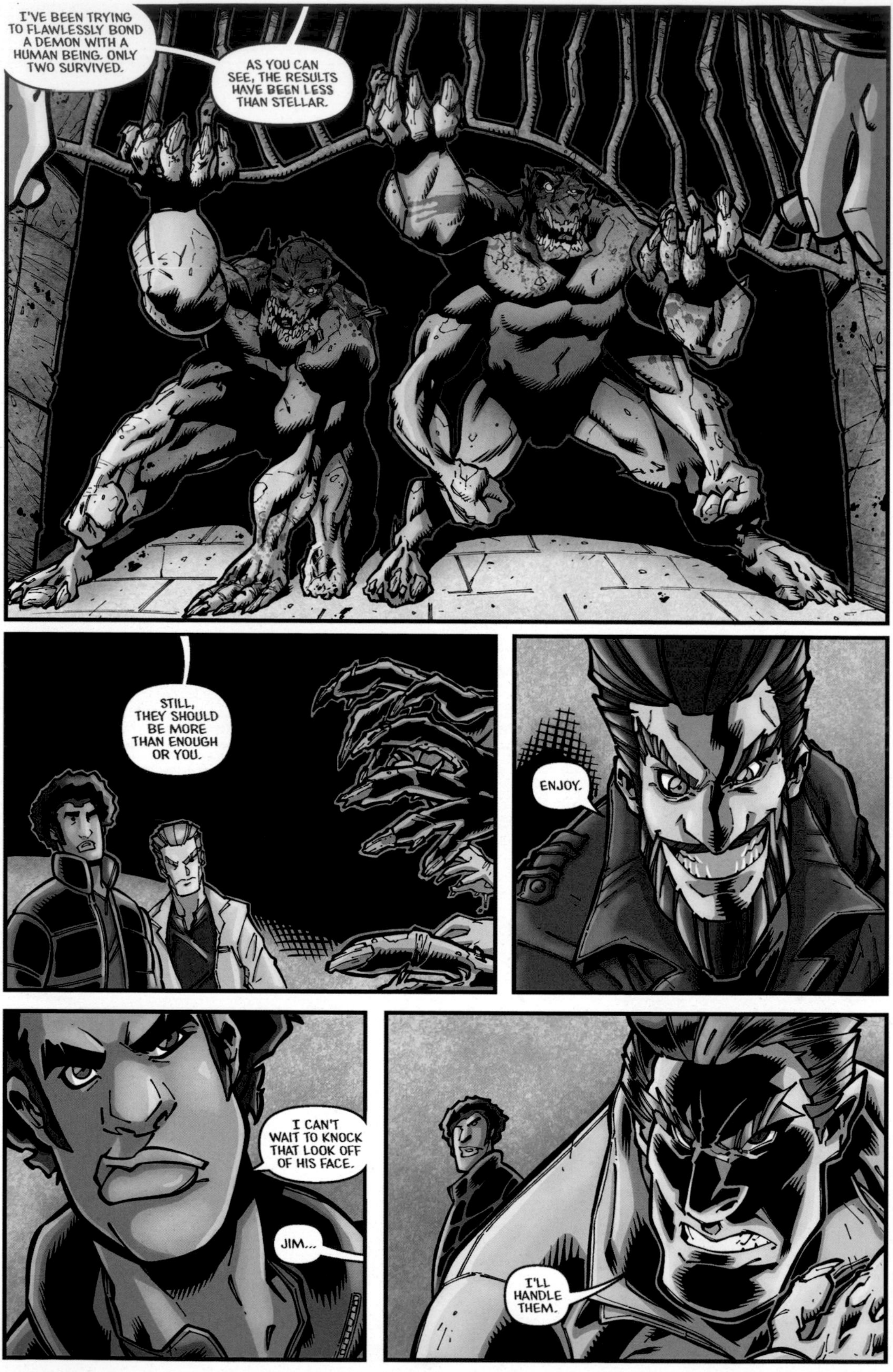
I'VE BEEN TRYING TO FLAWLESSLY BOND A DEMON WITH A HUMAN BEING. ONLY TWO SURVIVED.
AS YOU CAN SEE, THE RESULTS HAVE BEEN LESS THAN STELLAR.
STILL, THEY SHOULD BE MORE THAN ENOUGH OR YOU.
ENJOY.
I CAN'T WAIT TO KNOCK THAT LOOK OFF OF HIS FACE.
JIM...
I'LL HANDLE THEM.

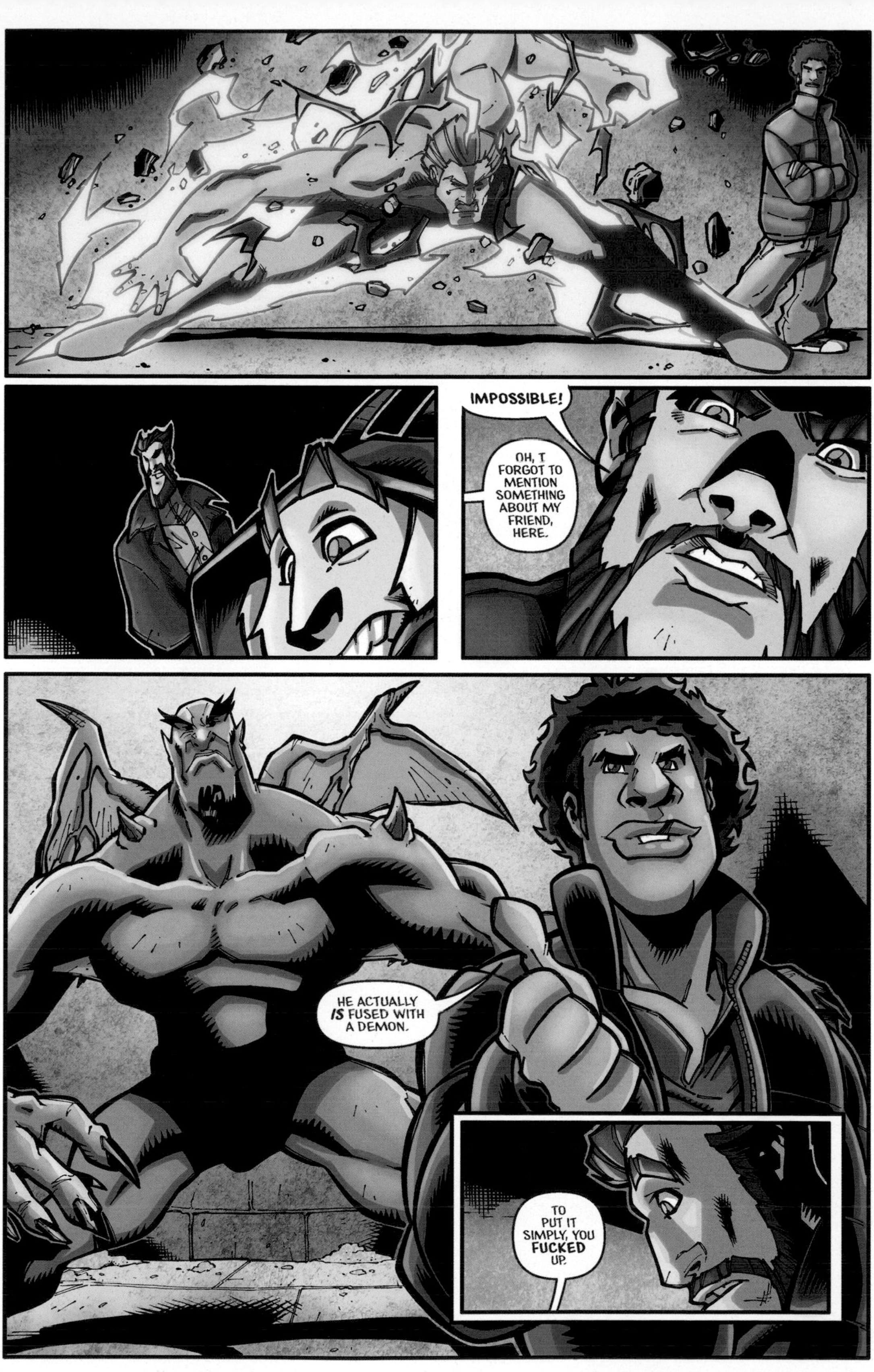
IMPOSSIBLE!
OH, I FORGOT TO MENTION SOMETHING ABOUT MY FRIEND, HERE.
HE ACTUALLY *IS* FUSED WITH A DEMON.
TO PUT IT SIMPLY, YOU **FUCKED** UP.

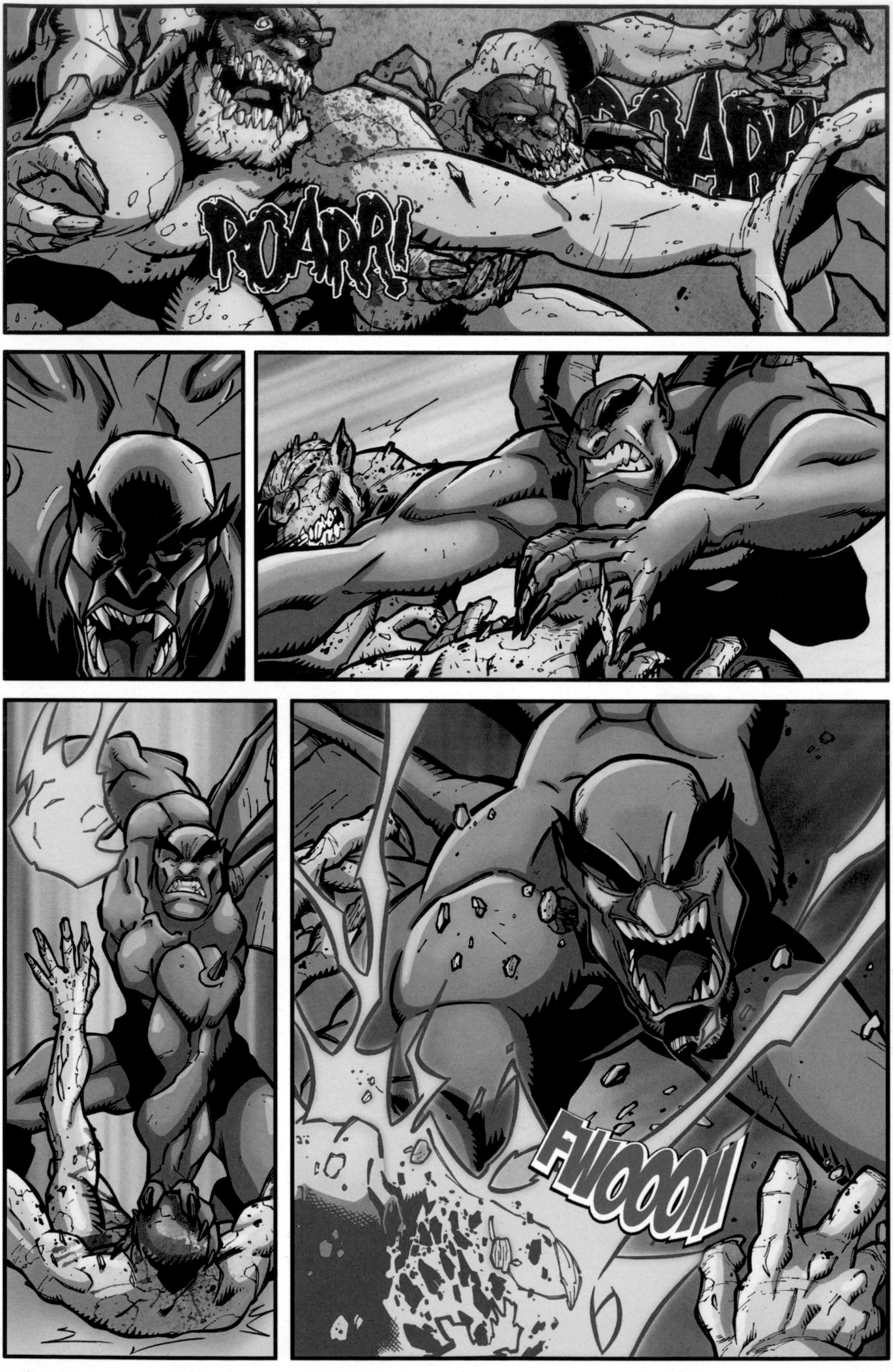
ROARR!
FWOOOM

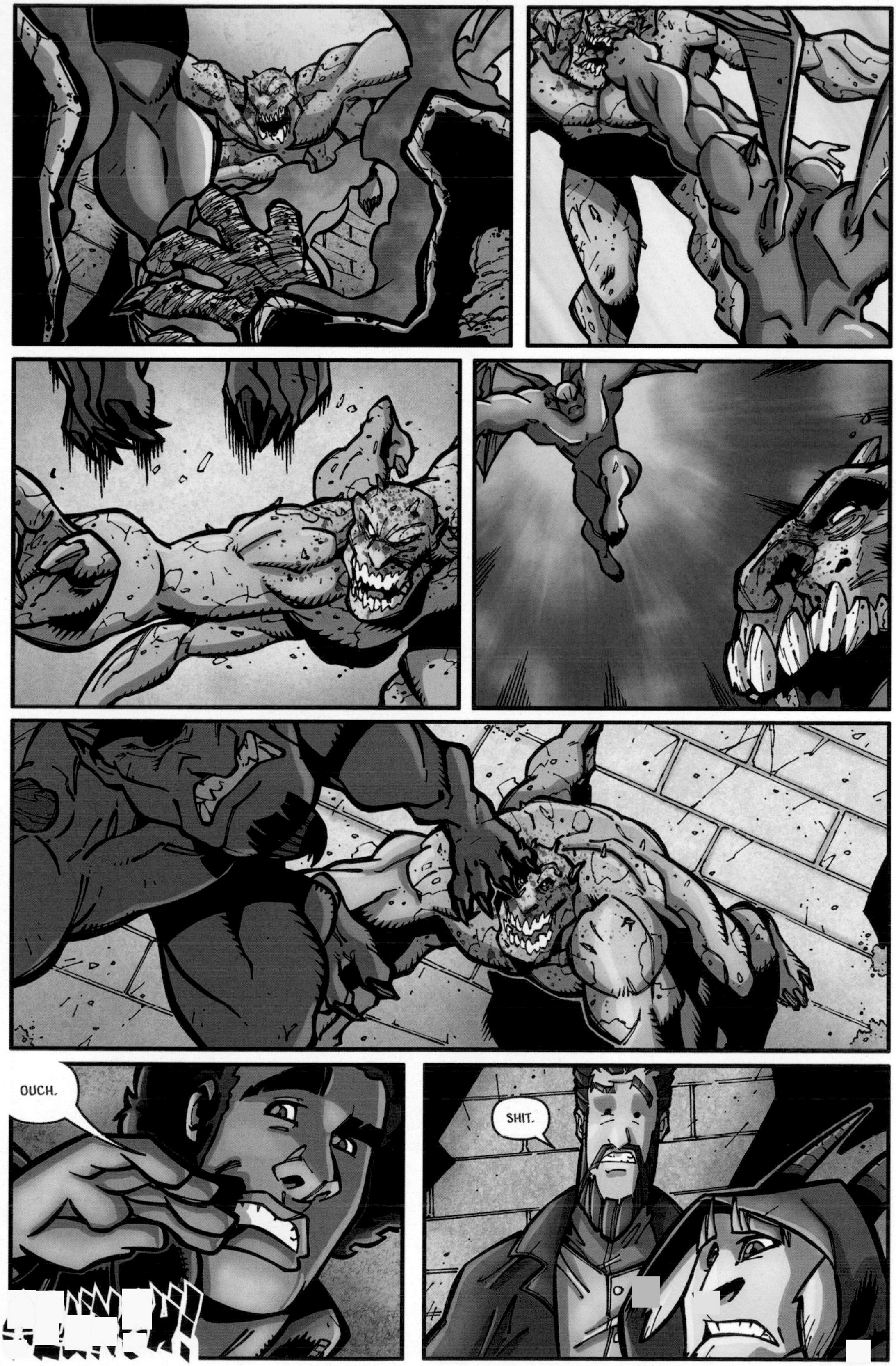
OUCH.
SHIT.

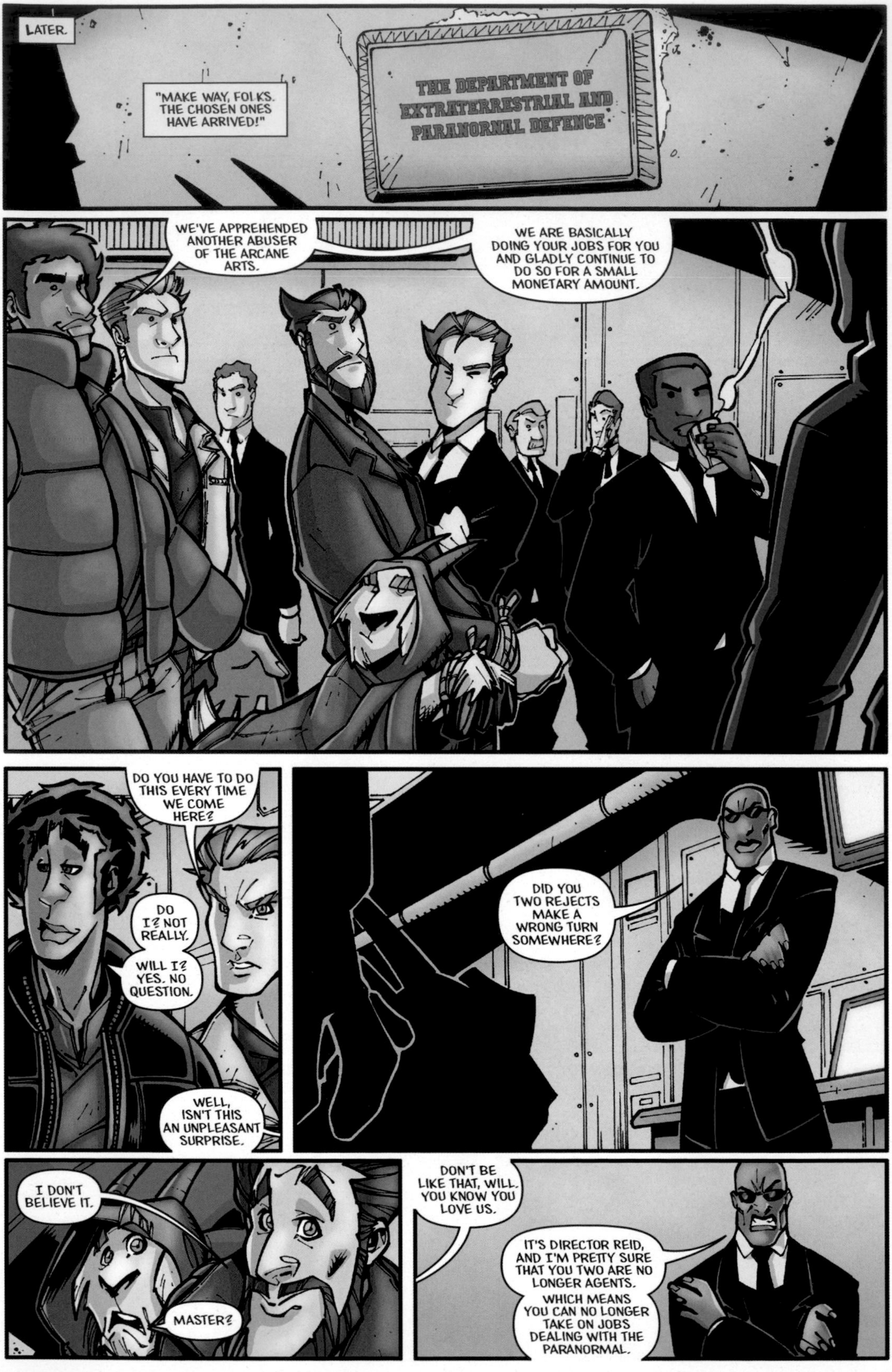
LATER.
"MAKE WAY, FOLKS. THE CHOSEN ONES HAVE ARRIVED!"
THE DEPARTMENT OF EXTRATERRESTRIAL AND PARANORMAL DEFENCE
WE'VE APPREHENDED ANOTHER ABUSER OF THE ARCANE ARTS.
WE ARE BASICALLY DOING YOUR JOBS FOR YOU AND GLADLY CONTINUE TO DO SO FOR A SMALL MONETARY AMOUNT.
DO YOU HAVE TO DO THIS EVERY TIME WE COME HERE?
DO I? NOT REALLY.
WILL I? YES. NO QUESTION.
WELL, ISN'T THIS AN UNPLEASANT SURPRISE.
DID YOU TWO REJECTS MAKE A WRONG TURN SOMEWHERE?
I DON'T BELIEVE IT.
MASTER?
DON'T BE LIKE THAT, WILL. YOU KNOW YOU LOVE US.
IT'S DIRECTOR REID, AND I'M PRETTY SURE THAT YOU TWO ARE NO LONGER AGENTS.
WHICH MEANS YOU CAN NO LONGER TAKE ON JOBS DEALING WITH THE PARANORMAL.

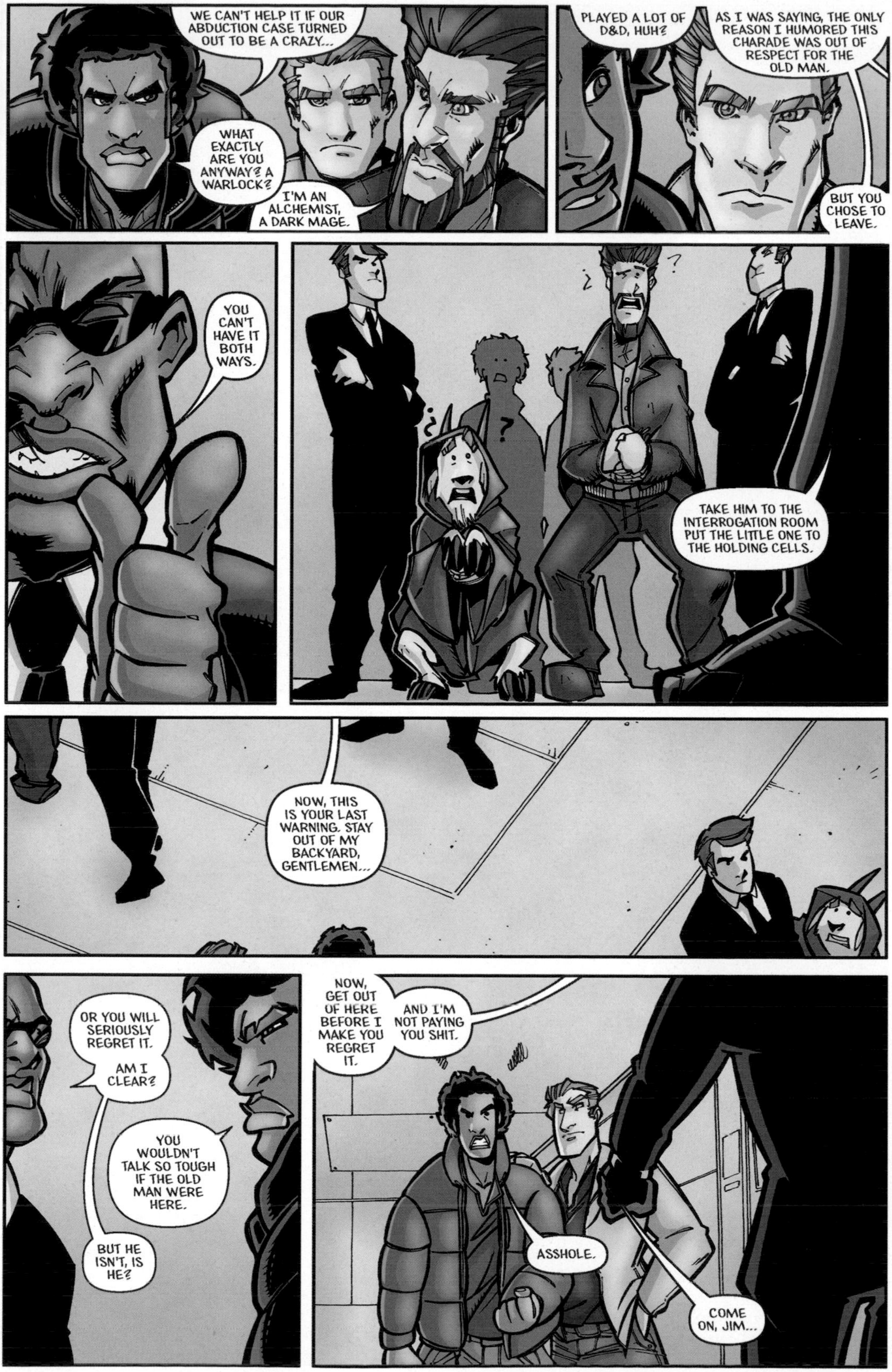
WE CAN'T HELP IT IF OUR ABDUCTION CASE TURNED OUT TO BE A CRAZY...
WHAT EXACTLY ARE YOU ANYWAY? A WARLOCK?
I'M AN ALCHEMIST, A DARK MAGE.
PLAYED A LOT OF D&D, HUH?
AS I WAS SAYING, THE ONLY REASON I HUMORED THIS CHARADE WAS OUT OF RESPECT FOR THE OLD MAN.
BUT YOU CHOSE TO LEAVE.
YOU CAN'T HAVE IT BOTH WAYS.
TAKE HIM TO THE INTERROGATION ROOM PUT THE LITTLE ONE TO THE HOLDING CELLS.
NOW, THIS IS YOUR LAST WARNING. STAY OUT OF MY BACKYARD, GENTLEMEN...
OR YOU WILL SERIOUSLY REGRET IT.
AM I CLEAR?
YOU WOULDN'T TALK SO TOUGH IF THE OLD MAN WERE HERE.
BUT HE ISN'T, IS HE?
NOW, GET OUT OF HERE BEFORE I MAKE YOU REGRET IT.
AND I'M NOT PAYING YOU SHIT.
ASSHOLE.
COME ON, JIM...

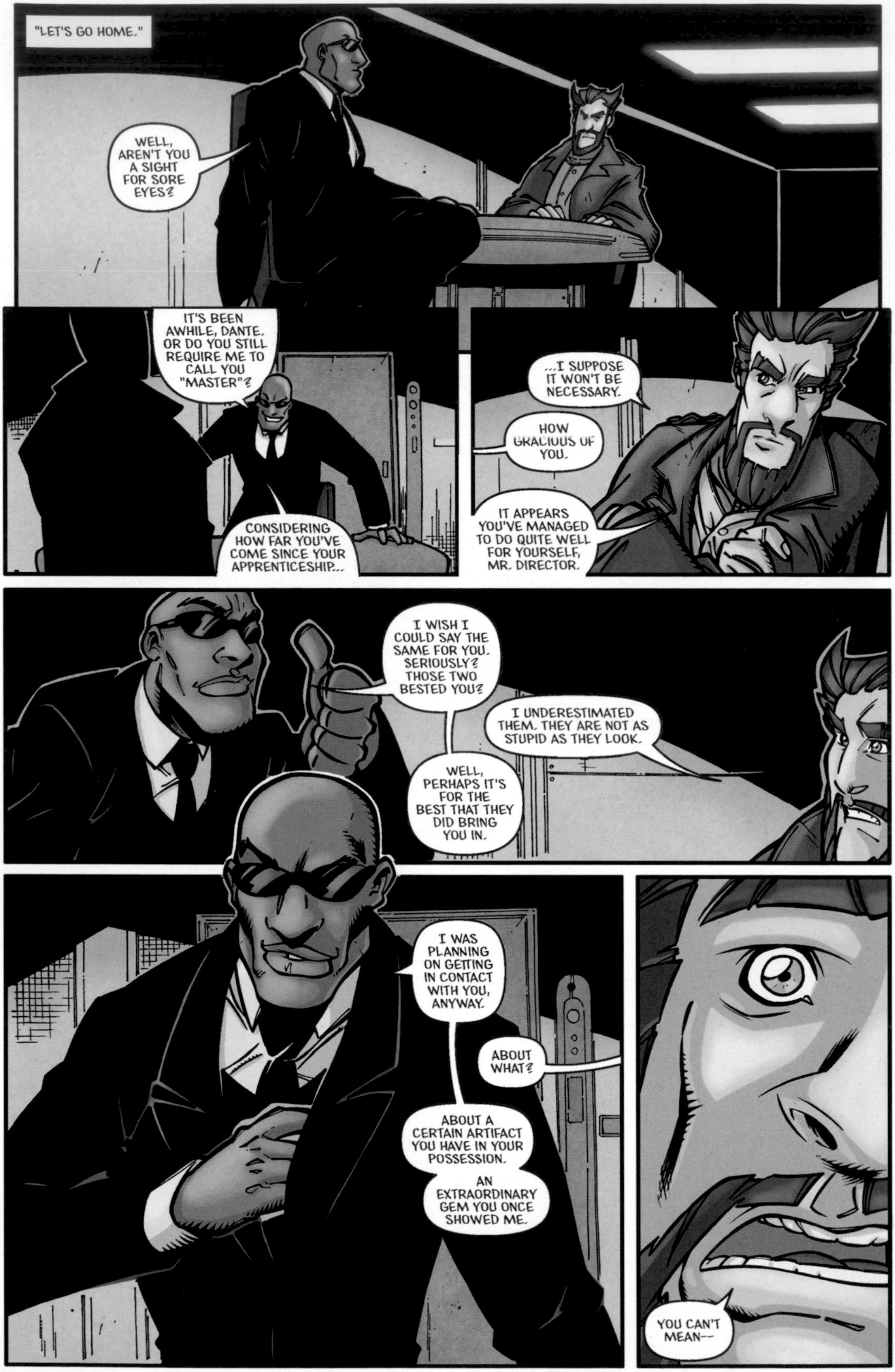
"LET'S GO HOME."
WELL, AREN'T YOU A SIGHT FOR SORE EYES?
IT'S BEEN AWHILE, DANTE. OR DO YOU STILL REQUIRE ME TO CALL YOU "MASTER"?
CONSIDERING HOW FAR YOU'VE COME SINCE YOUR APPRENTICESHIP...
...I SUPPOSE IT WON'T BE NECESSARY.
HOW GRACIOUS OF YOU.
IT APPEARS YOU'VE MANAGED TO DO QUITE WELL FOR YOURSELF, MR. DIRECTOR.
I WISH I COULD SAY THE SAME FOR YOU. SERIOUSLY? THOSE TWO BESTED YOU?
I UNDERESTIMATED THEM. THEY ARE NOT AS STUPID AS THEY LOOK.
WELL, PERHAPS IT'S FOR THE BEST THAT THEY DID BRING YOU IN.
I WAS PLANNING ON GETTING IN CONTACT WITH YOU, ANYWAY.
ABOUT WHAT?
ABOUT A CERTAIN ARTIFACT YOU HAVE IN YOUR POSSESSION.
AN EXTRAORDINARY GEM YOU ONCE SHOWED ME.
YOU CAN'T MEAN--

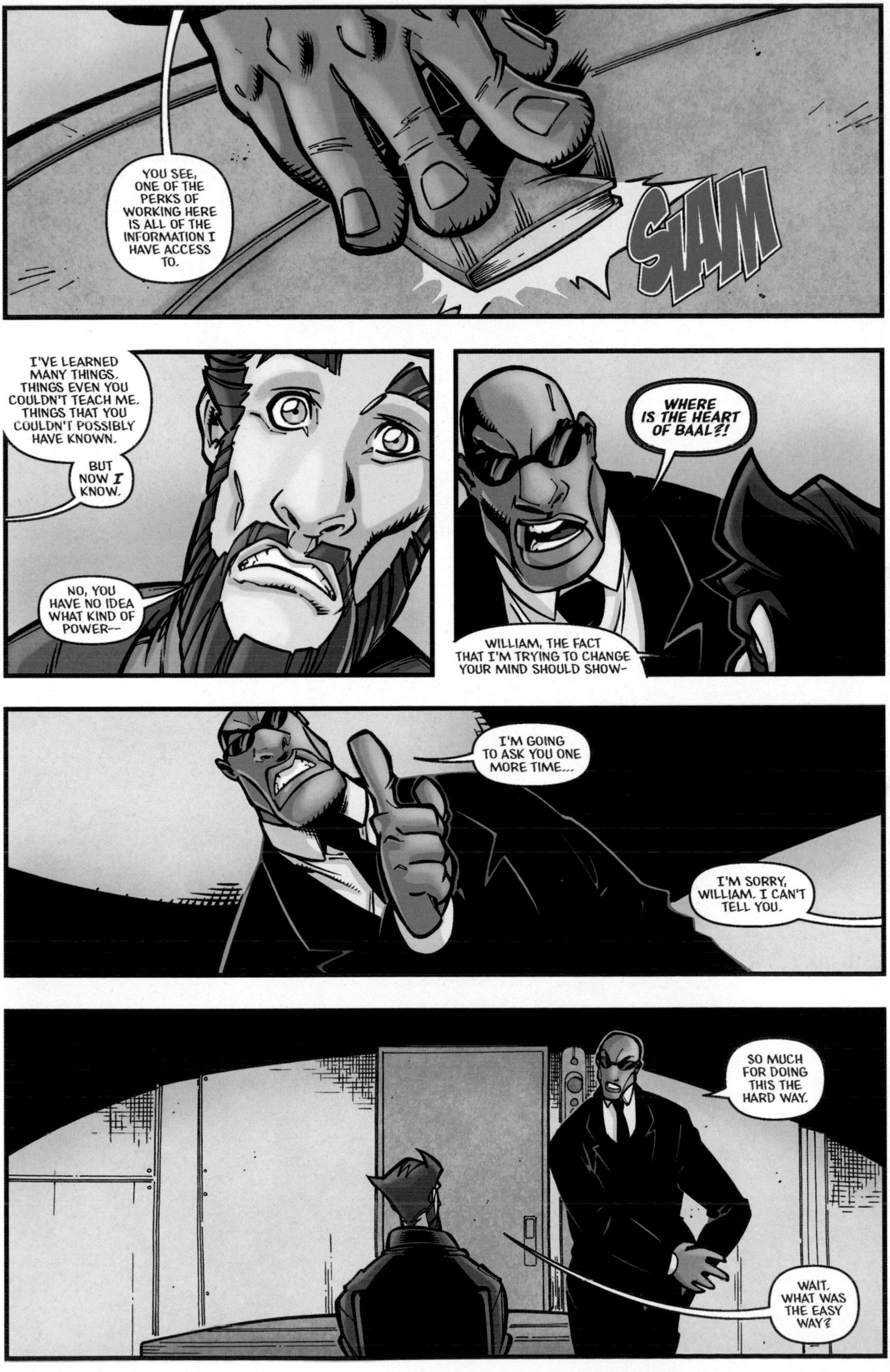
YOU SEE, ONE OF THE PERKS OF WORKING HERE IS ALL OF THE INFORMATION I HAVE ACCESS TO.
SLAM
I'VE LEARNED MANY THINGS. THINGS EVEN YOU COULDN'T TEACH ME. THINGS THAT YOU COULDN'T POSSIBLY HAVE KNOWN.
BUT NOW I KNOW.
NO, YOU HAVE NO IDEA WHAT KIND OF POWER--
WHERE IS THE HEART OF BAAL?!
WILLIAM, THE FACT THAT I'M TRYING TO CHANGE YOUR MIND SHOULD SHOW-
I'M GOING TO ASK YOU ONE MORE TIME...
I'M SORRY, WILLIAM. I CAN'T TELL YOU.
SO MUCH FOR DOING THIS THE HARD WAY.
WAIT. WHAT WAS THE EASY WAY?

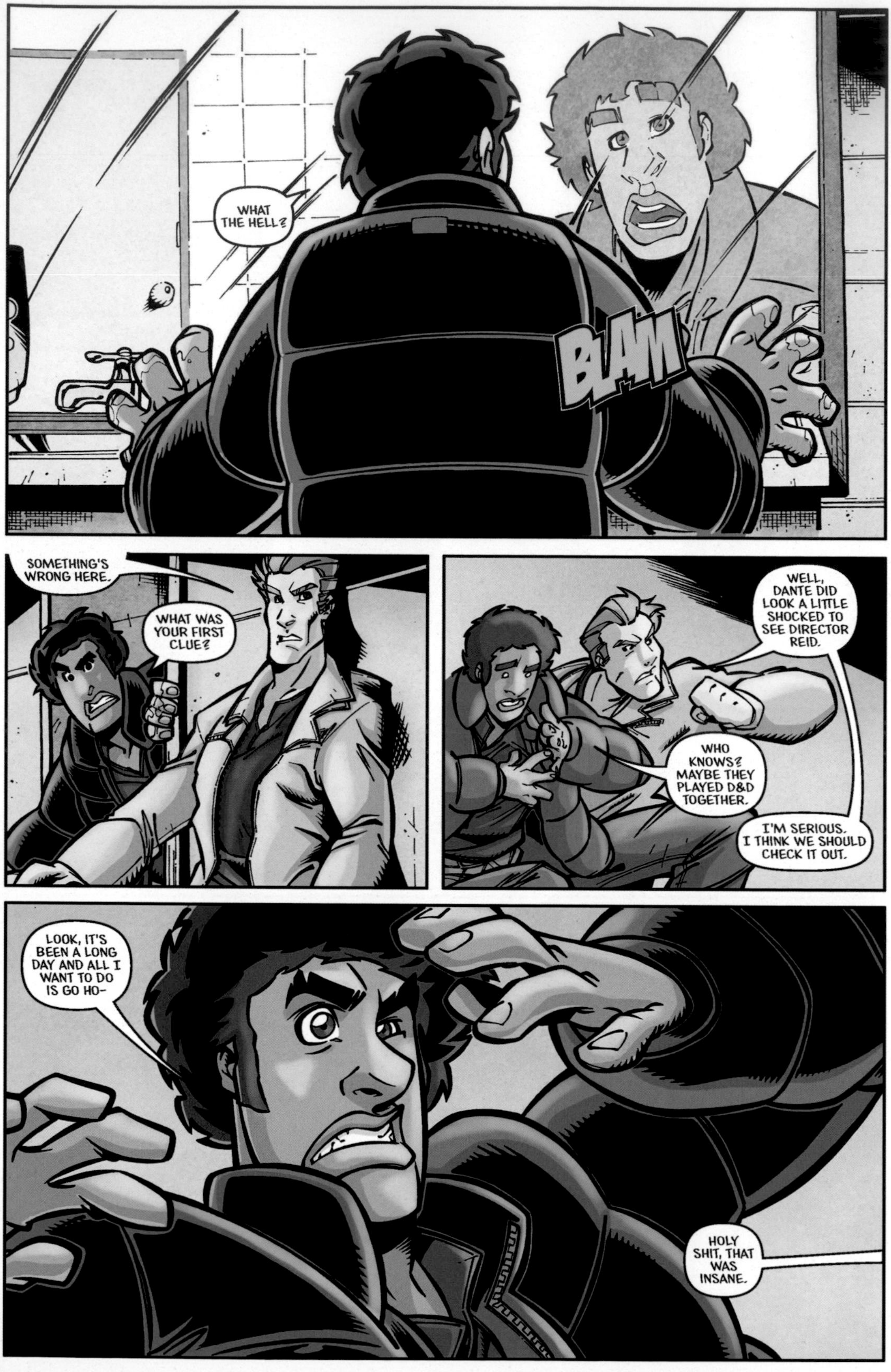
WHAT THE HELL?
BLAM
SOMETHING'S WRONG HERE.
WHAT WAS YOUR FIRST CLUE?
WELL, DANTE DID LOOK A LITTLE SHOCKED TO SEE DIRECTOR REID.
WHO KNOWS? MAYBE THEY PLAYED D&D TOGETHER.
I'M SERIOUS. I THINK WE SHOULD CHECK IT OUT.
LOOK, IT'S BEEN A LONG DAY AND ALL I WANT TO DO IS GO HO-
HOLY SHIT, THAT WAS INSANE.

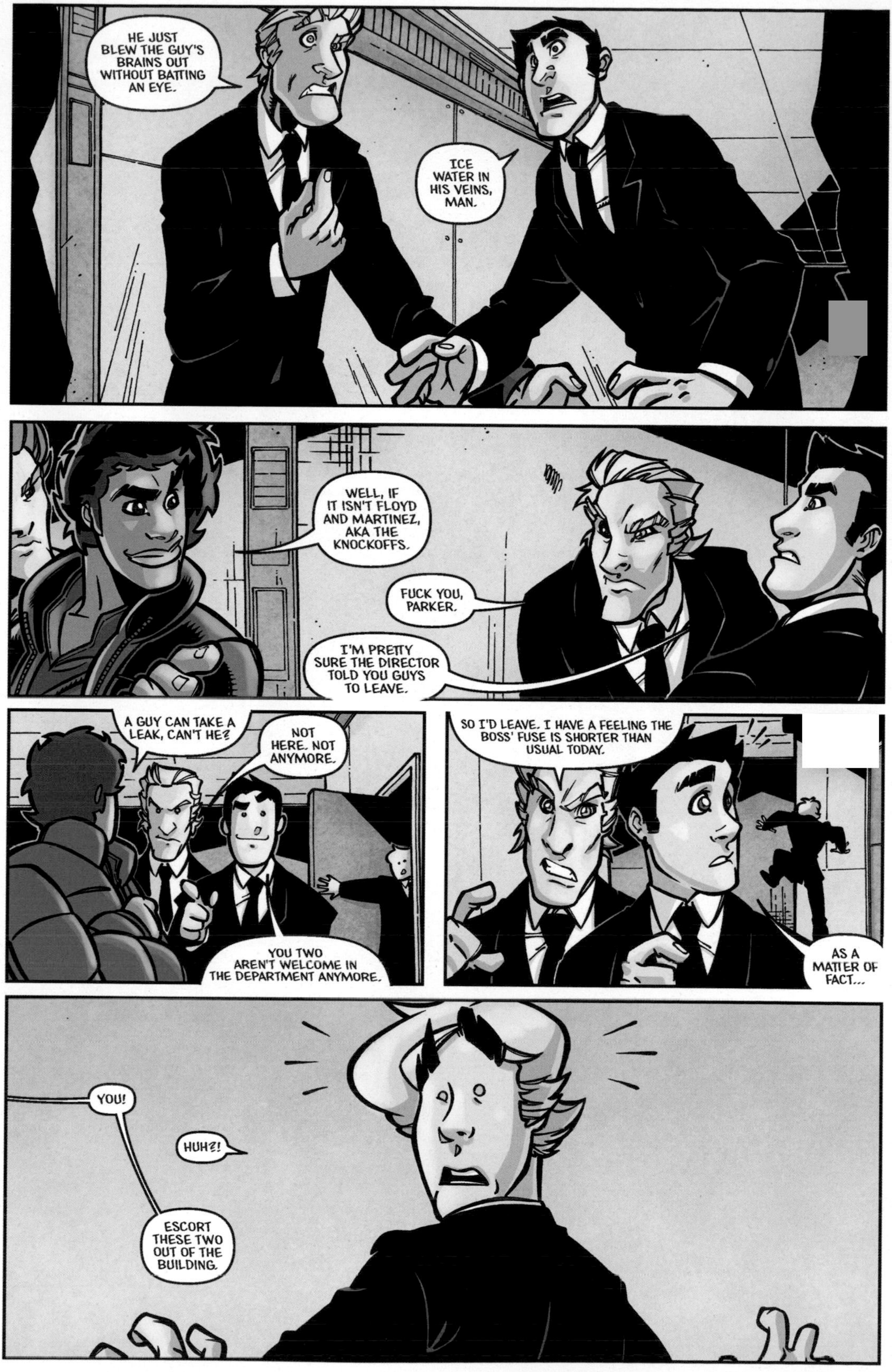
HE JUST BLEW THE GUY'S BRAINS OUT WITHOUT BATTING AN EYE.
ICE WATER IN HIS VEINS, MAN.
WELL, IF IT ISN'T FLOYD AND MARTINEZ, AKA THE KNOCKOFFS.
FUCK YOU, PARKER.
I'M PRETTY SURE THE DIRECTOR TOLD YOU GUYS TO LEAVE.
A GUY CAN TAKE A LEAK, CAN'T HE?
NOT HERE. NOT ANYMORE.
YOU TWO AREN'T WELCOME IN THE DEPARTMENT ANYMORE.
SO I'D LEAVE. I HAVE A FEELING THE BOSS' FUSE IS SHORTER THAN USUAL TODAY.
AS A MATTER OF FACT...
YOU!
HUH?!
ESCORT THESE TWO OUT OF THE BUILDING.

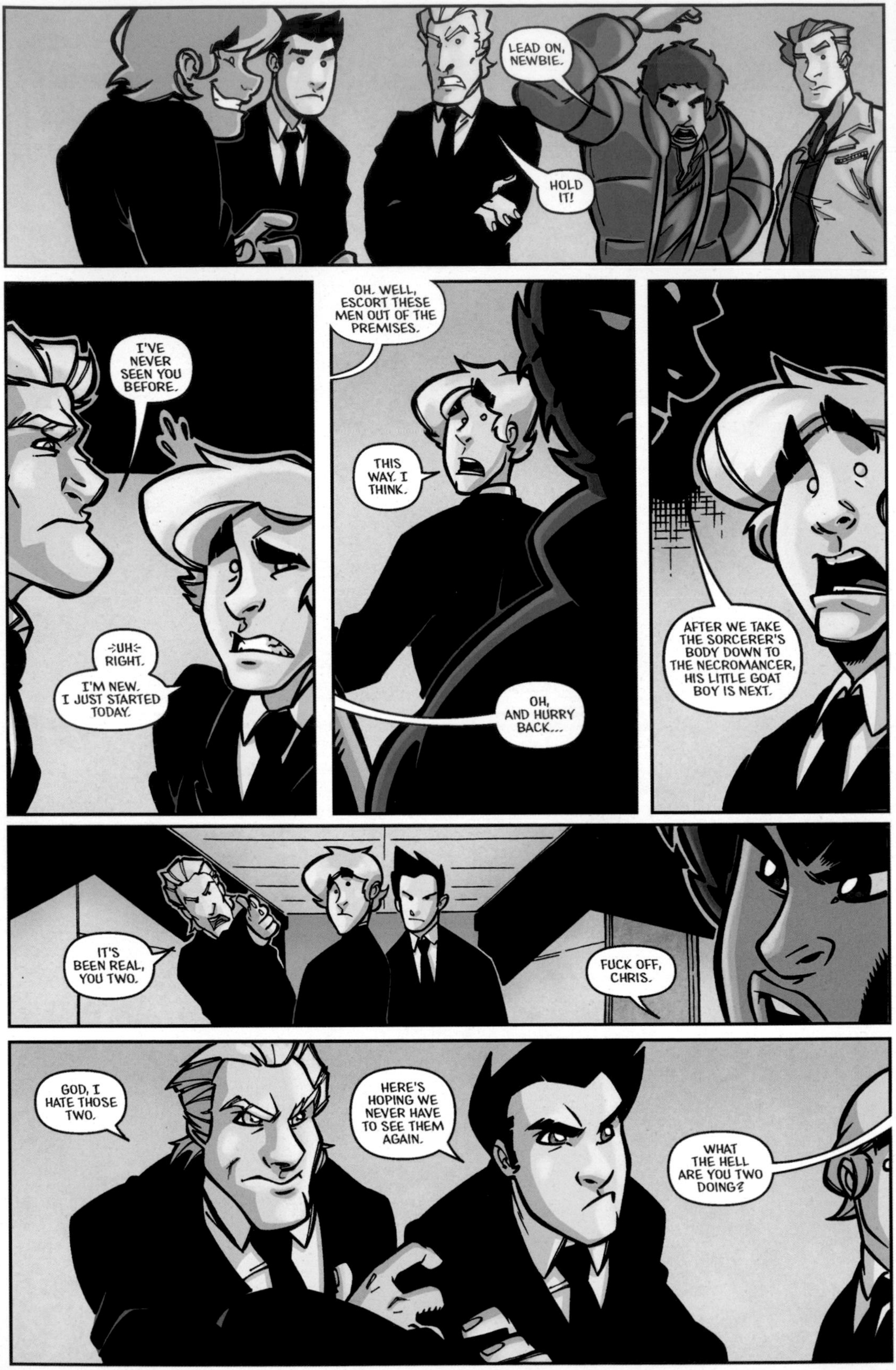
LEAD ON, NEWBIE.
HOLD IT!
I'VE NEVER SEEN YOU BEFORE.
-UH- RIGHT.
I'M NEW. I JUST STARTED TODAY.
OH. WELL, ESCORT THESE MEN OUT OF THE PREMISES.
THIS WAY. I THINK.
OH, AND HURRY BACK...
AFTER WE TAKE THE SORCERER'S BODY DOWN TO THE NECROMANCER, HIS LITTLE GOAT BOY IS NEXT.
IT'S BEEN REAL, YOU TWO.
FUCK OFF, CHRIS.
GOD, I HATE THOSE TWO.
HERE'S HOPING WE NEVER HAVE TO SEE THEM AGAIN.
WHAT THE HELL ARE YOU TWO DOING?

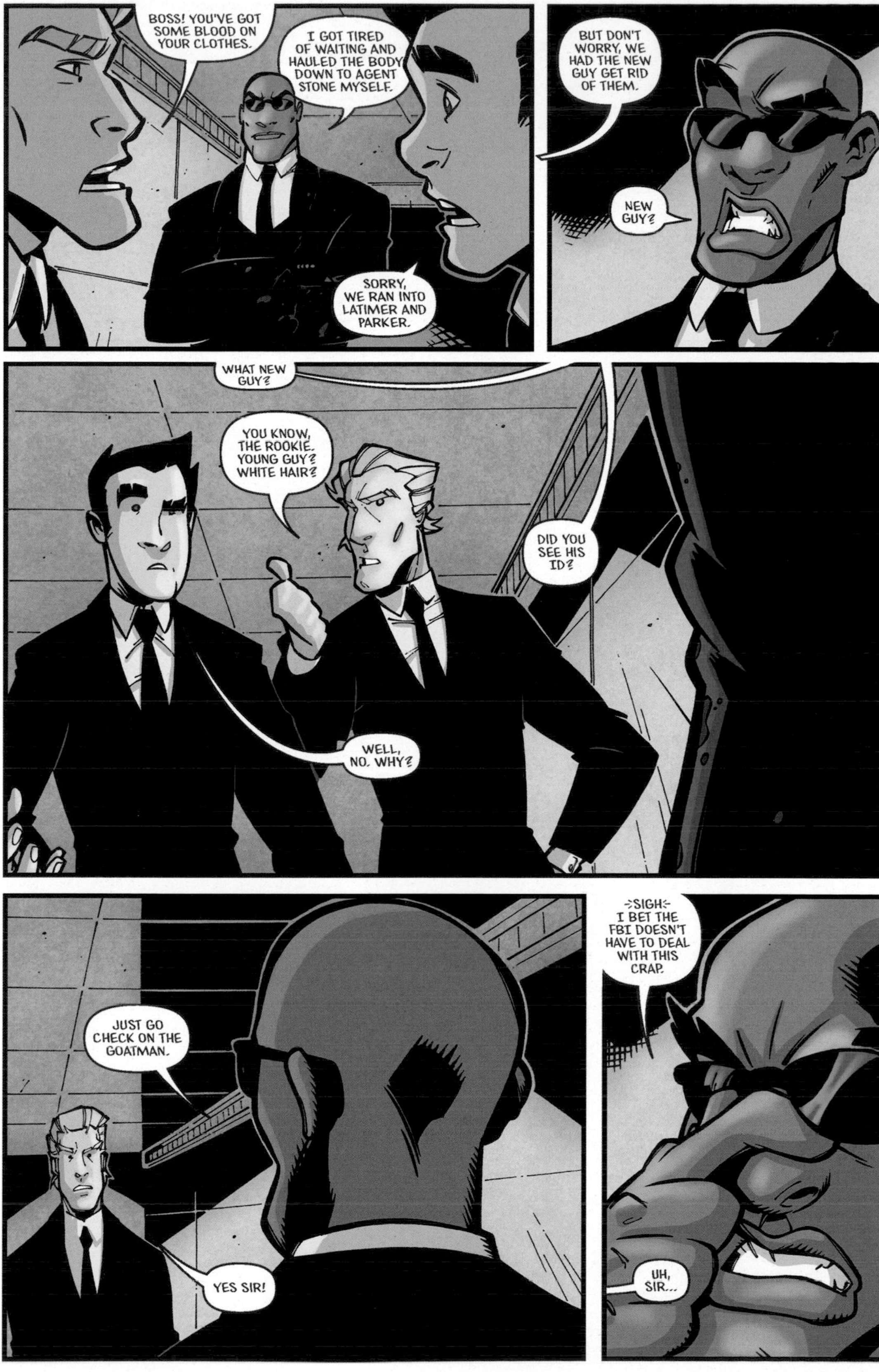
BOSS! YOU'VE GOT SOME BLOOD ON YOUR CLOTHES.
I GOT TIRED OF WAITING AND HAULED THE BODY DOWN TO AGENT STONE MYSELF.
SORRY, WE RAN INTO LATIMER AND PARKER.
BUT DON'T WORRY, WE HAD THE NEW GUY GET RID OF THEM.
NEW GUY?
WHAT NEW GUY?
YOU KNOW, THE ROOKIE. YOUNG GUY? WHITE HAIR?
DID YOU SEE HIS ID?
WELL, NO. WHY?
JUST GO CHECK ON THE GOATMAN.
YES SIR!
-SIGH- I BET THE FBI DOESN'T HAVE TO DEAL WITH THIS CRAP.
UH, SIR...

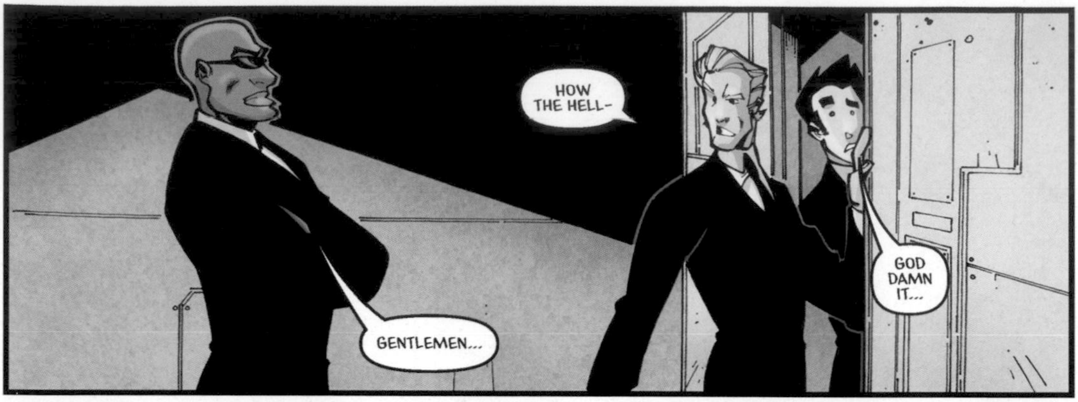
HOW THE HELL-
GOD DAMN IT...
GENTLEMEN...

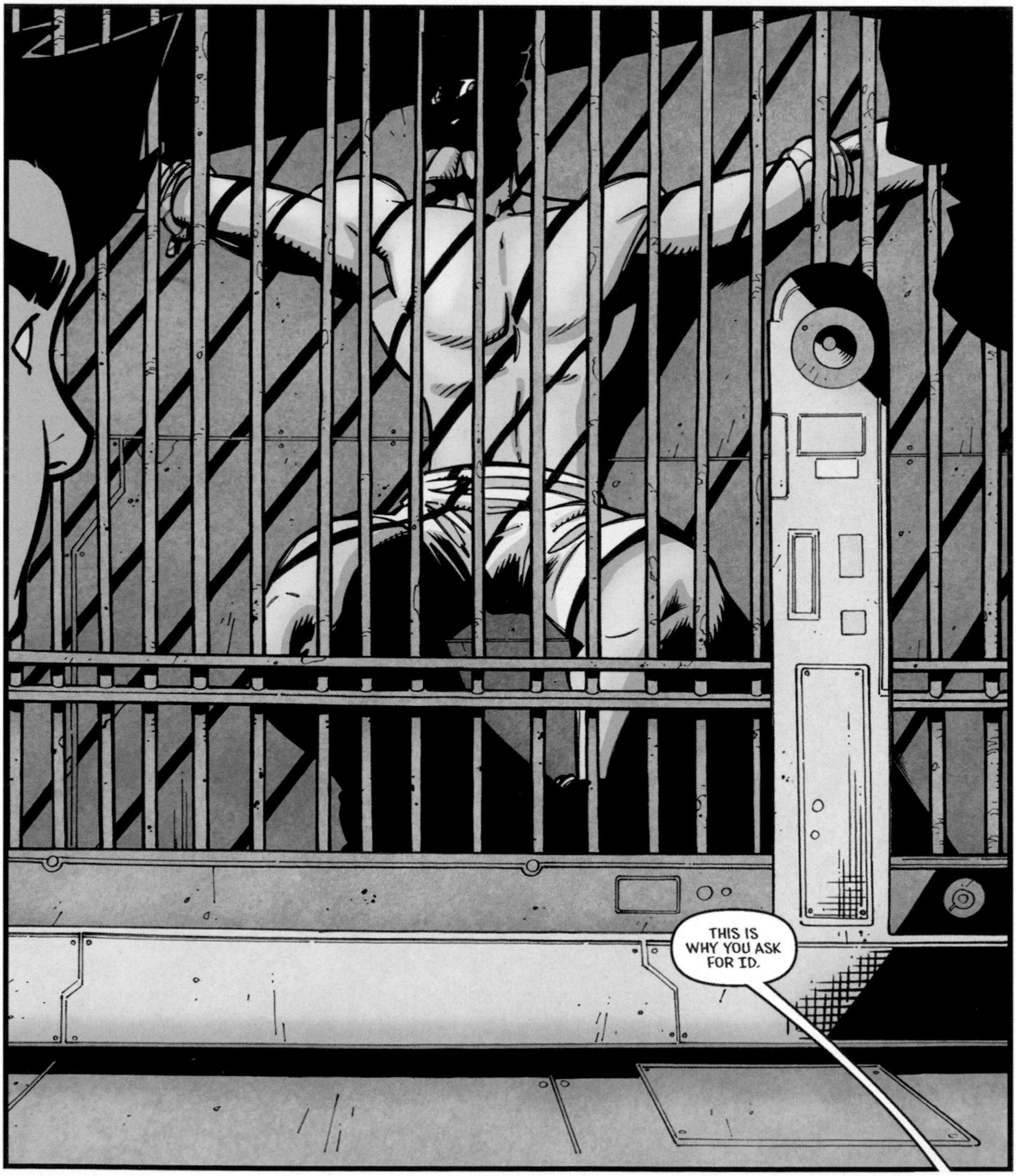
THIS IS WHY YOU ASK FOR ID.

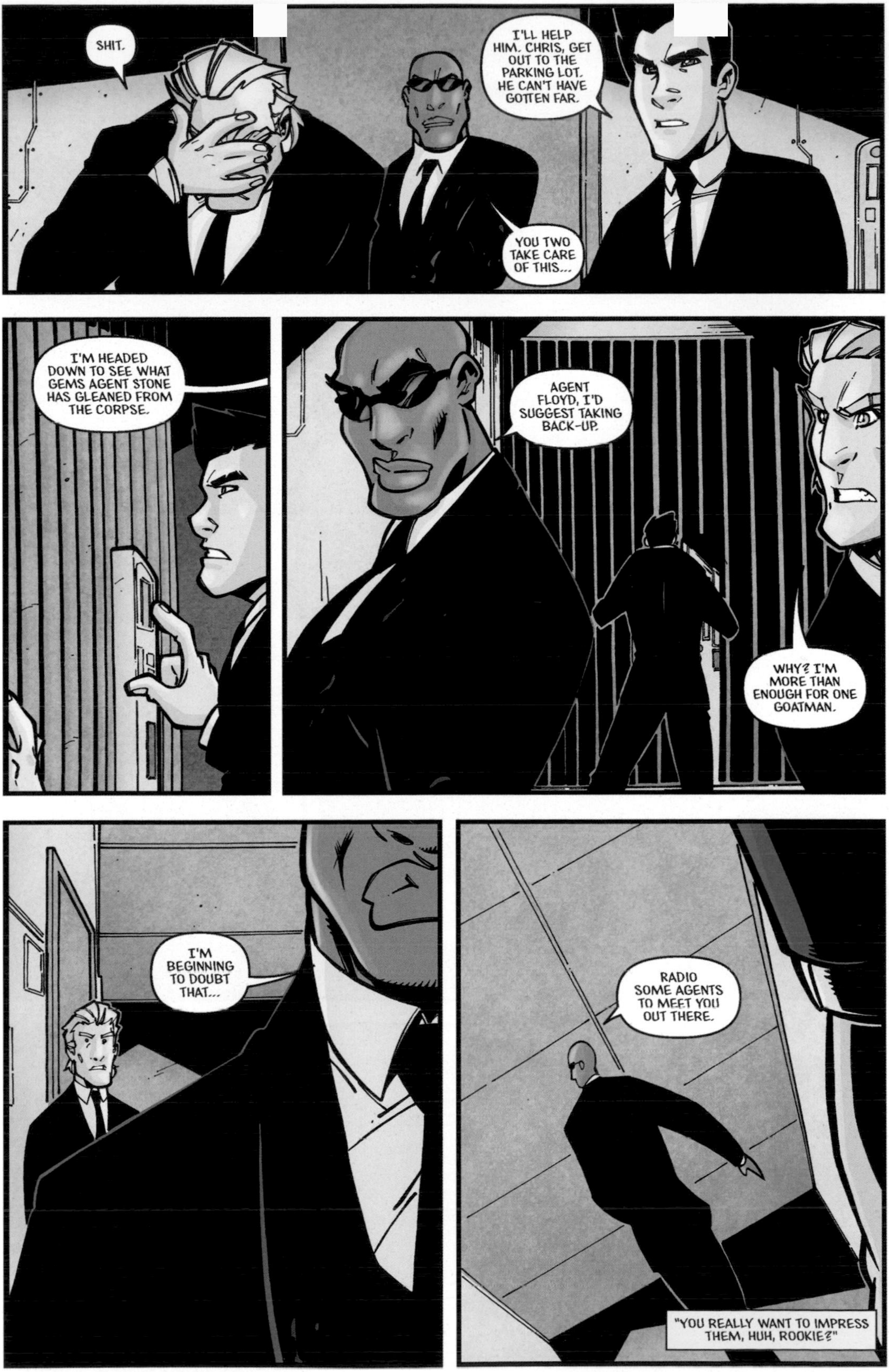
SHIT.
I'LL HELP HIM. CHRIS, GET OUT TO THE PARKING LOT. HE CAN'T HAVE GOTTEN FAR.
YOU TWO TAKE CARE OF THIS...
I'M HEADED DOWN TO SEE WHAT GEMS AGENT STONE HAS GLEANED FROM THE CORPSE.
AGENT FLOYD, I'D SUGGEST TAKING BACK-UP.
WHY? I'M MORE THAN ENOUGH FOR ONE GOATMAN.
I'M BEGINNING TO DOUBT THAT...
RADIO SOME AGENTS TO MEET YOU OUT THERE.
"YOU REALLY WANT TO IMPRESS THEM, HUH, ROOKIE?"

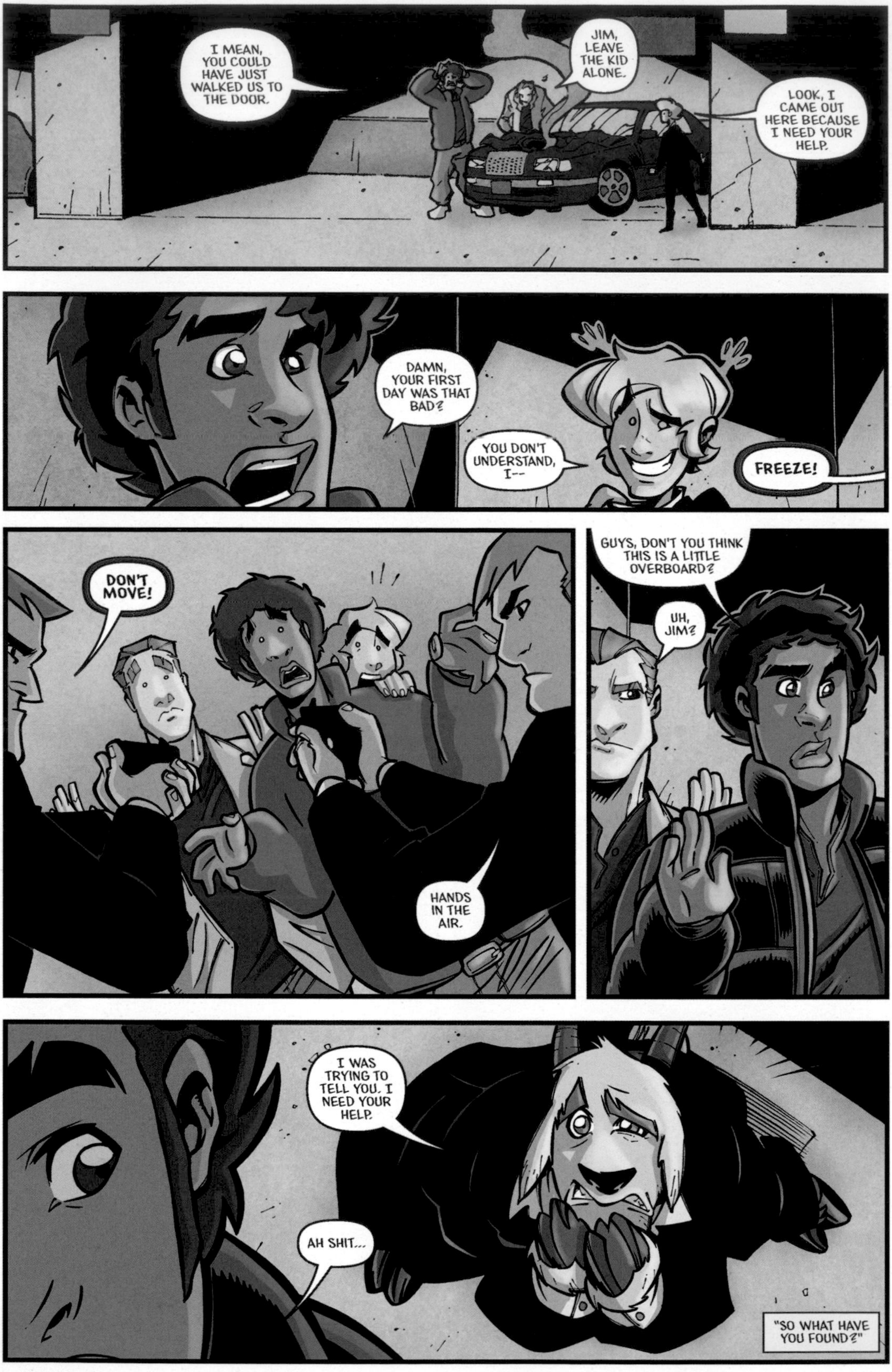
I MEAN, YOU COULD HAVE JUST WALKED US TO THE DOOR.
JIM, LEAVE THE KID ALONE.
LOOK, I CAME OUT HERE BECAUSE I NEED YOUR HELP.
DAMN, YOUR FIRST DAY WAS THAT BAD?
YOU DON'T UNDERSTAND, I--
FREEZE!
DON'T MOVE!
HANDS IN THE AIR.
GUYS, DON'T YOU THINK THIS IS A LITTLE OVERBOARD?
UH, JIM?
I WAS TRYING TO TELL YOU. I NEED YOUR HELP.
AH SHIT...
"SO WHAT HAVE YOU FOUND?"

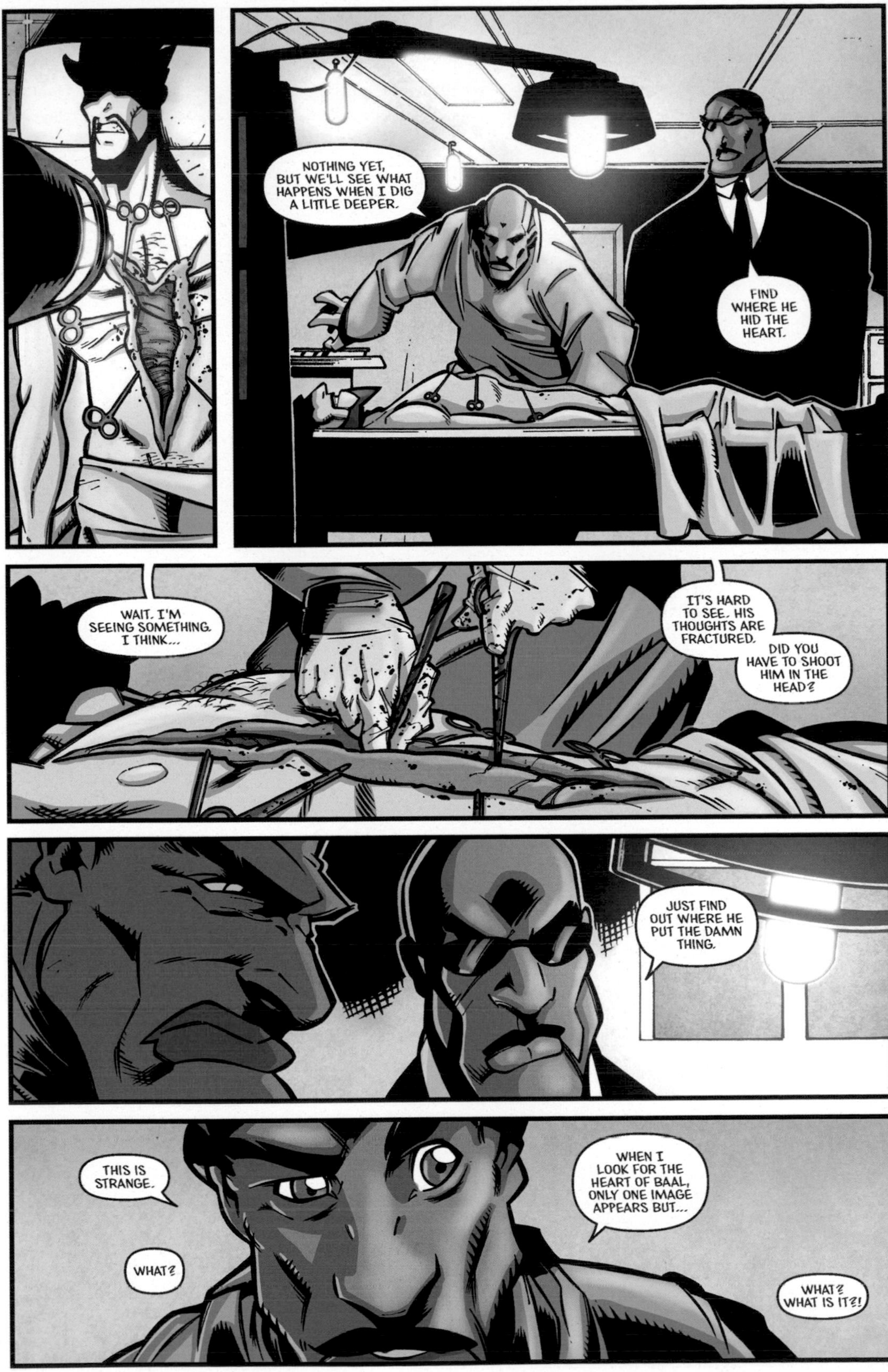
NOTHING YET, BUT WE'LL SEE WHAT HAPPENS WHEN I DIG A LITTLE DEEPER.
FIND WHERE HE HID THE HEART.
WAIT. I'M SEEING SOMETHING. I THINK...
IT'S HARD TO SEE. HIS THOUGHTS ARE FRACTURED.
DID YOU HAVE TO SHOOT HIM IN THE HEAD?
JUST FIND OUT WHERE HE PUT THE DAMN THING.
THIS IS STRANGE.
WHEN I LOOK FOR THE HEART OF BAAL, ONLY ONE IMAGE APPEARS BUT...
WHAT?
WHAT? WHAT IS IT?!

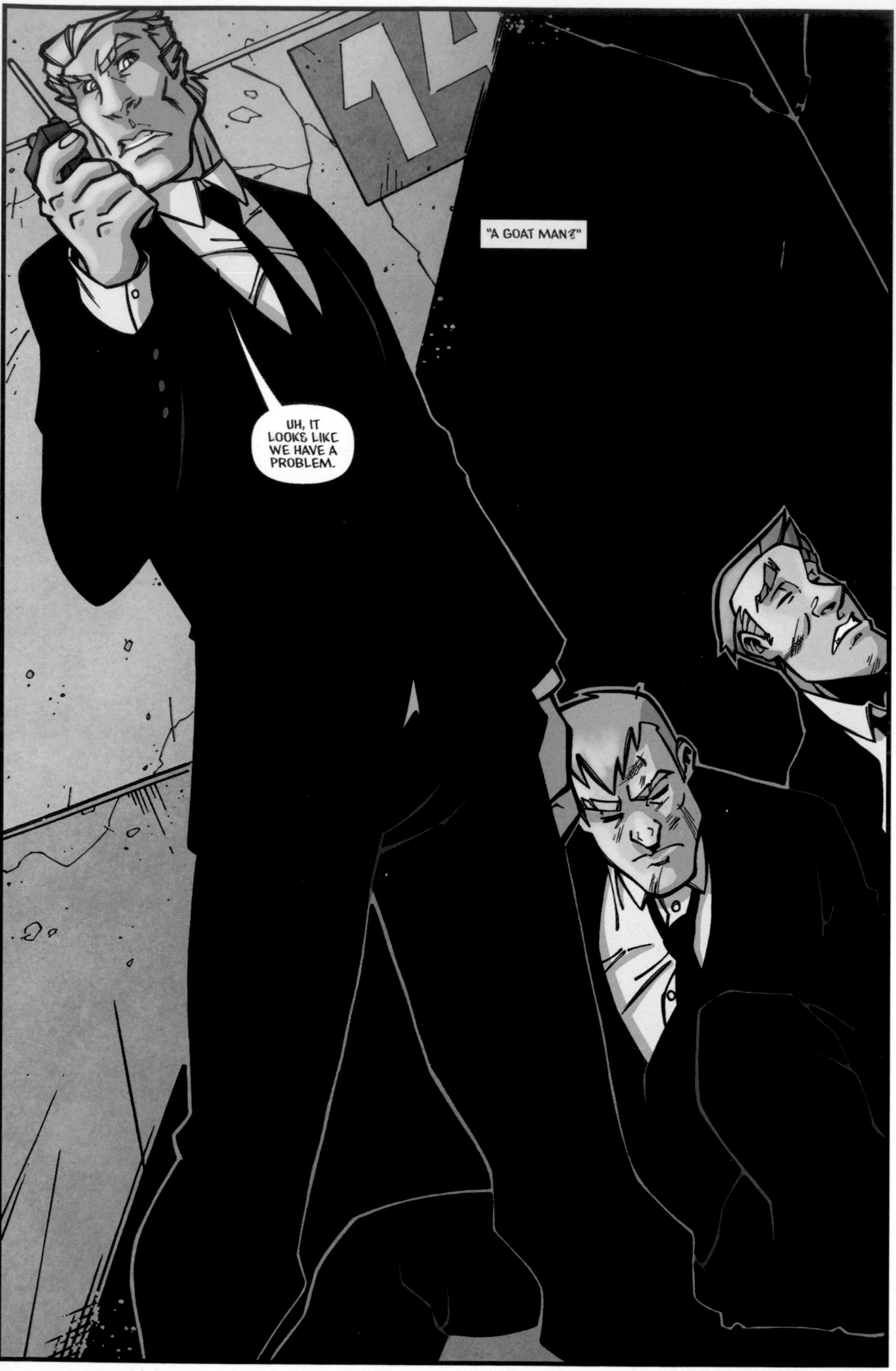
"A GOAT MAN?"
UH, IT LOOKS LIKE WE HAVE A PROBLEM.

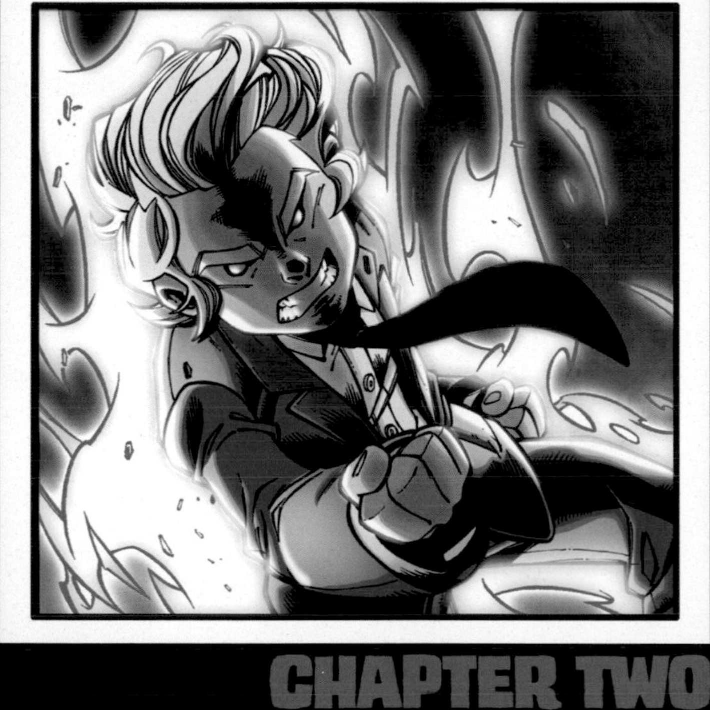

CHAPTER TWO

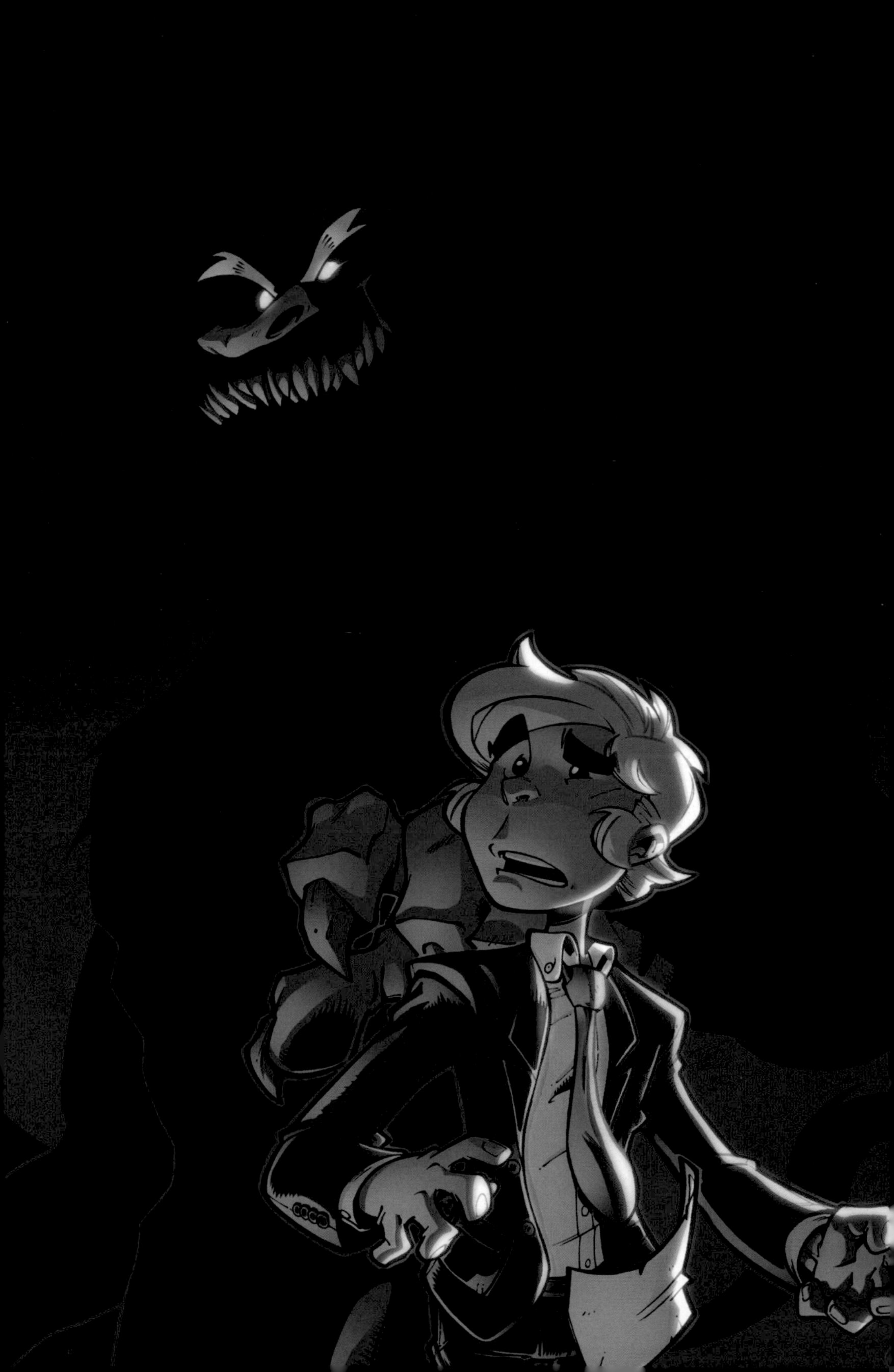

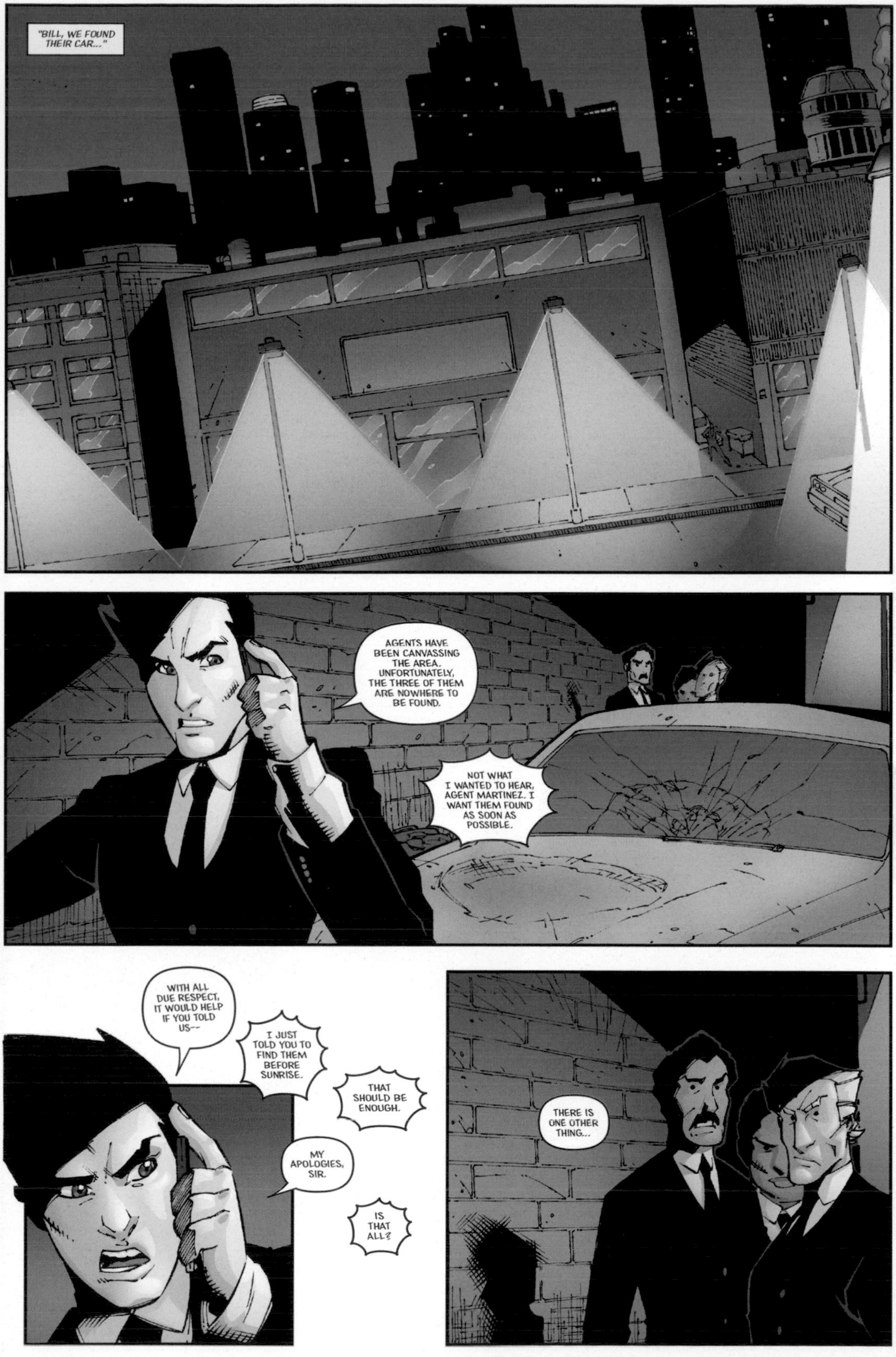
"BILL, WE FOUND THEIR CAR..."
AGENTS HAVE BEEN CANVASSING THE AREA. UNFORTUNATELY, THE THREE OF THEM ARE NOWHERE TO BE FOUND.
NOT WHAT I WANTED TO HEAR, AGENT MARTINEZ. I WANT THEM FOUND AS SOON AS POSSIBLE.
WITH ALL DUE RESPECT, IT WOULD HELP IF YOU TOLD US--
I JUST TOLD YOU TO FIND THEM BEFORE SUNRISE.
THAT SHOULD BE ENOUGH.
MY APOLOGIES, SIR.
IS THAT ALL?
THERE IS ONE OTHER THING...

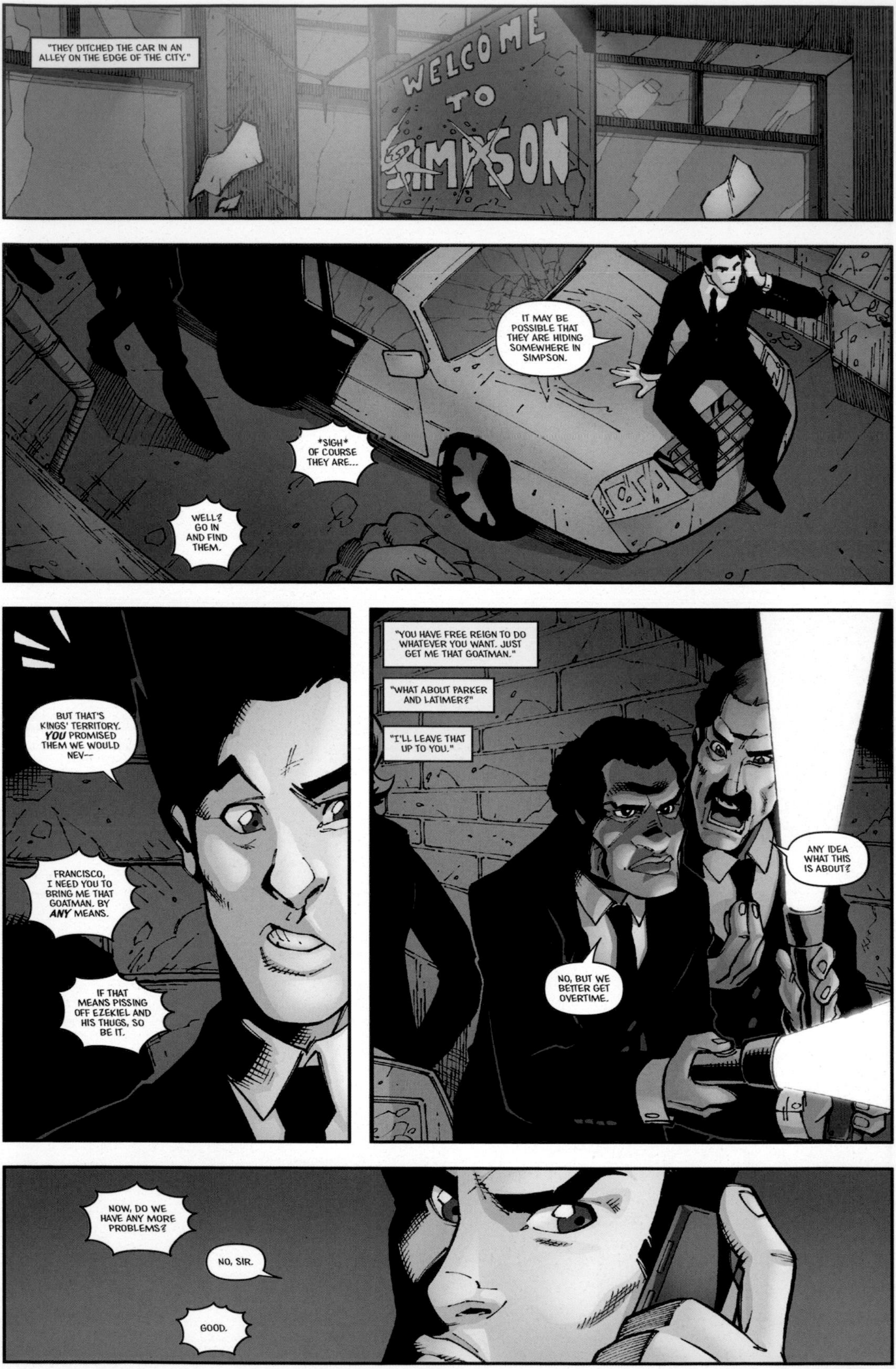
"THEY DITCHED THE CAR IN AN ALLEY ON THE EDGE OF THE CITY."
WELCOME TO SIMPSON
IT MAY BE POSSIBLE THAT THEY ARE HIDING SOMEWHERE IN SIMPSON.
SIGH OF COURSE THEY ARE...
WELL? GO IN AND FIND THEM.
BUT THAT'S KINGS' TERRITORY. YOU PROMISED THEM WE WOULD NEV--
FRANCISCO, I NEED YOU TO BRING ME THAT GOATMAN. BY ANY MEANS.
IF THAT MEANS PISSING OFF EZEKIEL AND HIS THUGS, SO BE IT.
"YOU HAVE FREE REIGN TO DO WHATEVER YOU WANT. JUST GET ME THAT GOATMAN."
"WHAT ABOUT PARKER AND LATIMER?"
"I'LL LEAVE THAT UP TO YOU."
ANY IDEA WHAT THIS IS ABOUT?
NO, BUT WE BETTER GET OVERTIME.
NOW, DO WE HAVE ANY MORE PROBLEMS?
NO, SIR.
GOOD.

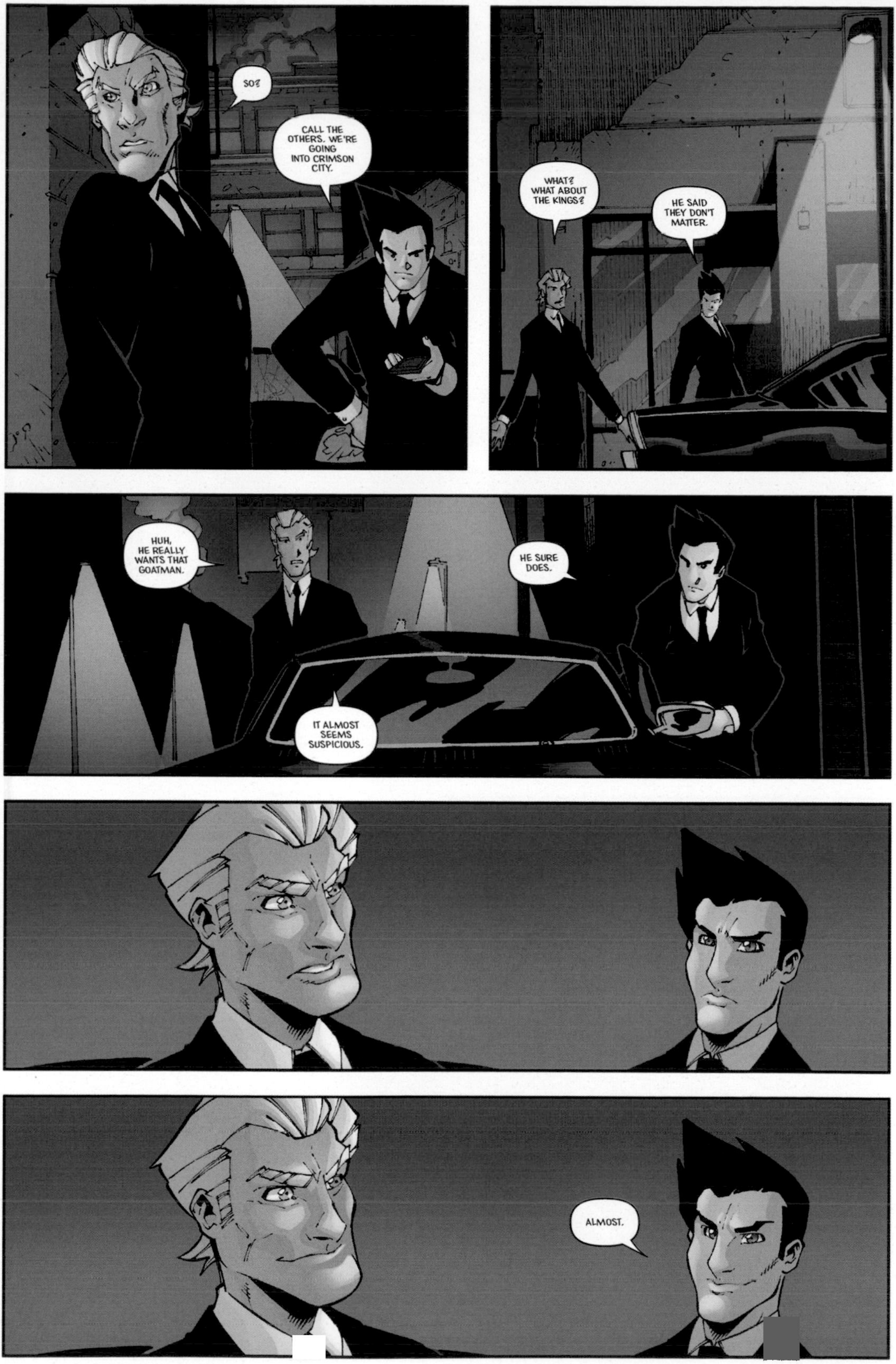
SO?
CALL THE OTHERS. WE'RE GOING INTO CRIMSON CITY.
WHAT? WHAT ABOUT THE KINGS?
HE SAID THEY DON'T MATTER.
HUH, HE REALLY WANTS THAT GOATMAN.
HE SURE DOES.
IT ALMOST SEEMS SUSPICIOUS.
ALMOST.

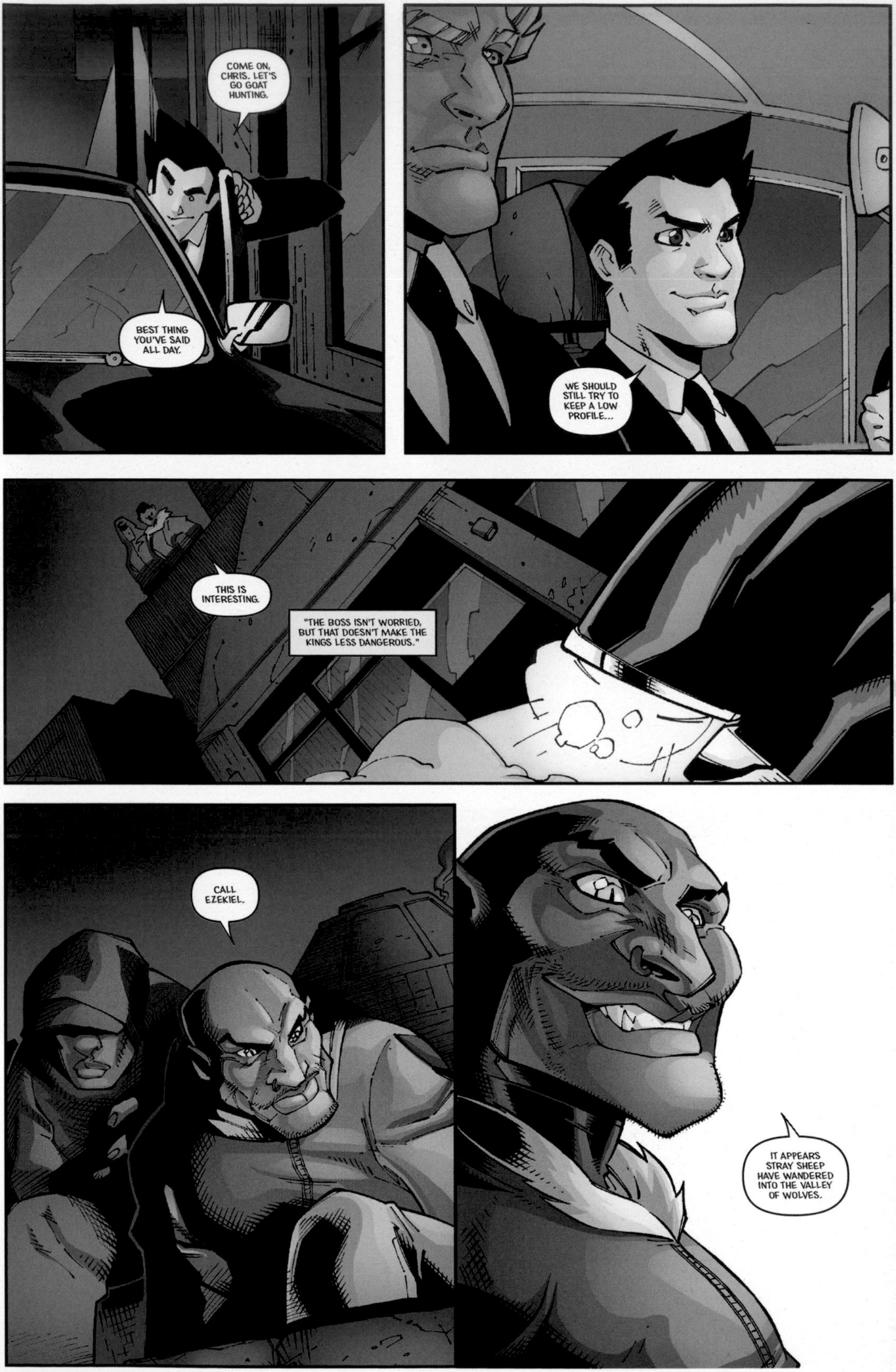
COME ON, CHRIS. LET'S GO GOAT HUNTING.
BEST THING YOU'VE SAID ALL DAY.
WE SHOULD STILL TRY TO KEEP A LOW PROFILE...
THIS IS INTERESTING.
"THE BOSS ISN'T WORRIED, BUT THAT DOESN'T MAKE THE KINGS LESS DANGEROUS."
CALL EZEKIEL.
IT APPEARS STRAY SHEEP HAVE WANDERED INTO THE VALLEY OF WOLVES.

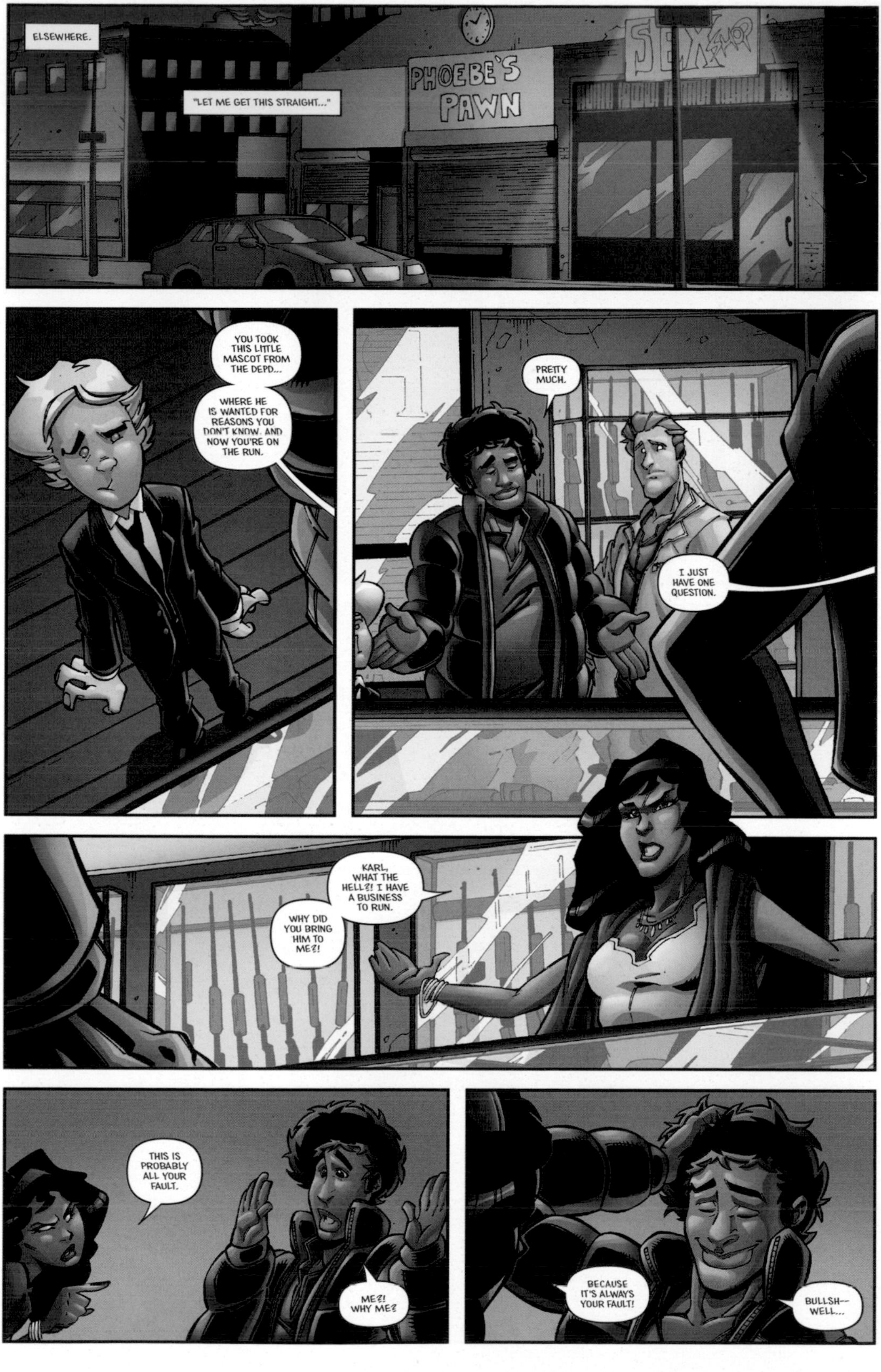
ELSEWHERE.
"LET ME GET THIS STRAIGHT..."
PHOEBE'S PAWN
SEX SHOP
YOU TOOK THIS LITTLE MASCOT FROM THE DEPD...
WHERE HE IS WANTED FOR REASONS YOU DON'T KNOW. AND NOW YOU'RE ON THE RUN.
PRETTY MUCH.
I JUST HAVE ONE QUESTION.
KARL, WHAT THE HELL?! I HAVE A BUSINESS TO RUN.
WHY DID YOU BRING HIM TO ME?!
THIS IS PROBABLY ALL YOUR FAULT.
ME?! WHY ME?
BECAUSE IT'S ALWAYS YOUR FAULT!
BULLSH-- WELL...

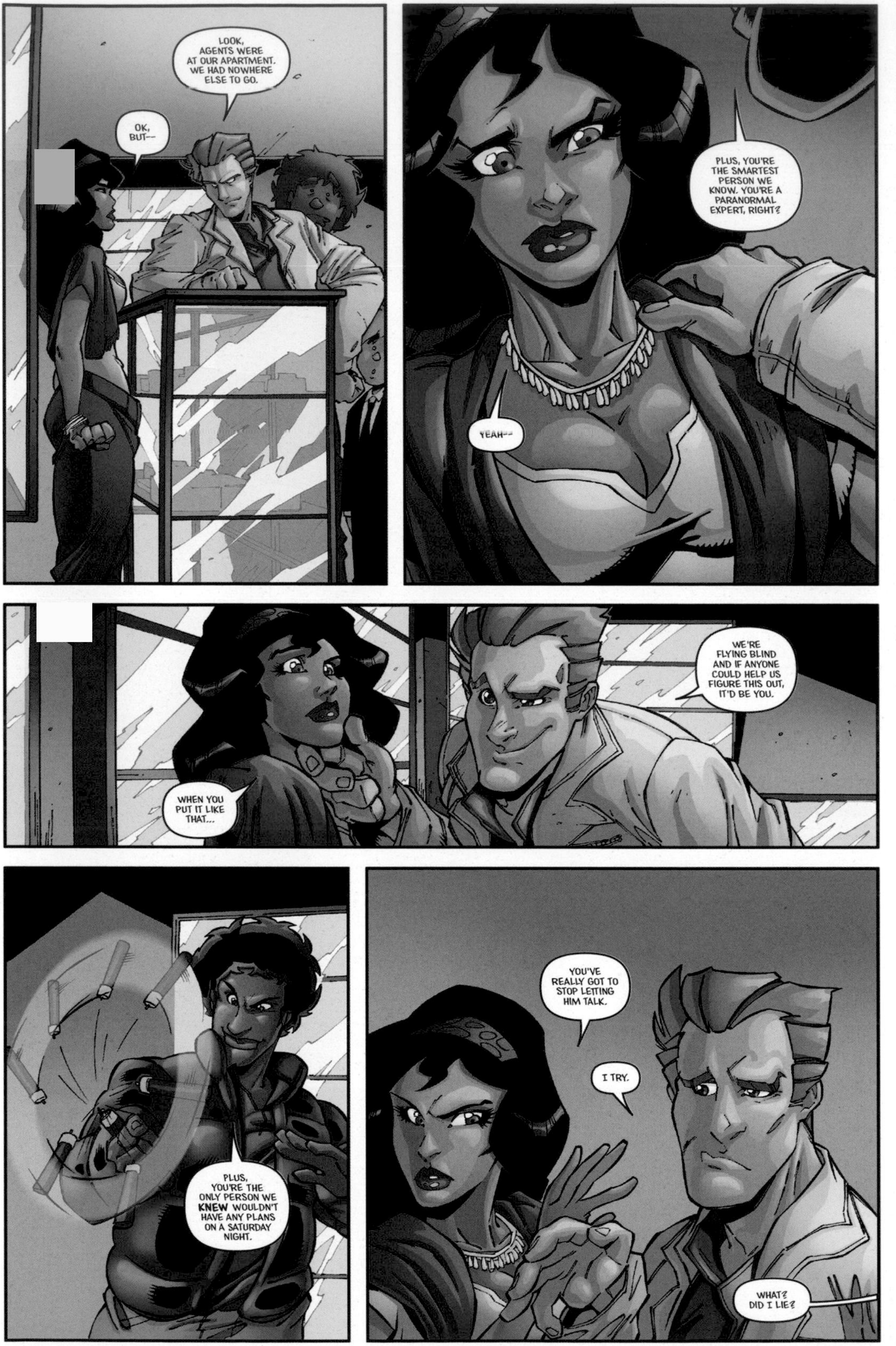
LOOK, AGENTS WERE AT OUR APARTMENT. WE HAD NOWHERE ELSE TO GO.
OK, BUT--
PLUS, YOU'RE THE SMARTEST PERSON WE KNOW. YOU'RE A PARANORMAL EXPERT, RIGHT?
YEAH--
WE'RE FLYING BLIND AND IF ANYONE COULD HELP US FIGURE THIS OUT, IT'D BE YOU.
WHEN YOU PUT IT LIKE THAT...
PLUS, YOU'RE THE ONLY PERSON WE KNEW WOULDN'T HAVE ANY PLANS ON A SATURDAY NIGHT.
YOU'VE REALLY GOT TO STOP LETTING HIM TALK.
I TRY.
WHAT? DID I LIE?

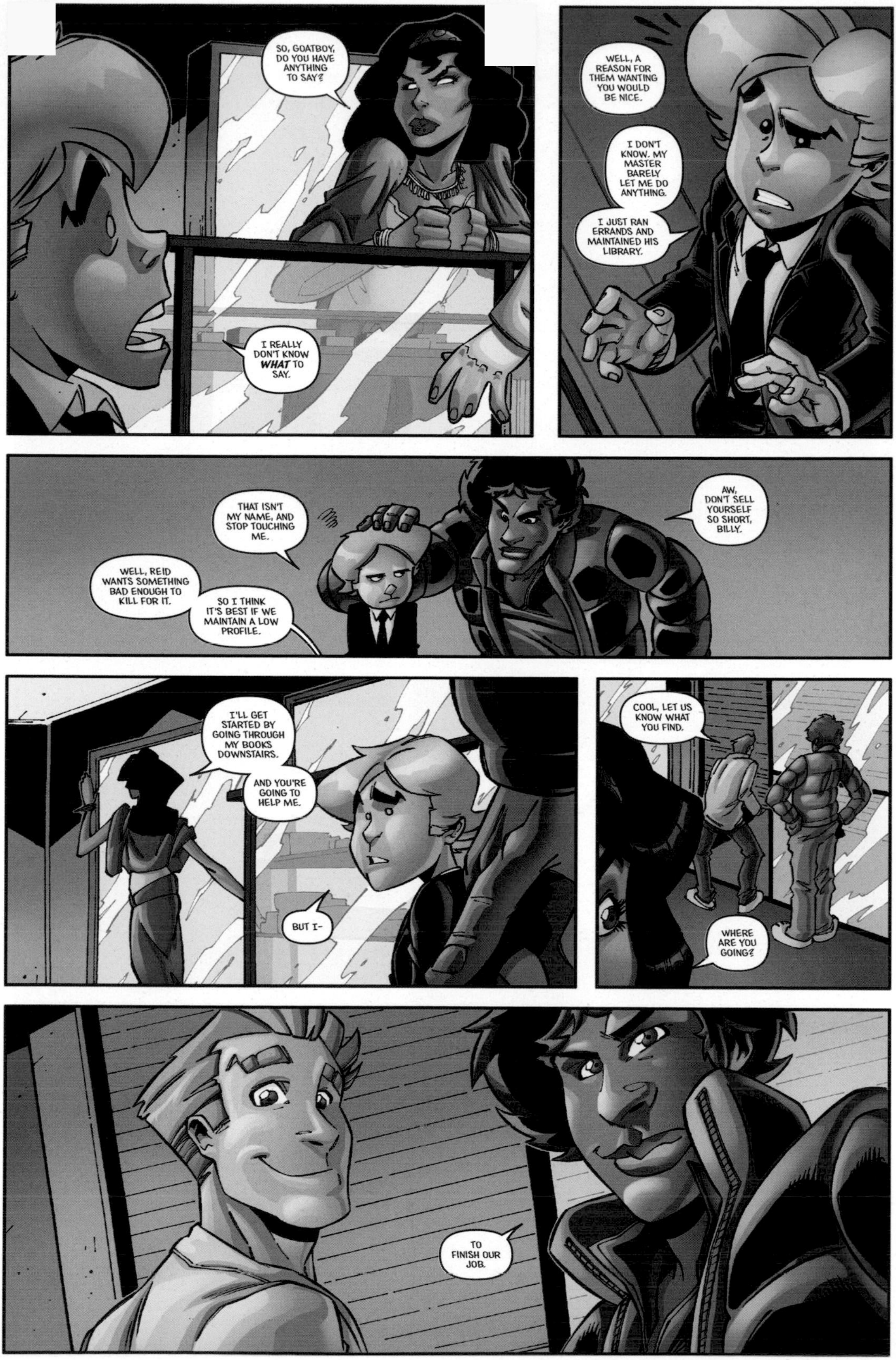
SO, GOATBOY, DO YOU HAVE ANYTHING TO SAY?
I REALLY DON'T KNOW WHAT TO SAY.
WELL, A REASON FOR THEM WANTING YOU WOULD BE NICE.
I DON'T KNOW. MY MASTER BARELY LET ME DO ANYTHING.
I JUST RAN ERRANDS AND MAINTAINED HIS LIBRARY.
AW, DON'T SELL YOURSELF SO SHORT, BILLY.
THAT ISN'T MY NAME, AND STOP TOUCHING ME.
WELL, REID WANTS SOMETHING BAD ENOUGH TO KILL FOR IT.
SO I THINK IT'S BEST IF WE MAINTAIN A LOW PROFILE.
I'LL GET STARTED BY GOING THROUGH MY BOOKS DOWNSTAIRS.
AND YOU'RE GOING TO HELP ME.
BUT I-
COOL, LET US KNOW WHAT YOU FIND.
WHERE ARE YOU GOING?
TO FINISH OUR JOB.

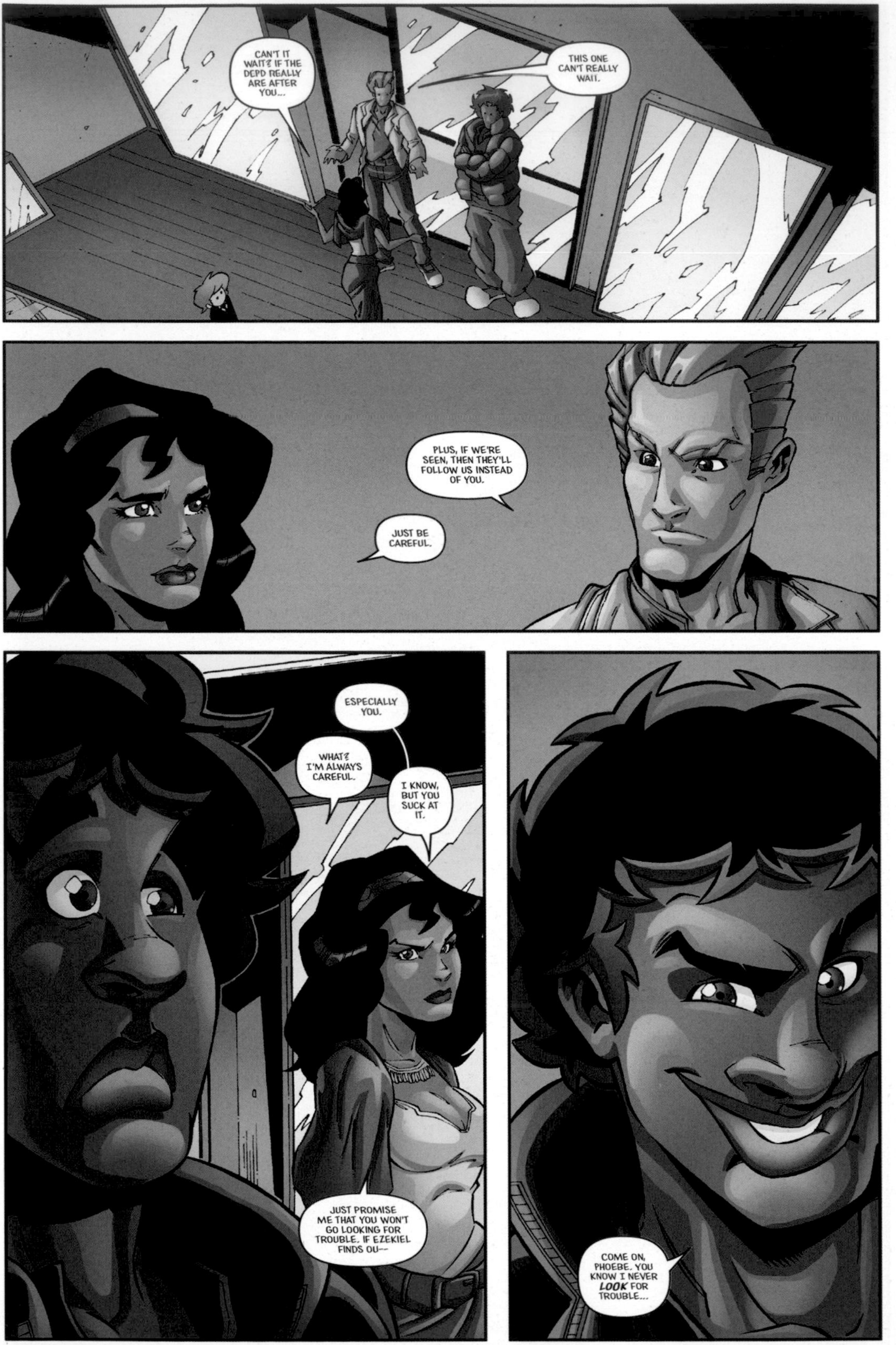
CAN'T IT WAIT? IF THE DEPD REALLY ARE AFTER YOU...
THIS ONE CAN'T REALLY WAIT.
PLUS, IF WE'RE SEEN, THEN THEY'LL FOLLOW US INSTEAD OF YOU.
JUST BE CAREFUL.
ESPECIALLY YOU.
WHAT? I'M ALWAYS CAREFUL.
I KNOW, BUT YOU SUCK AT IT.
JUST PROMISE ME THAT YOU WON'T GO LOOKING FOR TROUBLE. IF EZEKIEL FINDS OU--
COME ON, PHOEBE. YOU KNOW I NEVER LOOK FOR TROUBLE...

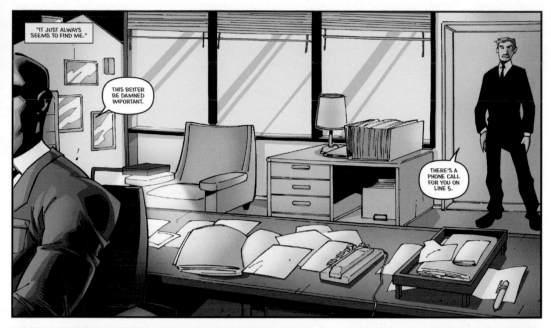

"IT JUST ALWAYS SEEMS TO FIND ME."

THIS BETTER BE DAMNED IMPORTANT.

THERE'S A PHONE CALL FOR YOU ON LINE 5.

WHY DIDN'T THEY CALL MY CELL?

HE SAID HE DIDN'T KNOW IT.

THEN *HE* PROBABLY ISN'T ANYONE IMPORTANT.

HE SAYS HIS NAME IS EZEKIEL.

SHIT.

I'LL TAKE IT FROM HERE.

I CAN EXPLAIN.

I HAVE YOUR AGENTS COMPLETELY SURROUNDED, AND THEY DON'T EVEN KNOW IT.

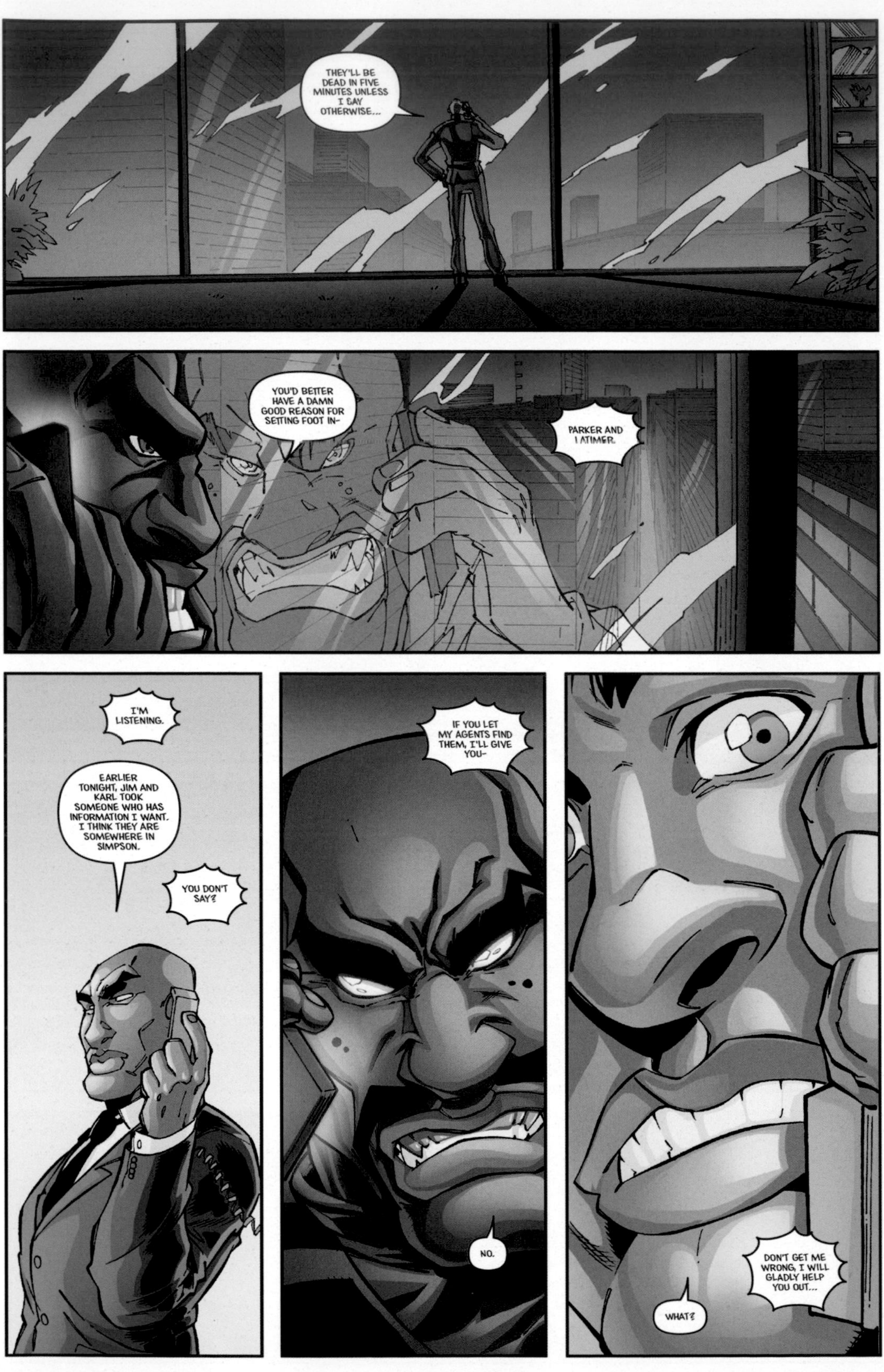
THEY'LL BE DEAD IN FIVE MINUTES UNLESS I SAY OTHERWISE...
YOU'D BETTER HAVE A DAMN GOOD REASON FOR SETTING FOOT IN-
PARKER AND LATIMER.
I'M LISTENING.
EARLIER TONIGHT, JIM AND KARL TOOK SOMEONE WHO HAS INFORMATION I WANT. I THINK THEY ARE SOMEWHERE IN SIMPSON.
YOU DON'T SAY?
IF YOU LET MY AGENTS FIND THEM, I'LL GIVE YOU-
NO.
WHAT?
DON'T GET ME WRONG, I WILL GLADLY HELP YOU OUT...

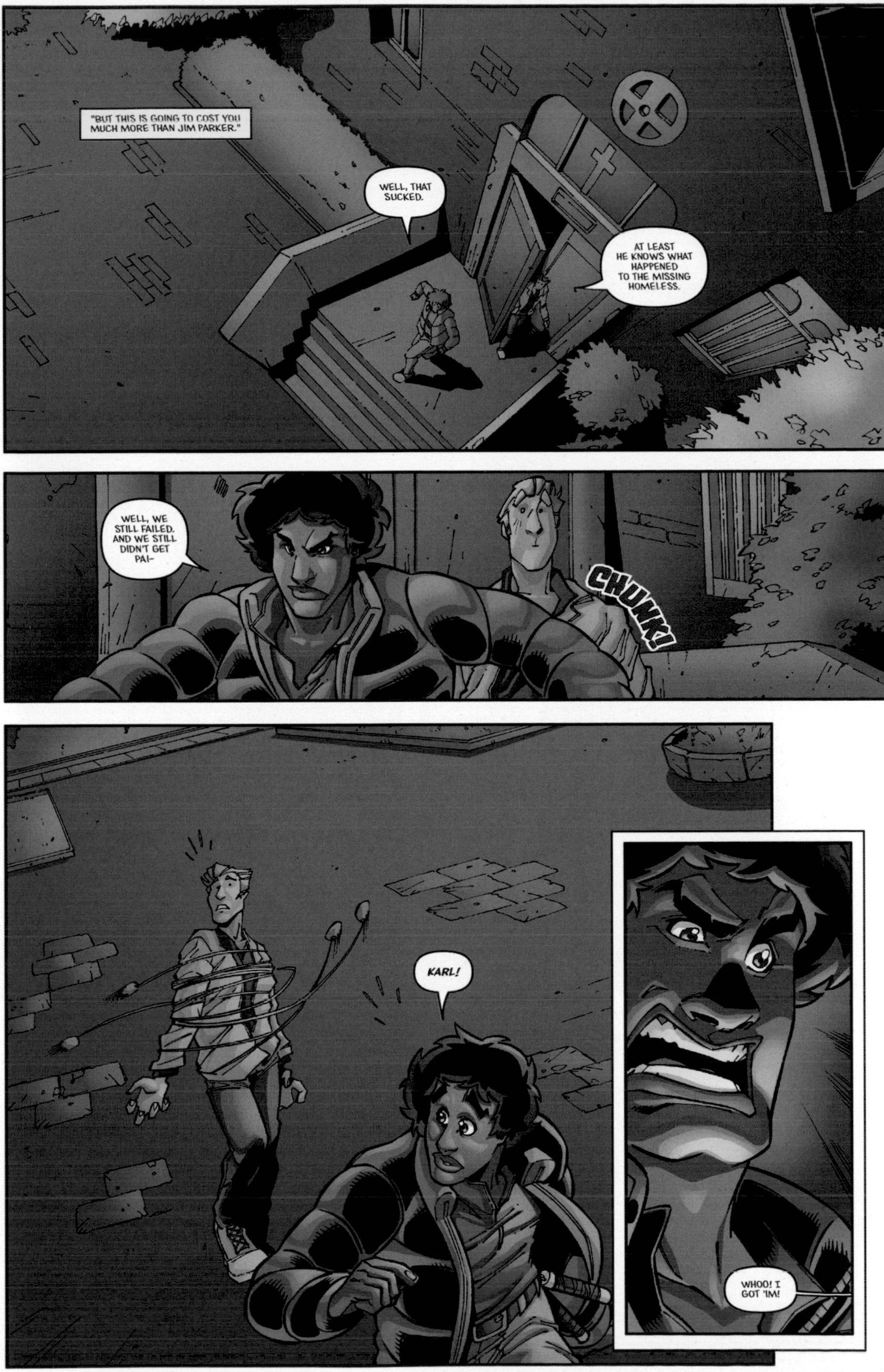
"BUT THIS IS GOING TO COST YOU MUCH MORE THAN JIM PARKER."
WELL, THAT SUCKED.
AT LEAST HE KNOWS WHAT HAPPENED TO THE MISSING HOMELESS.
WELL, WE STILL FAILED. AND WE STILL DIDN'T GET PAI-
CHUNK!
KARL!
WHOO! I GOT 'IM!

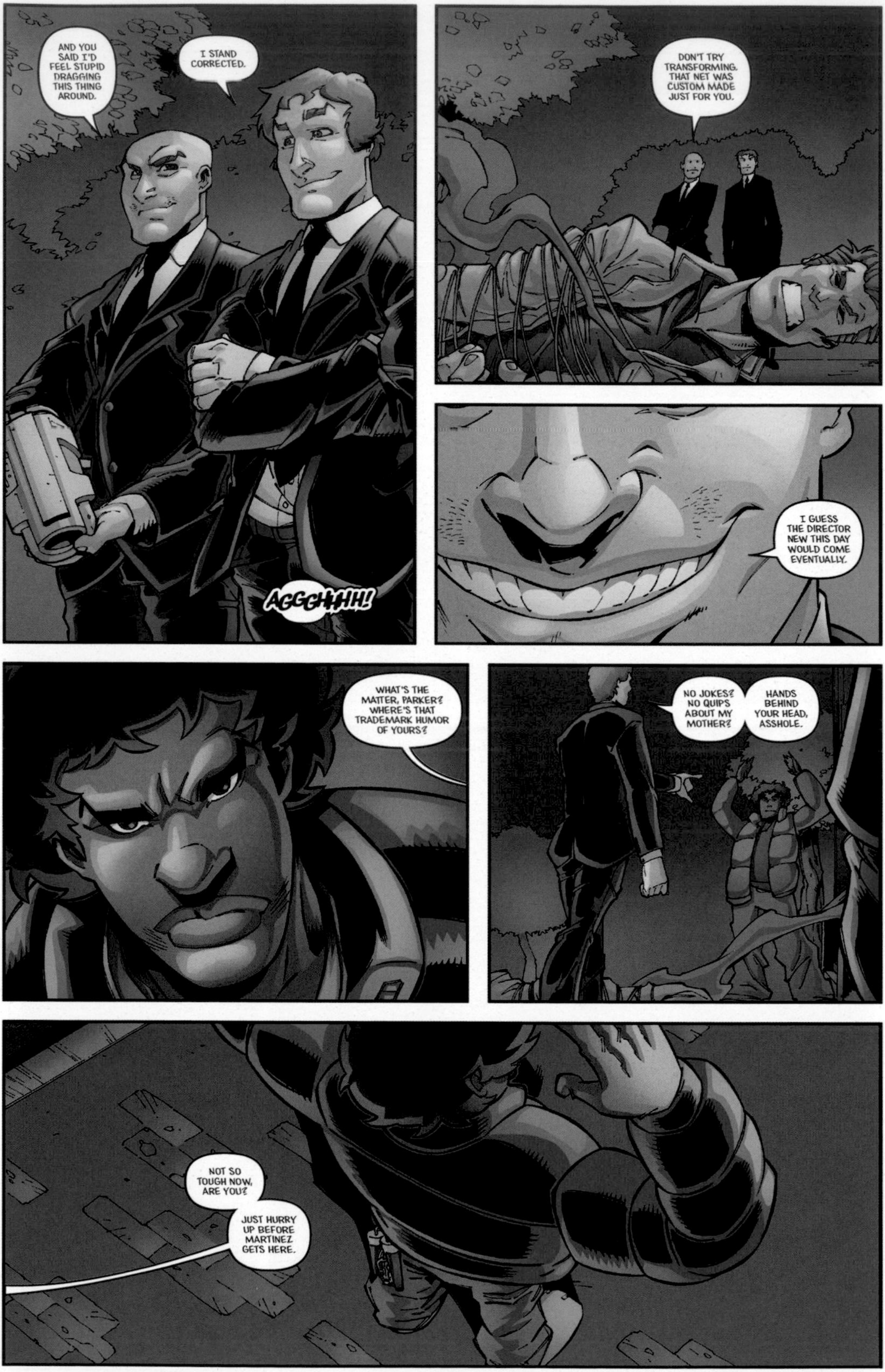
AND YOU SAID I'D FEEL STUPID DRAGGING THIS THING AROUND.
I STAND CORRECTED.
AGGGHHHH!
DON'T TRY TRANSFORMING. THAT NET WAS CUSTOM MADE JUST FOR YOU.
I GUESS THE DIRECTOR NEW THIS DAY WOULD COME EVENTUALLY.
WHAT'S THE MATTER, PARKER? WHERE'S THAT TRADEMARK HUMOR OF YOURS?
NO JOKES? NO QUIPS ABOUT MY MOTHER?
HANDS BEHIND YOUR HEAD, ASSHOLE.
NOT SO TOUGH NOW, ARE YOU?
JUST HURRY UP BEFORE MARTINEZ GETS HERE.

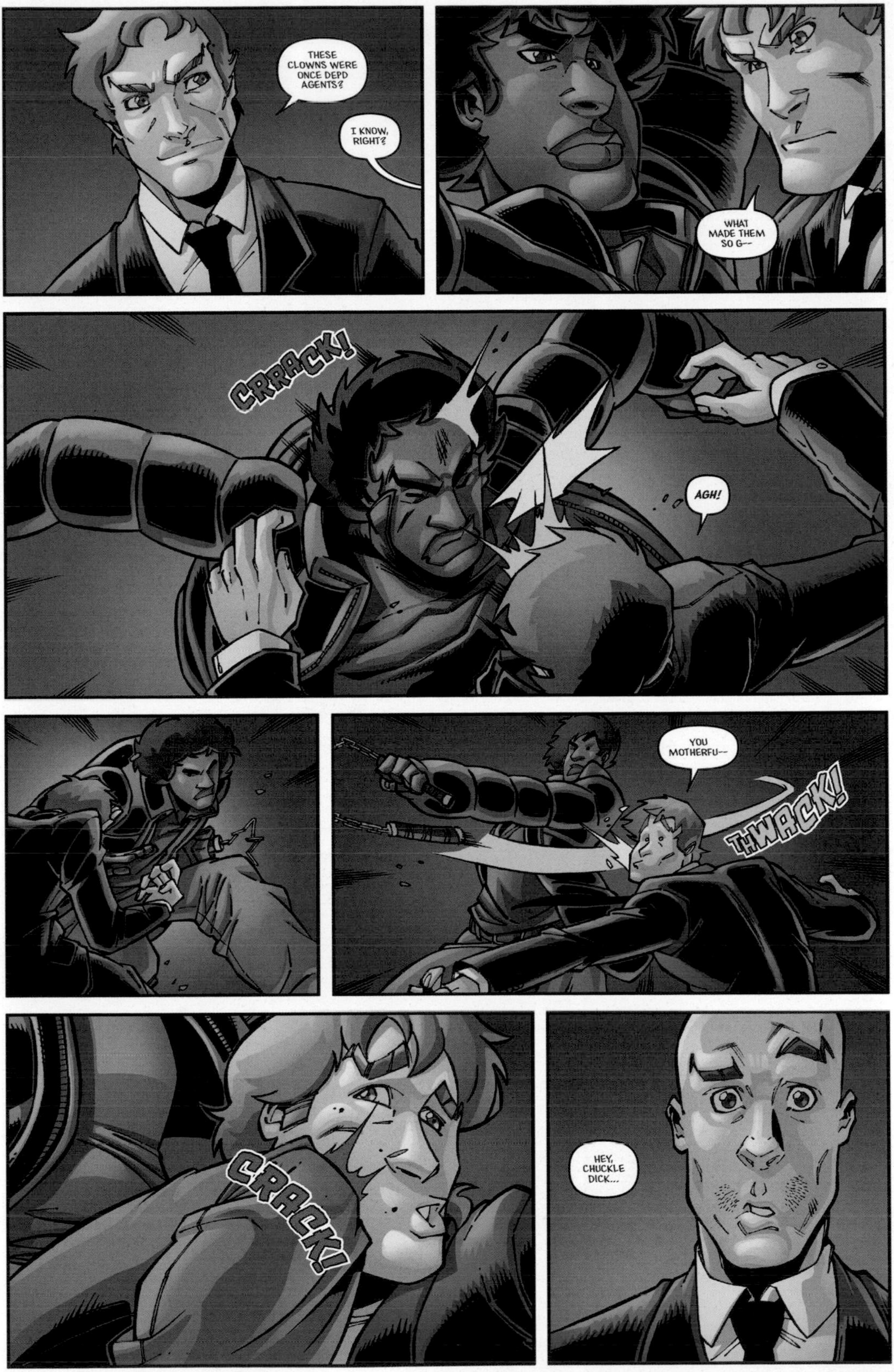
THESE CLOWNS WERE ONCE DEPD AGENTS?
I KNOW, RIGHT?
WHAT MADE THEM SO G--
CRRACK!
AGH!
YOU MOTHERFU--
THWACK!
CRACK!
HEY, CHUCKLE DICK...

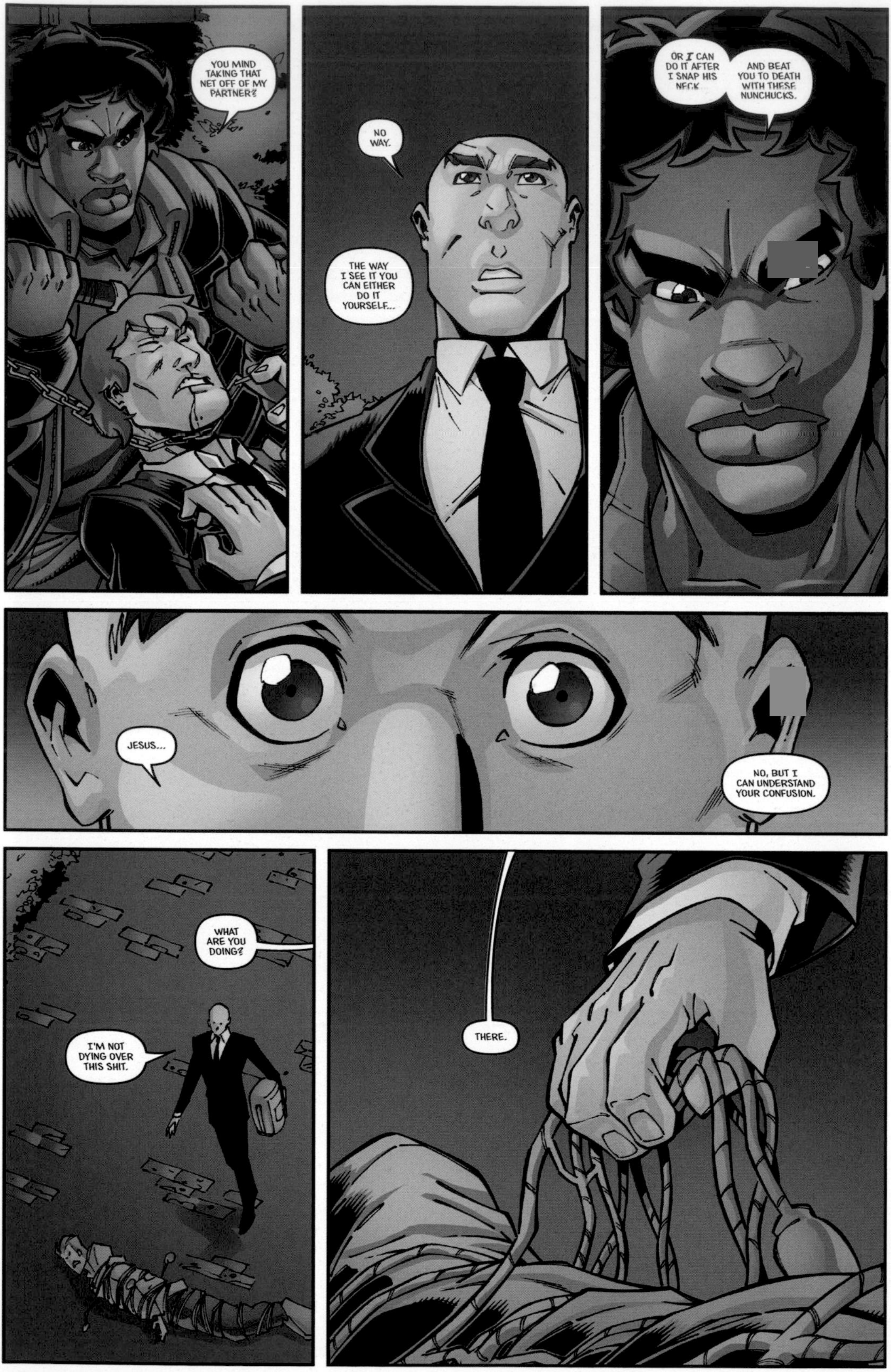

YOU MIND TAKING THAT NET OFF OF MY PARTNER?
NO WAY.
THE WAY I SEE IT YOU CAN EITHER DO IT YOURSELF...
OR I CAN DO IT AFTER I SNAP HIS NECK
AND BEAT YOU TO DEATH WITH THESE NUNCHUCKS.
JESUS...
NO, BUT I CAN UNDERSTAND YOUR CONFUSION.
WHAT ARE YOU DOING?
I'M NOT DYING OVER THIS SHIT.
THERE.

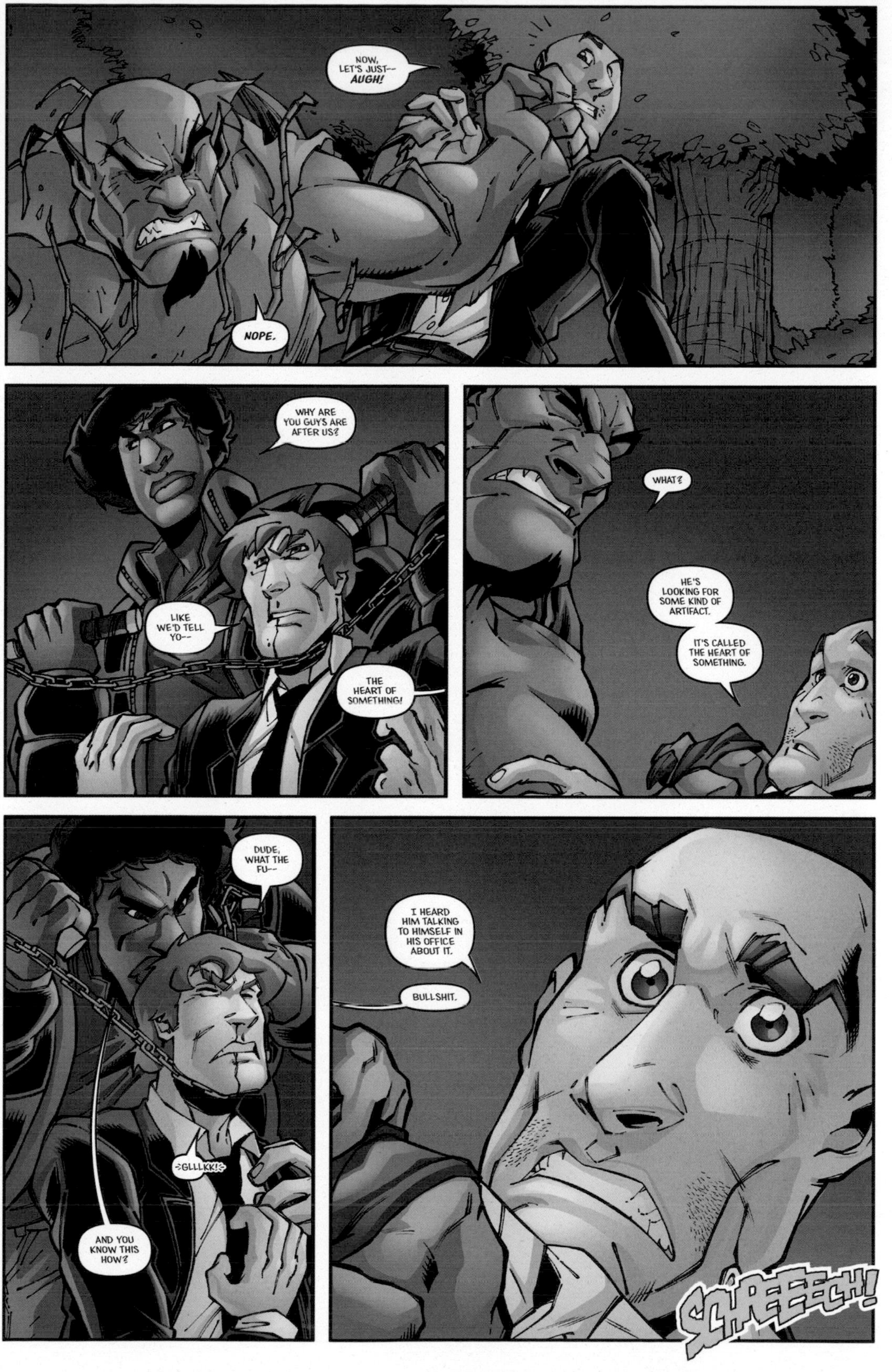
NOW, LET'S JUST-- AUGH!
NOPE.
WHY ARE YOU GUYS ARE AFTER US?
LIKE WE'D TELL YO--
THE HEART OF SOMETHING!
WHAT?
HE'S LOOKING FOR SOME KIND OF ARTIFACT.
IT'S CALLED THE HEART OF SOMETHING.
DUDE, WHAT THE FU--
-GLLLKK!-
AND YOU KNOW THIS HOW?
I HEARD HIM TALKING TO HIMSELF IN HIS OFFICE ABOUT IT.
BULLSHIT.
SCHREEECH!

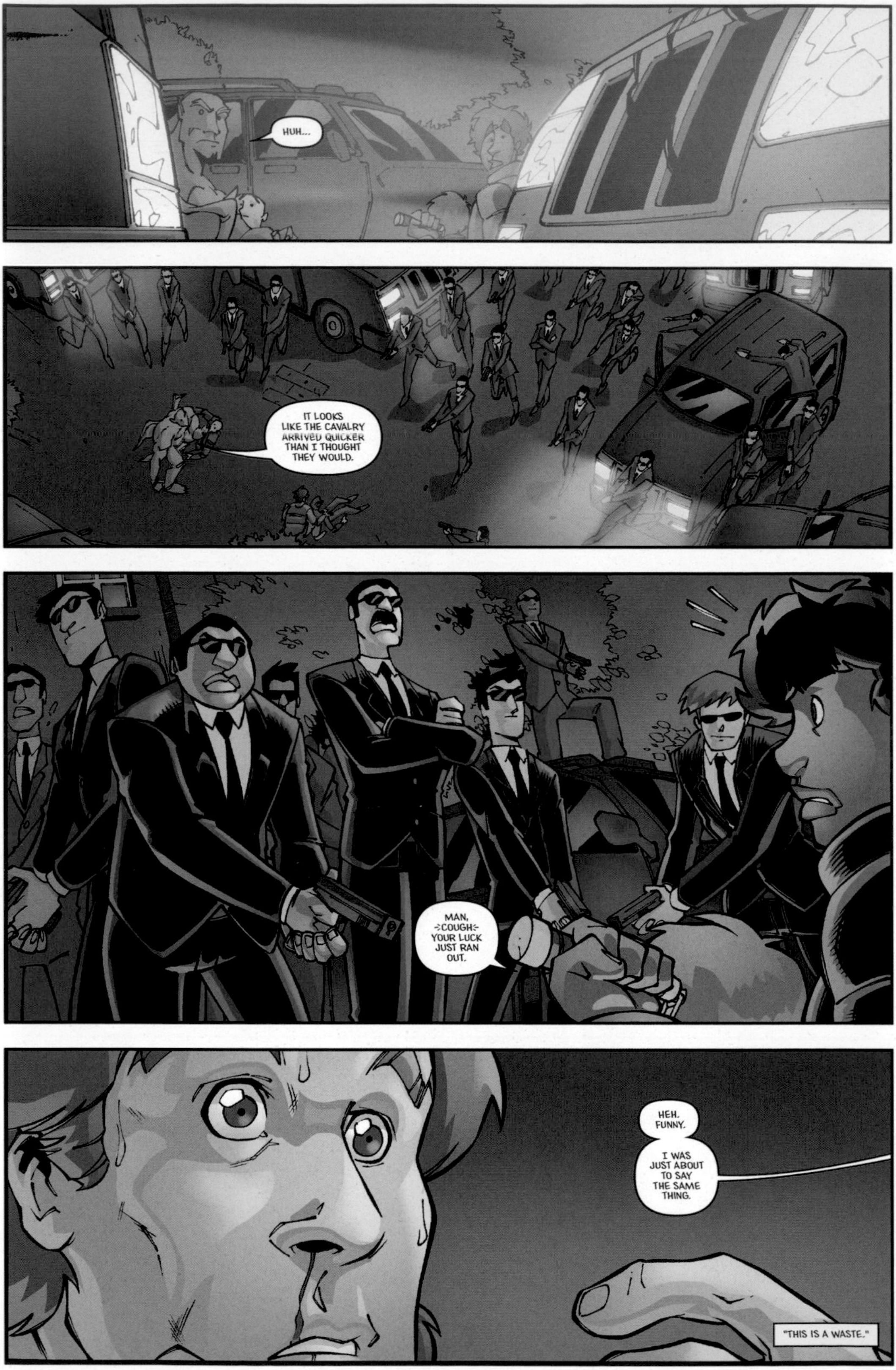
HUH...
IT LOOKS LIKE THE CAVALRY ARRIVED QUICKER THAN I THOUGHT THEY WOULD.
MAN, -COUGH- YOUR LUCK JUST RAN OUT.
HEH. FUNNY.
I WAS JUST ABOUT TO SAY THE SAME THING.
"THIS IS A WASTE."

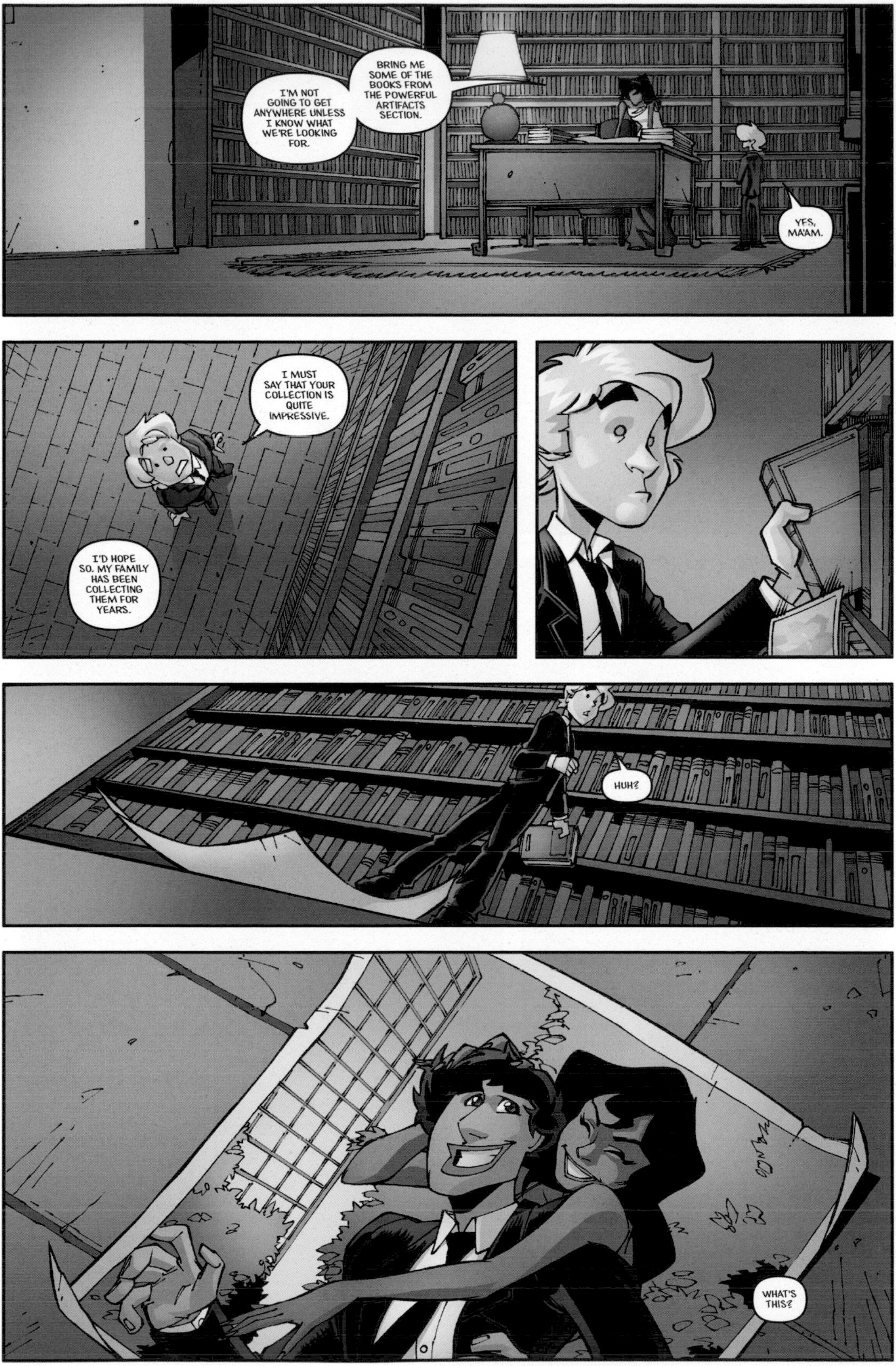
I'M NOT GOING TO GET ANYWHERE UNLESS I KNOW WHAT WE'RE LOOKING FOR.
BRING ME SOME OF THE BOOKS FROM THE POWERFUL ARTIFACTS SECTION.
YES, MA'AM.
I MUST SAY THAT YOUR COLLECTION IS QUITE IMPRESSIVE.
I'D HOPE SO. MY FAMILY HAS BEEN COLLECTING THEM FOR YEARS.
HUH?
WHAT'S THIS?

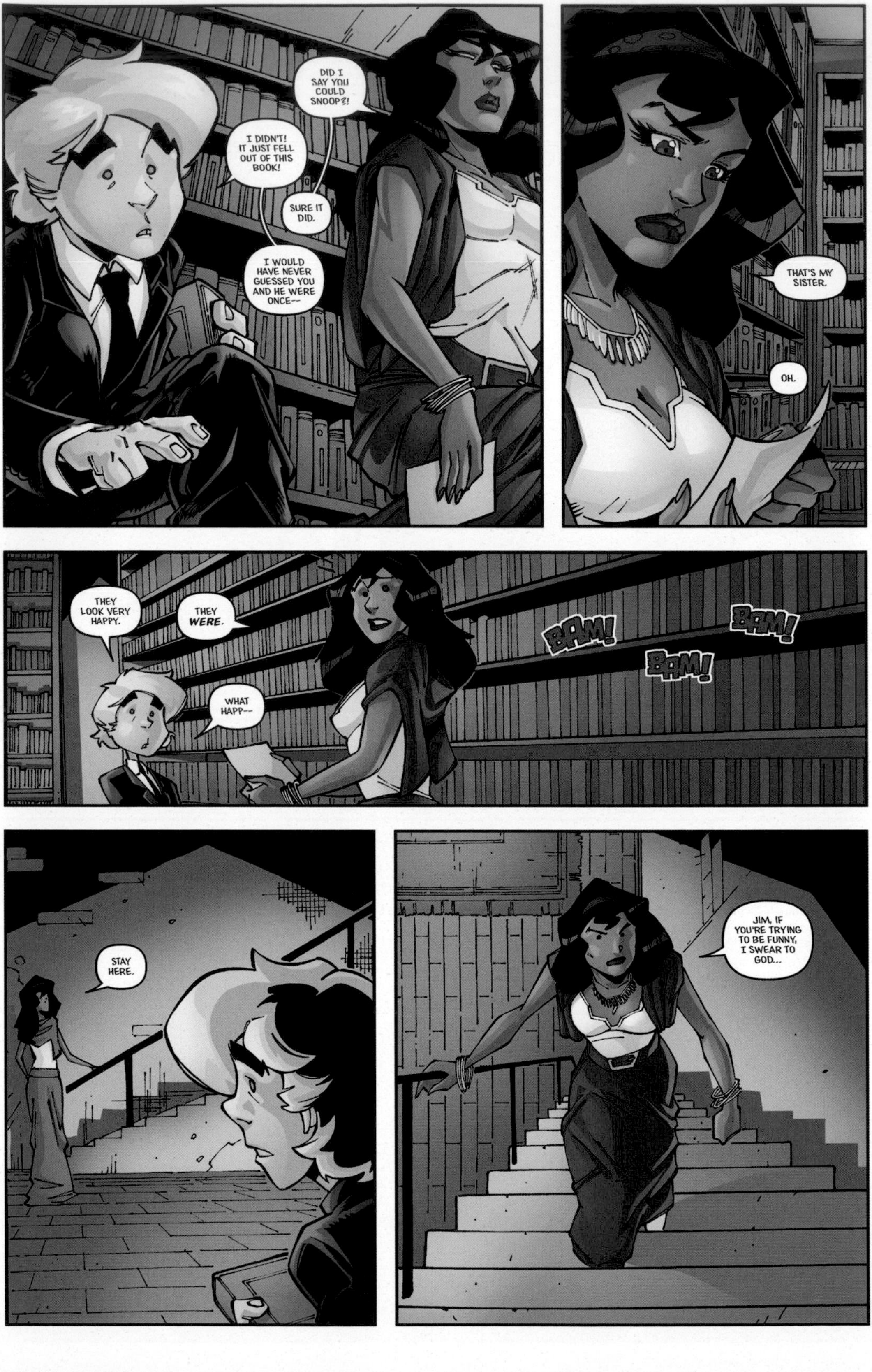
DID I SAY YOU COULD SNOOP?!
I DIDN'T! IT JUST FELL OUT OF THIS BOOK!
SURE IT DID.
I WOULD HAVE NEVER GUESSED YOU AND HE WERE ONCE--
THAT'S MY SISTER.
OH.
THEY LOOK VERY HAPPY.
THEY *WERE*.
WHAT HAPP--
BAM!
BAM!
BAM!
STAY HERE.
JIM, IF YOU'RE TRYING TO BE FUNNY, I SWEAR TO GOD...

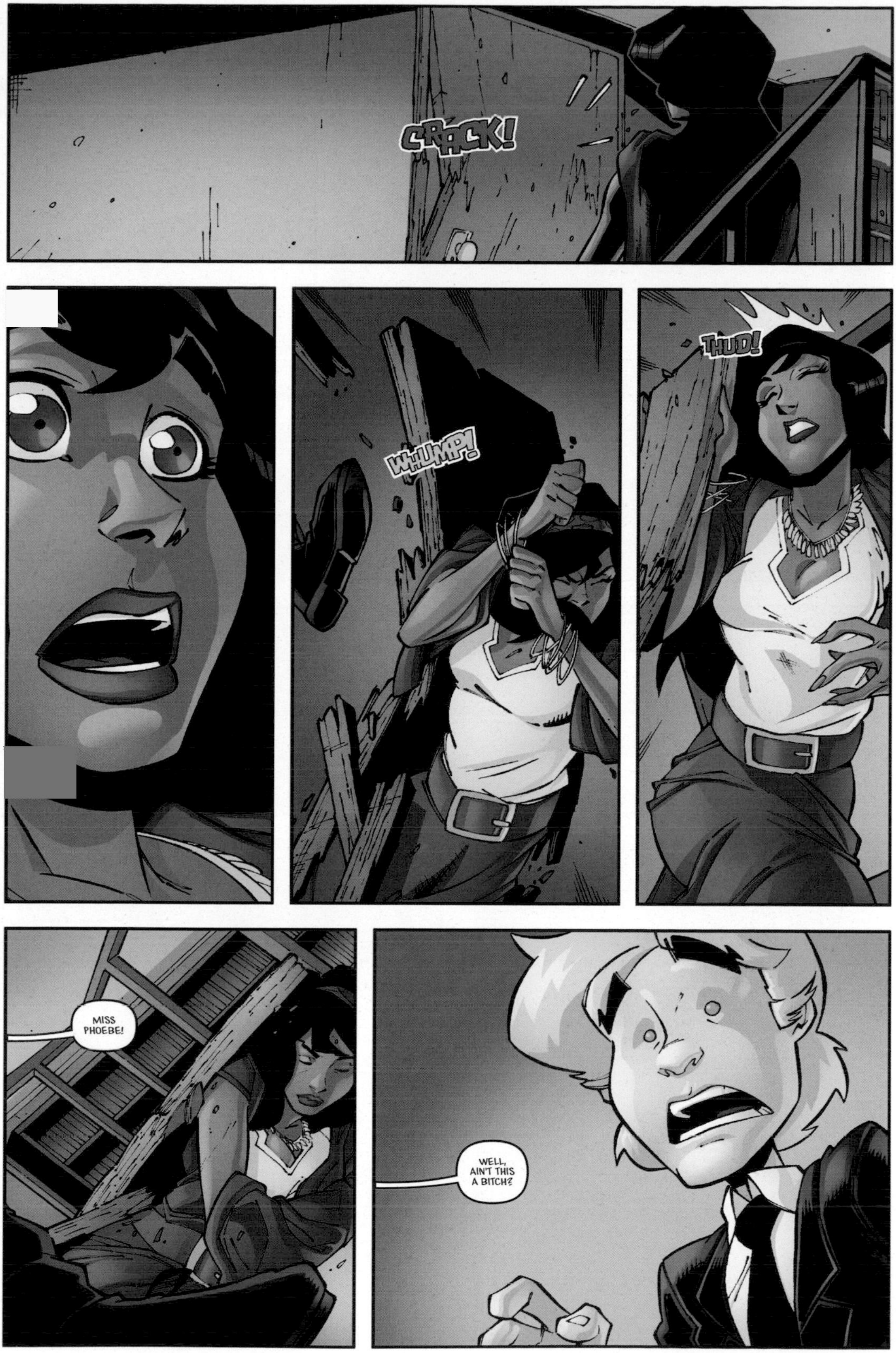
CRACK!
WHUMP!
THUD!
MISS PHOEBE!
WELL, AIN'T THIS A BITCH?

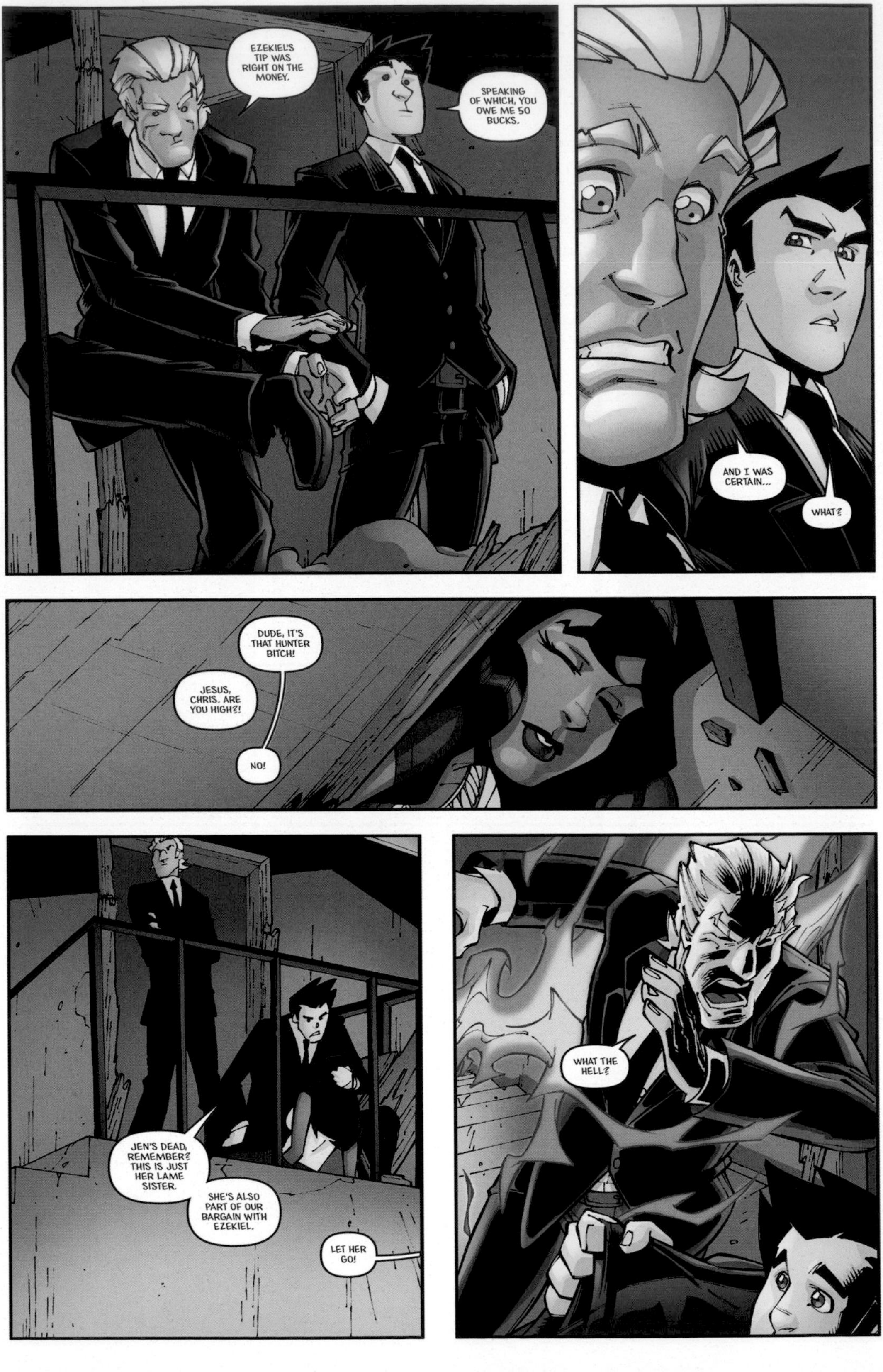
EZEKIEL'S TIP WAS RIGHT ON THE MONEY.
SPEAKING OF WHICH, YOU OWE ME 50 BUCKS.
AND I WAS CERTAIN...
WHAT?
DUDE, IT'S THAT HUNTER BITCH!
JESUS, CHRIS. ARE YOU HIGH?!
NO!
JEN'S DEAD, REMEMBER? THIS IS JUST HER LAME SISTER.
SHE'S ALSO PART OF OUR BARGAIN WITH EZEKIEL.
LET HER GO!
WHAT THE HELL?

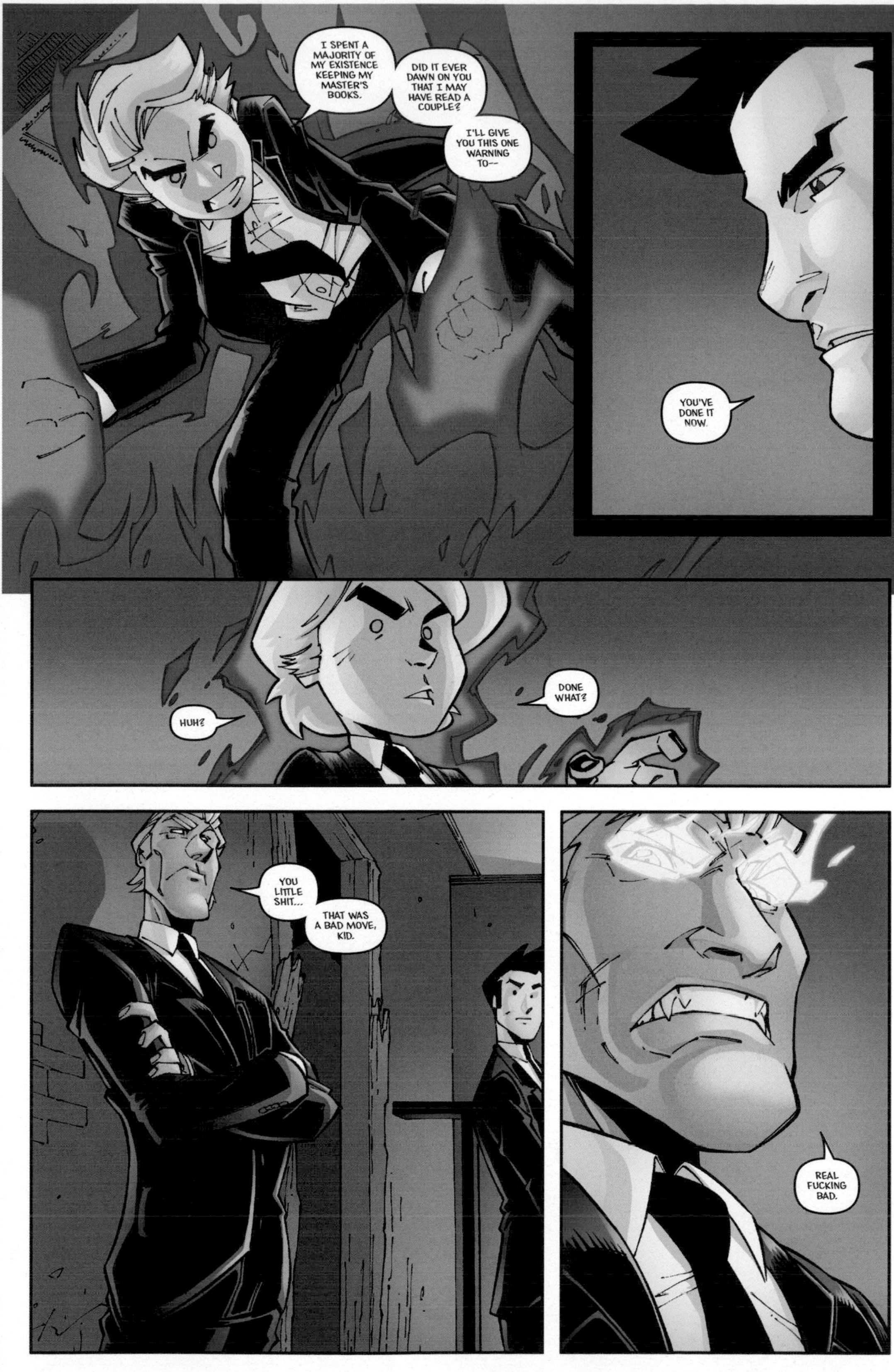
I SPENT A MAJORITY OF MY EXISTENCE KEEPING MY MASTER'S BOOKS.
DID IT EVER DAWN ON YOU THAT I MAY HAVE READ A COUPLE?
I'LL GIVE YOU THIS ONE WARNING TO--
YOU'VE DONE IT NOW.
HUH?
DONE WHAT?
YOU LITTLE SHIT...
THAT WAS A BAD MOVE, KID.
REAL FUCKING BAD.

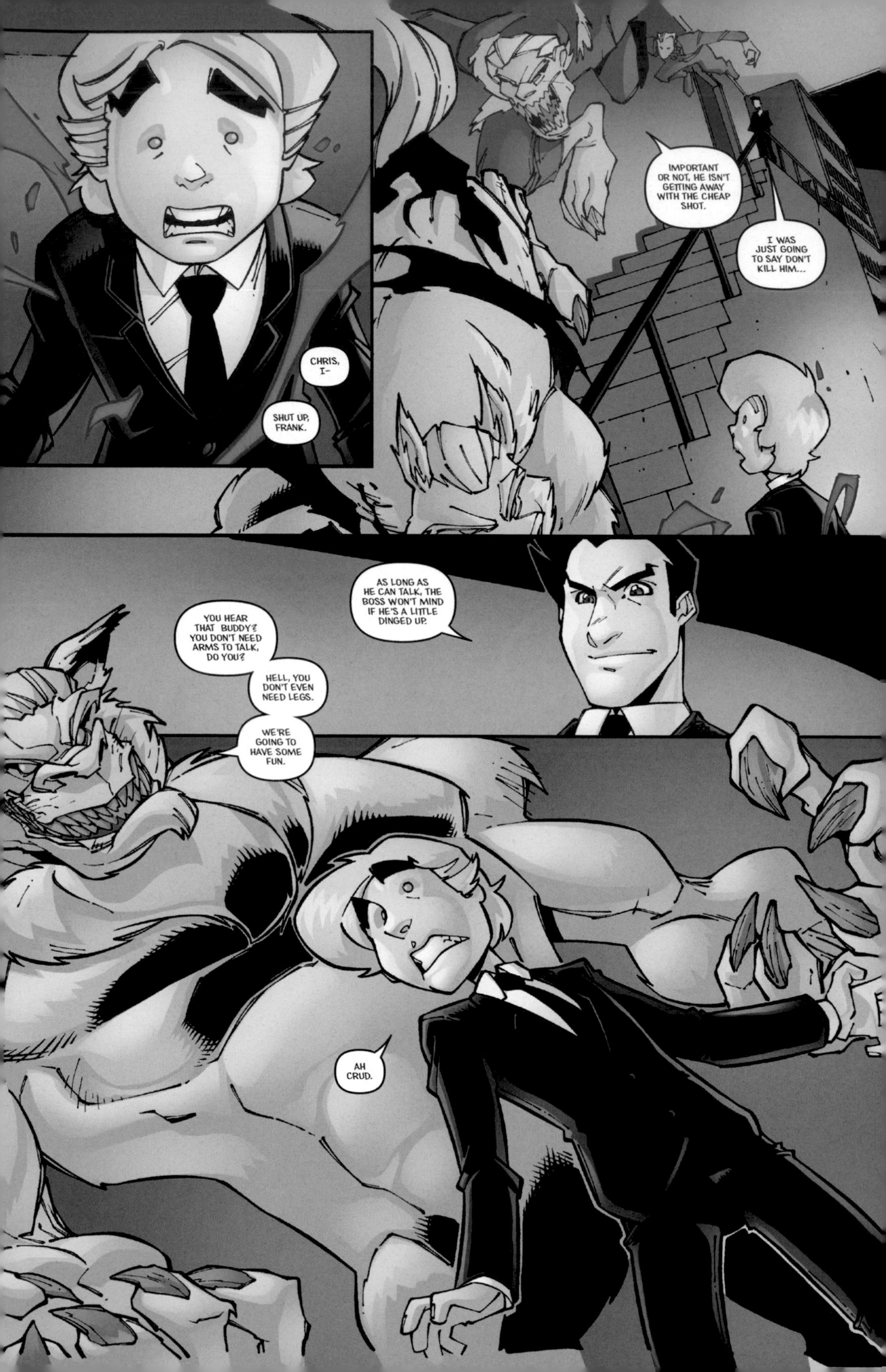
CHRIS, I-
SHUT UP, FRANK.
IMPORTANT OR NOT, HE ISN'T GETTING AWAY WITH THE CHEAP SHOT.
I WAS JUST GOING TO SAY DON'T KILL HIM...
AS LONG AS HE CAN TALK, THE BOSS WON'T MIND IF HE'S A LITTLE DINGED UP.
YOU HEAR THAT BUDDY? YOU DON'T NEED ARMS TO TALK, DO YOU?
HELL, YOU DON'T EVEN NEED LEGS.
WE'RE GOING TO HAVE SOME FUN.
AH CRUD.

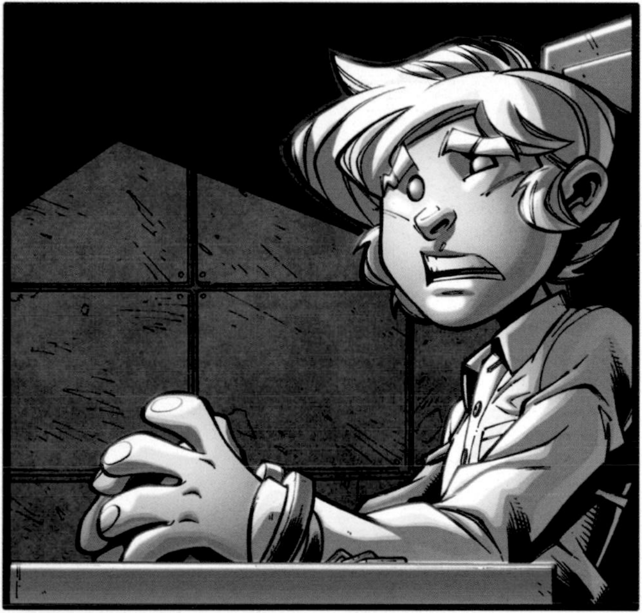

CHAPTER THREE

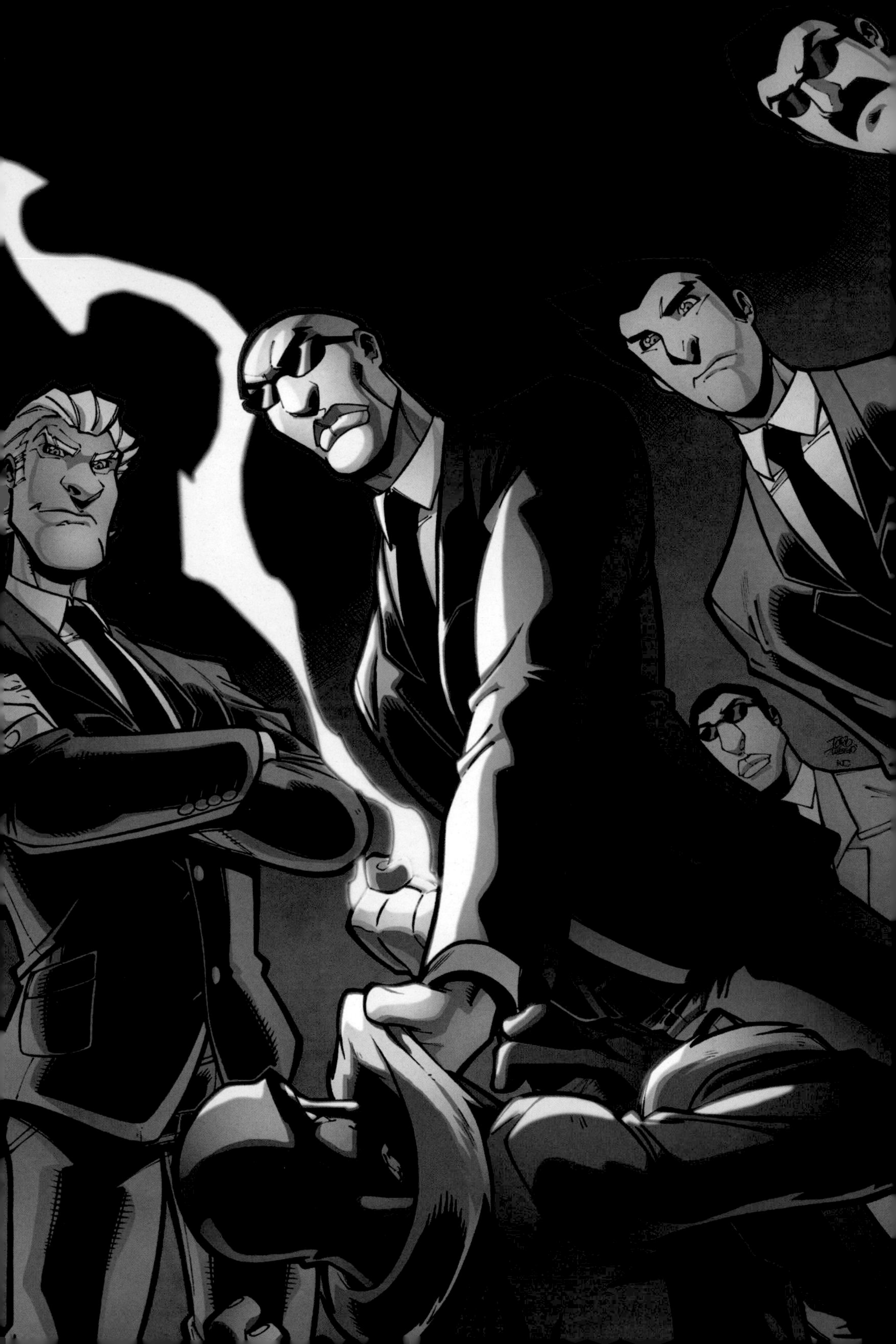

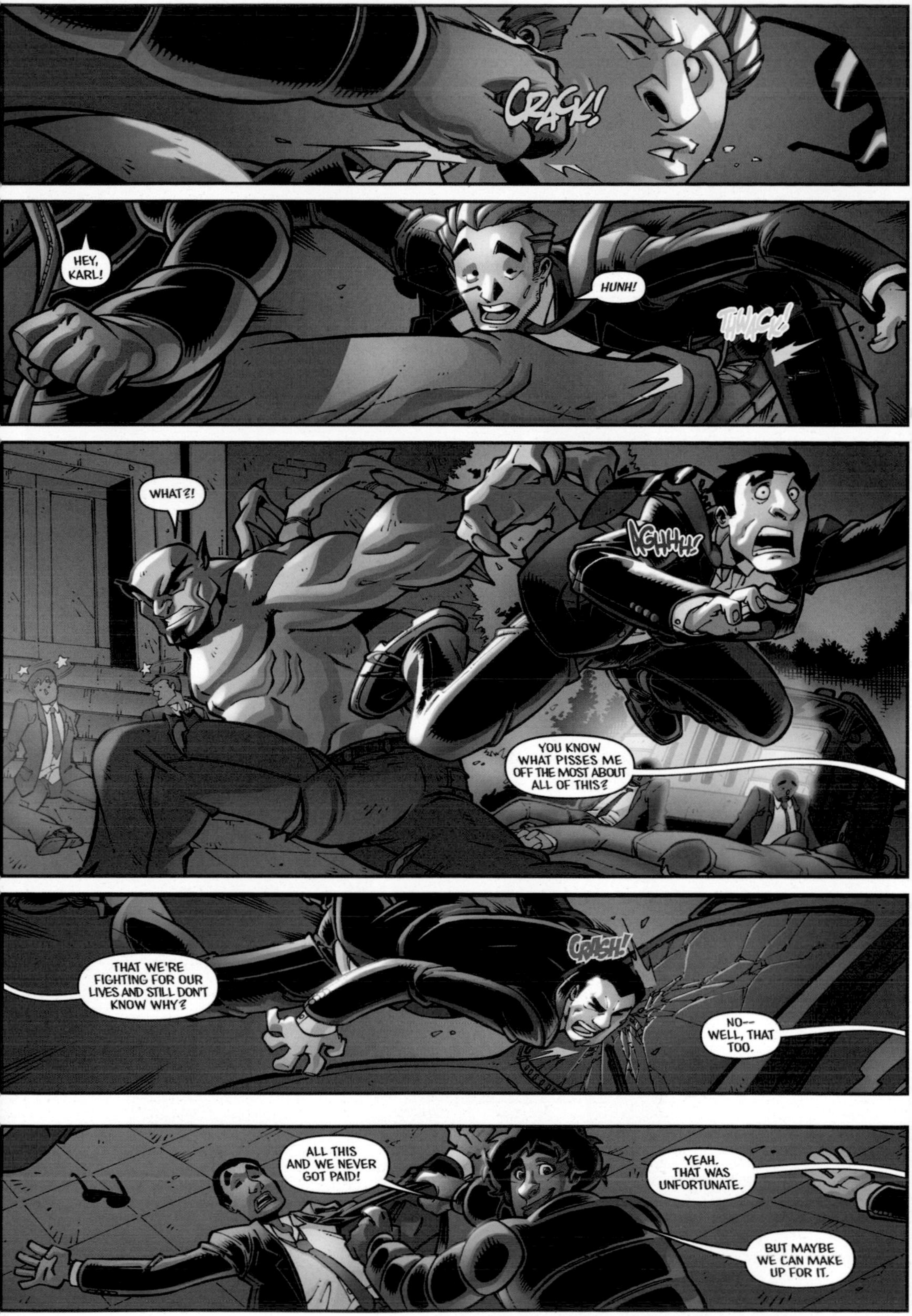
CRACK!
HEY, KARL!
HUNH!
THWACK!
WHAT?!
AGHHH!
YOU KNOW WHAT PISSES ME OFF THE MOST ABOUT ALL OF THIS?
CRASH!
THAT WE'RE FIGHTING FOR OUR LIVES AND STILL DON'T KNOW WHY?
NO-- WELL, THAT TOO.
ALL THIS AND WE NEVER GOT PAID!
YEAH. THAT WAS UNFORTUNATE.
BUT MAYBE WE CAN MAKE UP FOR IT.

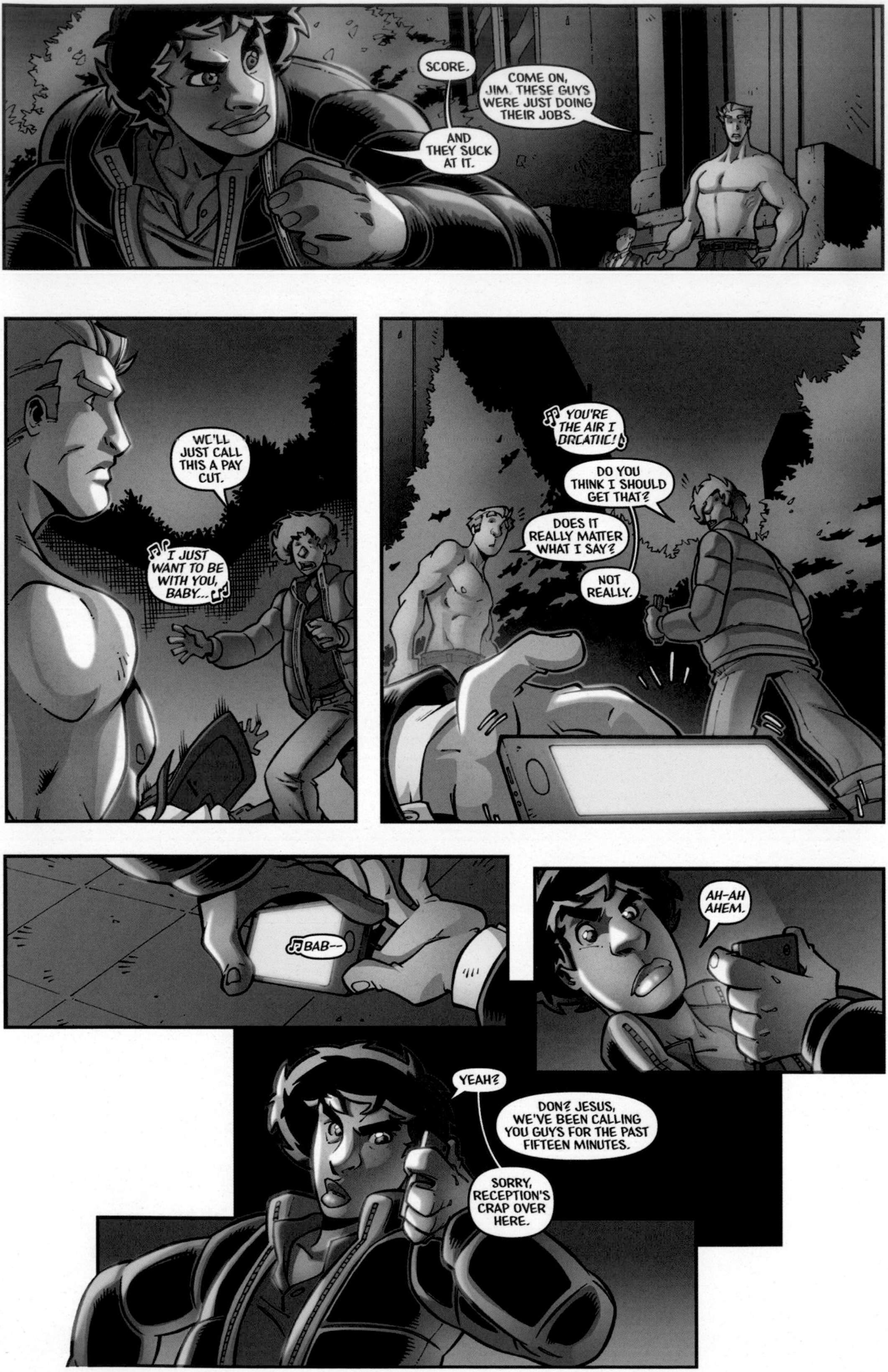
SCORE.
COME ON, JIM. THESE GUYS WERE JUST DOING THEIR JOBS.
AND THEY SUCK AT IT.
WE'LL JUST CALL THIS A PAY CUT.
I JUST WANT TO BE WITH YOU, BABY...
YOU'RE THE AIR I BREATHE!
DO YOU THINK I SHOULD GET THAT?
DOES IT REALLY MATTER WHAT I SAY?
NOT REALLY.
BAB--
AH-AH AHEM.
YEAH?
DON? JESUS, WE'VE BEEN CALLING YOU GUYS FOR THE PAST FIFTEEN MINUTES.
SORRY, RECEPTION'S CRAP OVER HERE.

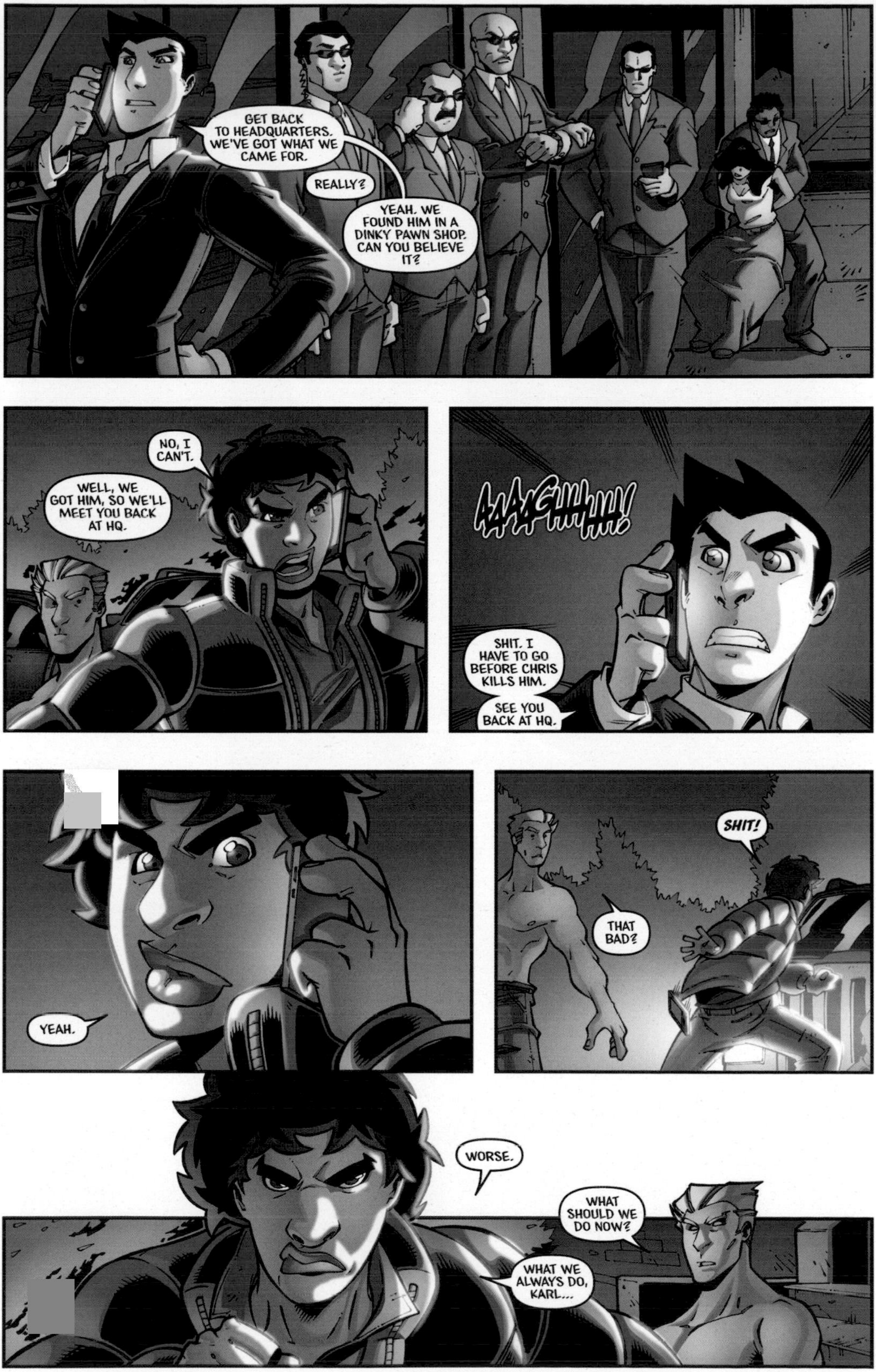
GET BACK TO HEADQUARTERS. WE'VE GOT WHAT WE CAME FOR.
REALLY?
YEAH. WE FOUND HIM IN A DINKY PAWN SHOP. CAN YOU BELIEVE IT?
NO, I CAN'T.
WELL, WE GOT HIM, SO WE'LL MEET YOU BACK AT HQ.
AAAAGHHHHH!
SHIT. I HAVE TO GO BEFORE CHRIS KILLS HIM.
SEE YOU BACK AT HQ.
YEAH.
SHIT!
THAT BAD?
WORSE.
WHAT SHOULD WE DO NOW?
WHAT WE ALWAYS DO, KARL...

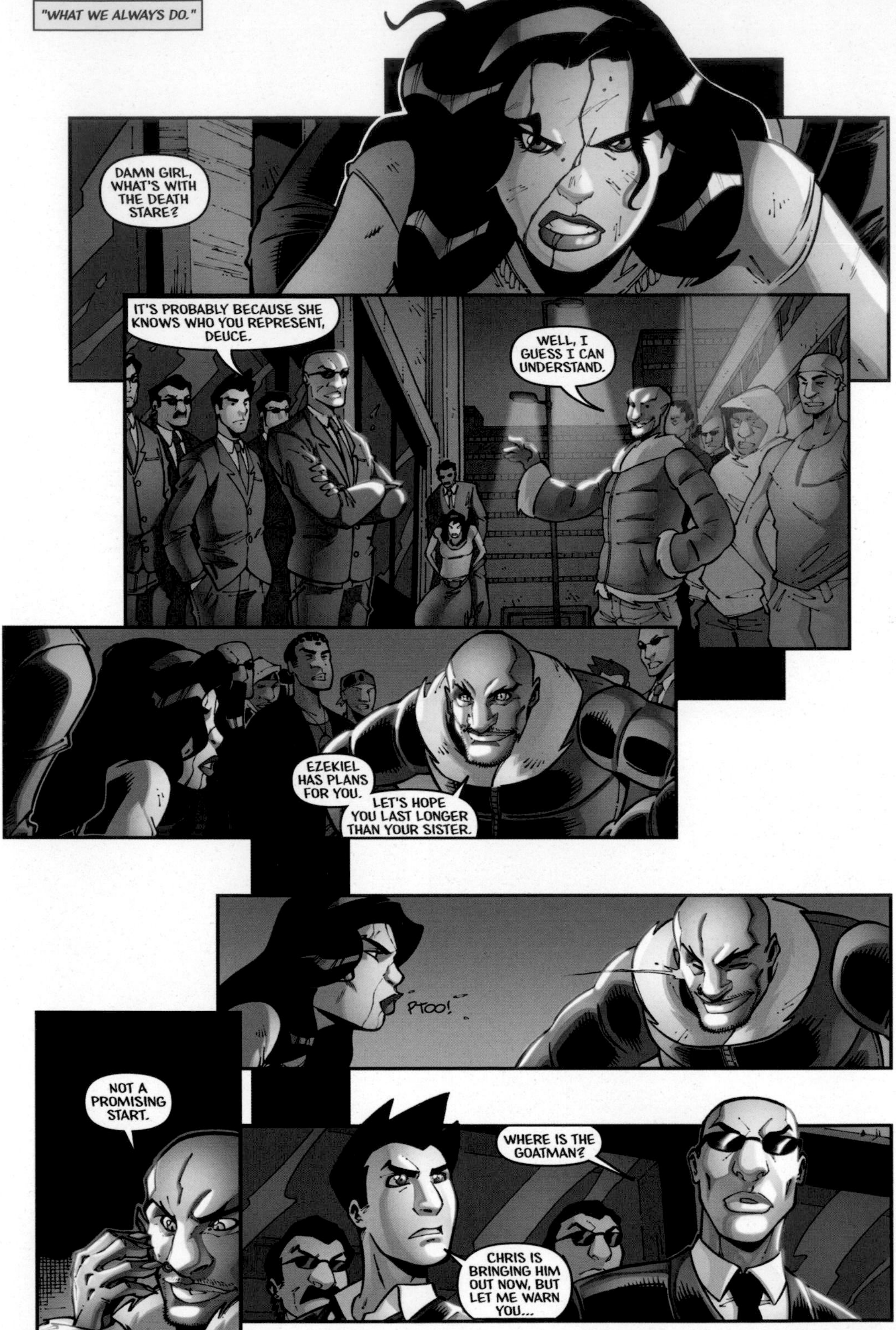
"WHAT WE ALWAYS DO."
DAMN GIRL, WHAT'S WITH THE DEATH STARE?
IT'S PROBABLY BECAUSE SHE KNOWS WHO YOU REPRESENT, DEUCE.
WELL, I GUESS I CAN UNDERSTAND.
EZEKIEL HAS PLANS FOR YOU.
LET'S HOPE YOU LAST LONGER THAN YOUR SISTER.
PTOO!
NOT A PROMISING START.
WHERE IS THE GOATMAN?
CHRIS IS BRINGING HIM OUT NOW, BUT LET ME WARN YOU...

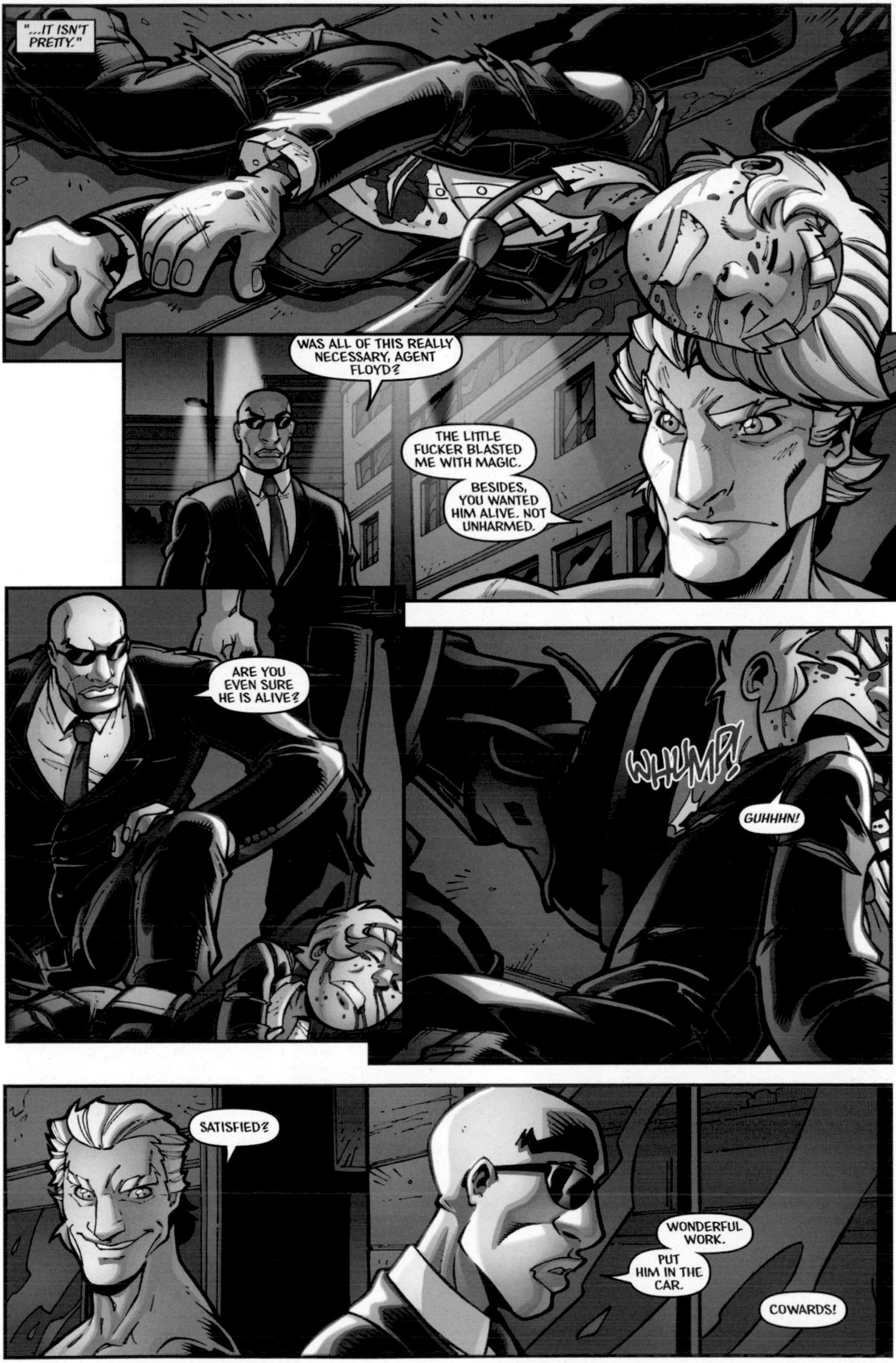
"...IT ISN'T PRETTY."
WAS ALL OF THIS REALLY NECESSARY, AGENT FLOYD?
THE LITTLE FUCKER BLASTED ME WITH MAGIC.
BESIDES, YOU WANTED HIM ALIVE. NOT UNHARMED.
ARE YOU EVEN SURE HE IS ALIVE?
WHUMP!
GUHHHN!
SATISFIED?
WONDERFUL WORK.
PUT HIM IN THE CAR.
COWARDS!

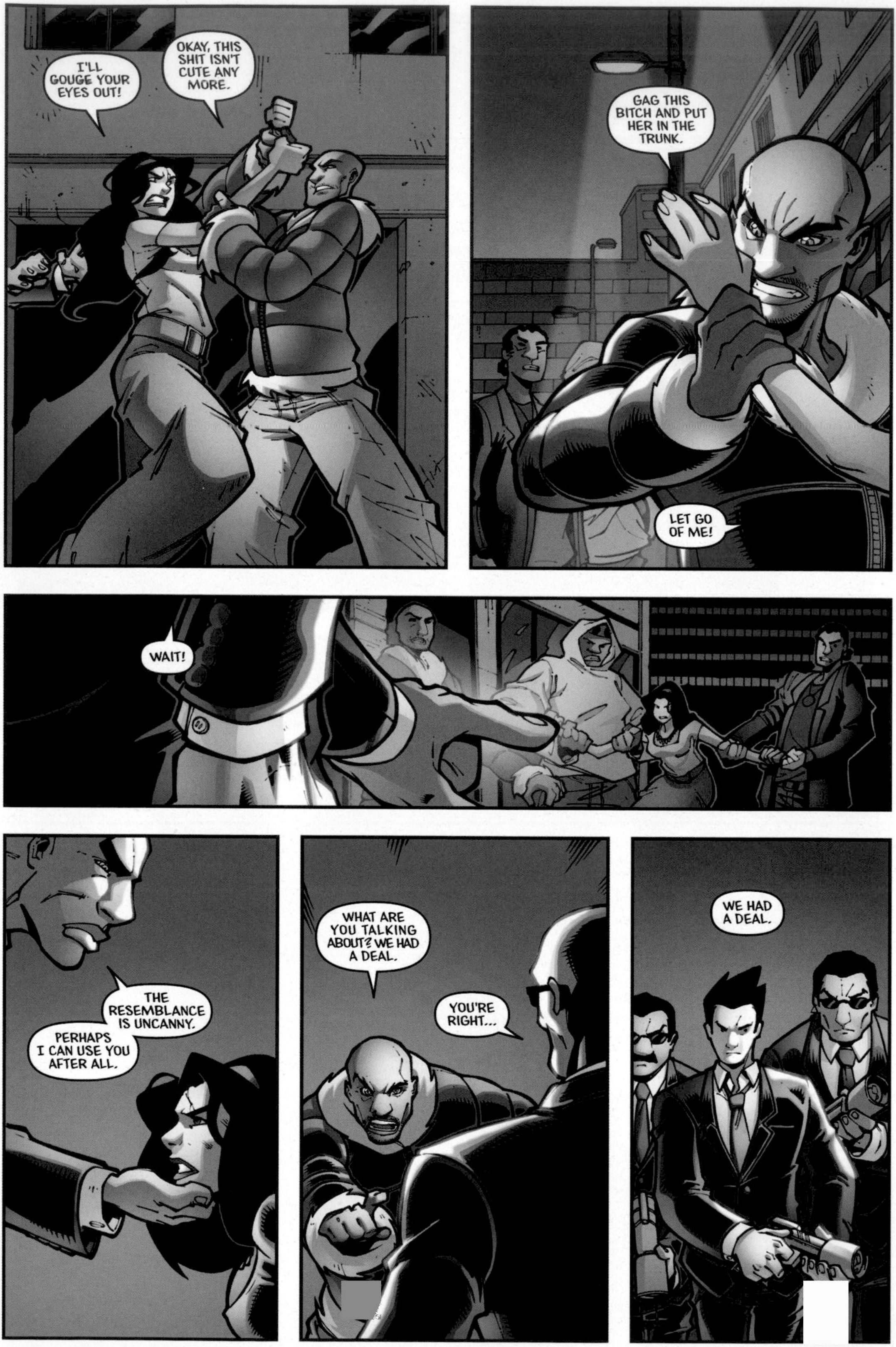
I'LL GOUGE YOUR EYES OUT!
OKAY, THIS SHIT ISN'T CUTE ANY MORE.
GAG THIS BITCH AND PUT HER IN THE TRUNK.
LET GO OF ME!
WAIT!
THE RESEMBLANCE IS UNCANNY.
PERHAPS I CAN USE YOU AFTER ALL.
WHAT ARE YOU TALKING ABOUT? WE HAD A DEAL.
YOU'RE RIGHT...
WE HAD A DEAL.

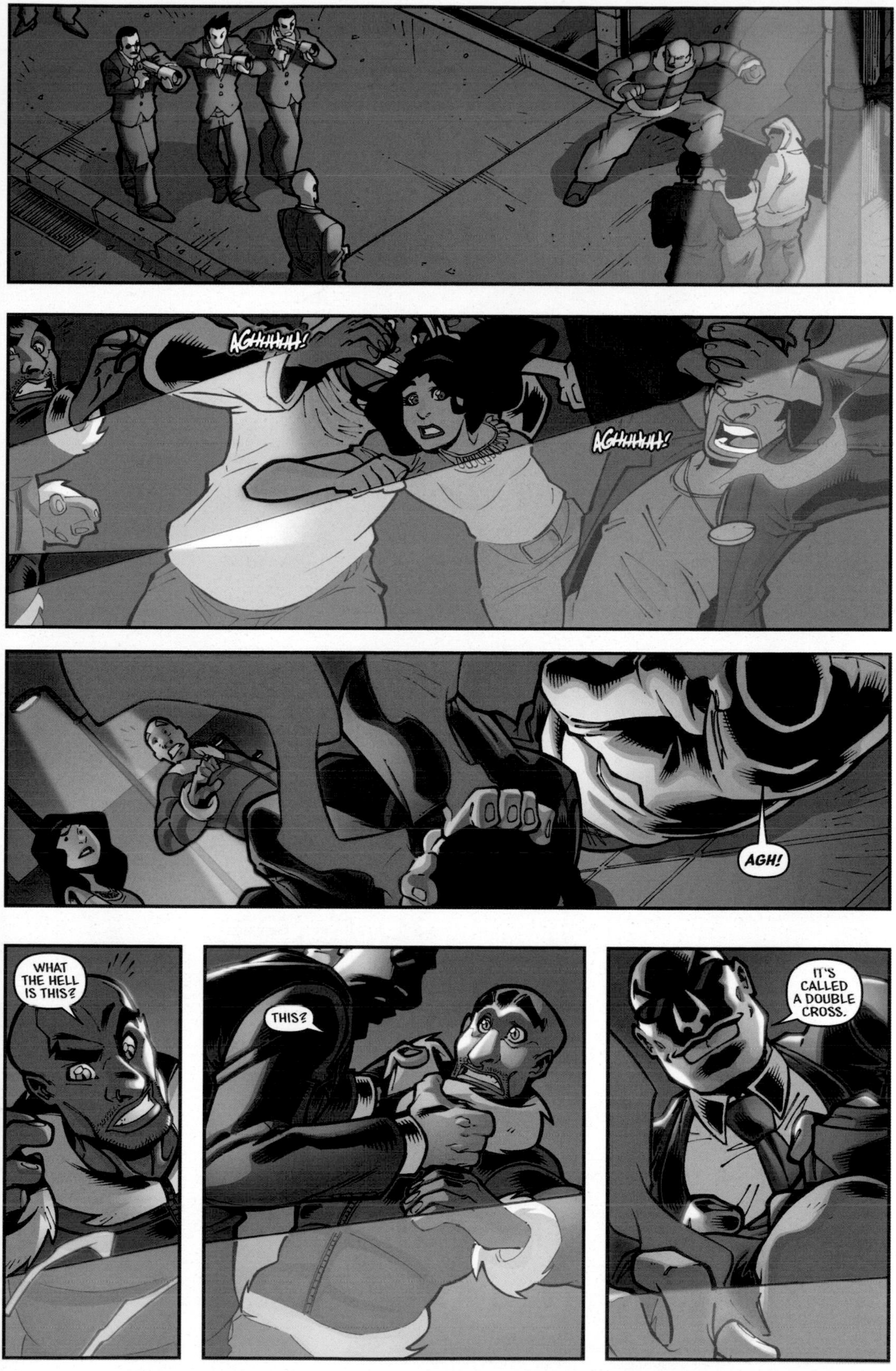
AGHHHHHH!
AGHHHHHH!
AGH!
WHAT THE HELL IS THIS?
THIS?
IT'S CALLED A DOUBLE CROSS.

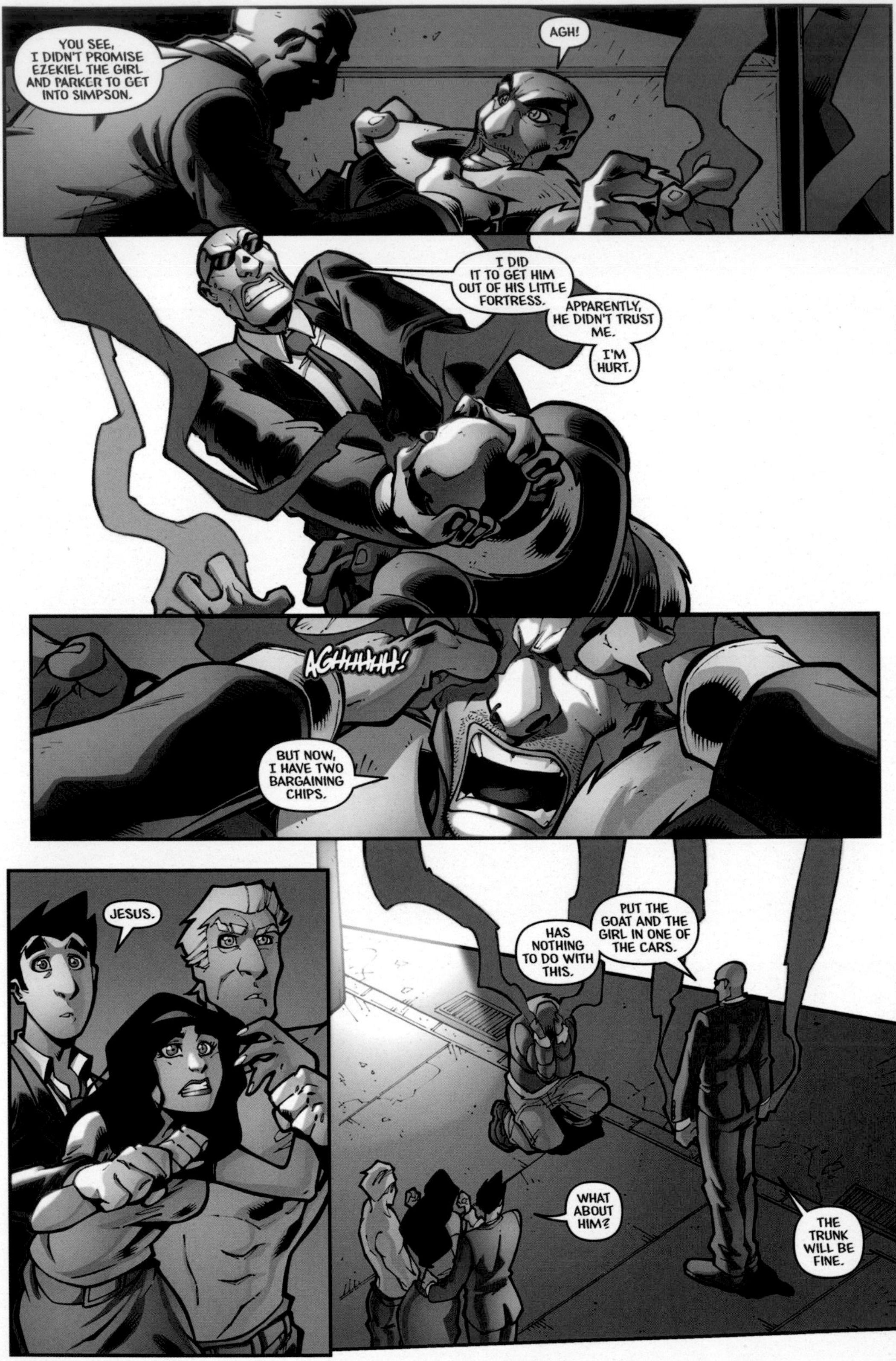
YOU SEE, I DIDN'T PROMISE EZEKIEL THE GIRL AND PARKER TO GET INTO SIMPSON.
AGH!
I DID IT TO GET HIM OUT OF HIS LITTLE FORTRESS.
APPARENTLY, HE DIDN'T TRUST ME.
I'M HURT.
AGHHHHH!
BUT NOW, I HAVE TWO BARGAINING CHIPS.
JESUS.
PUT THE GOAT AND THE GIRL IN ONE OF THE CARS.
HAS NOTHING TO DO WITH THIS.
WHAT ABOUT HIM?
THE TRUNK WILL BE FINE.

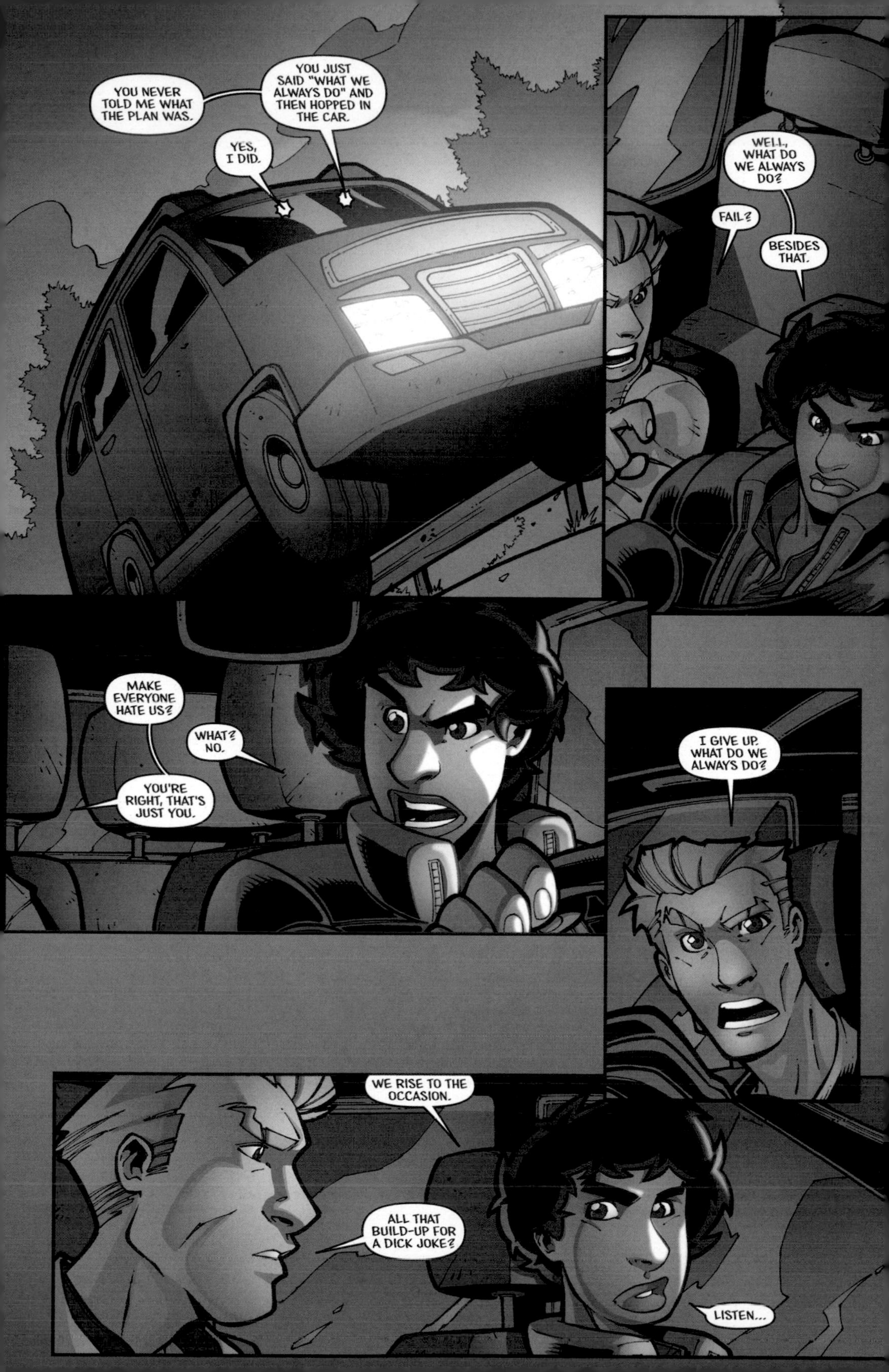
YOU NEVER TOLD ME WHAT THE PLAN WAS.
YOU JUST SAID "WHAT WE ALWAYS DO" AND THEN HOPPED IN THE CAR.
YES, I DID.
WELL, WHAT DO WE ALWAYS DO?
FAIL?
BESIDES THAT.
MAKE EVERYONE HATE US?
WHAT? NO.
YOU'RE RIGHT, THAT'S JUST YOU.
I GIVE UP. WHAT DO WE ALWAYS DO?
WE RISE TO THE OCCASION.
ALL THAT BUILD-UP FOR A DICK JOKE?
LISTEN...

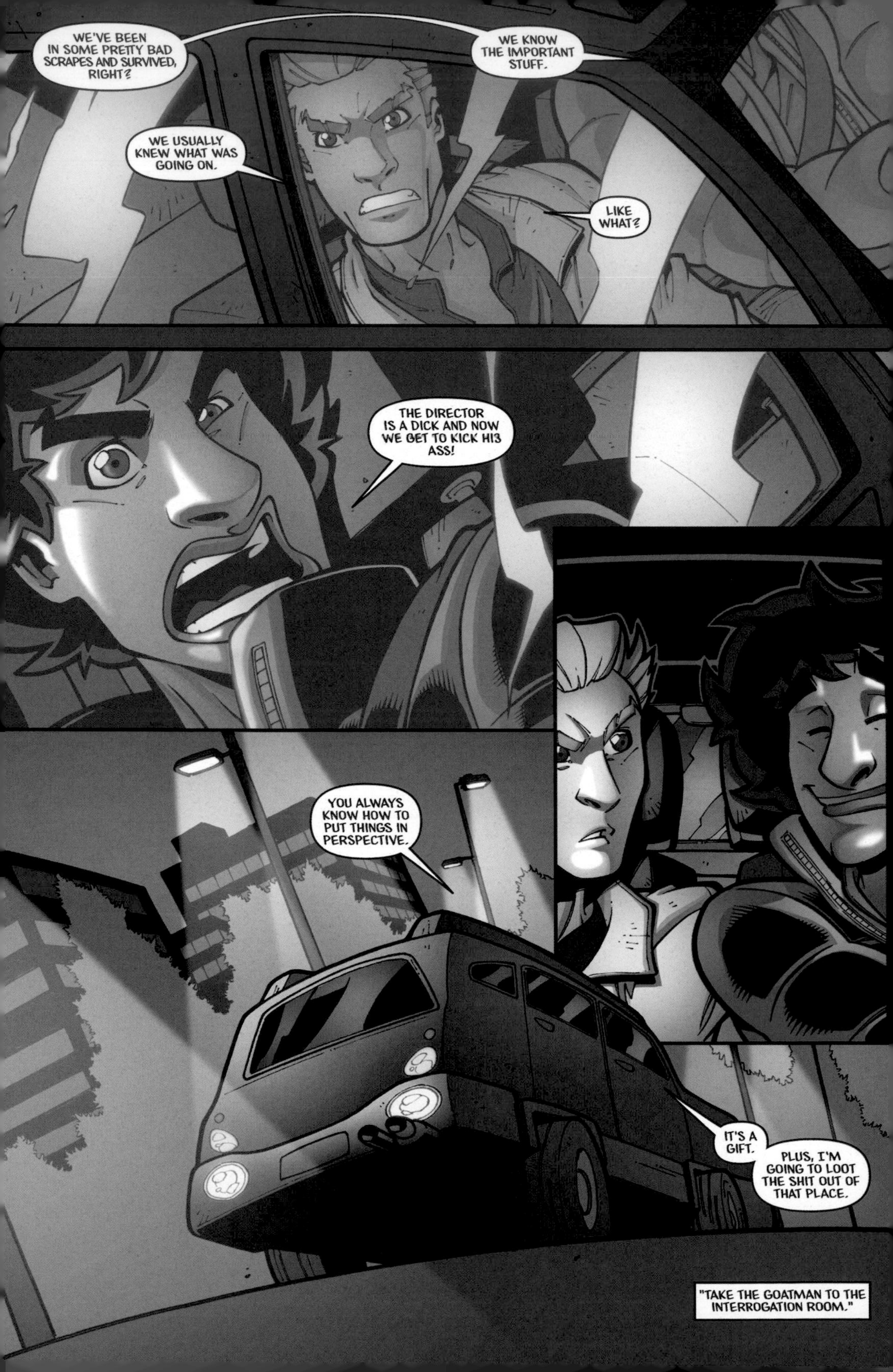
WE'VE BEEN IN SOME PRETTY BAD SCRAPES AND SURVIVED, RIGHT?
WE KNOW THE IMPORTANT STUFF.
WE USUALLY KNEW WHAT WAS GOING ON.
LIKE WHAT?
THE DIRECTOR IS A DICK AND NOW WE GET TO KICK HIS ASS!
YOU ALWAYS KNOW HOW TO PUT THINGS IN PERSPECTIVE.
IT'S A GIFT.
PLUS, I'M GOING TO LOOT THE SHIT OUT OF THAT PLACE.
"TAKE THE GOATMAN TO THE INTERROGATION ROOM."

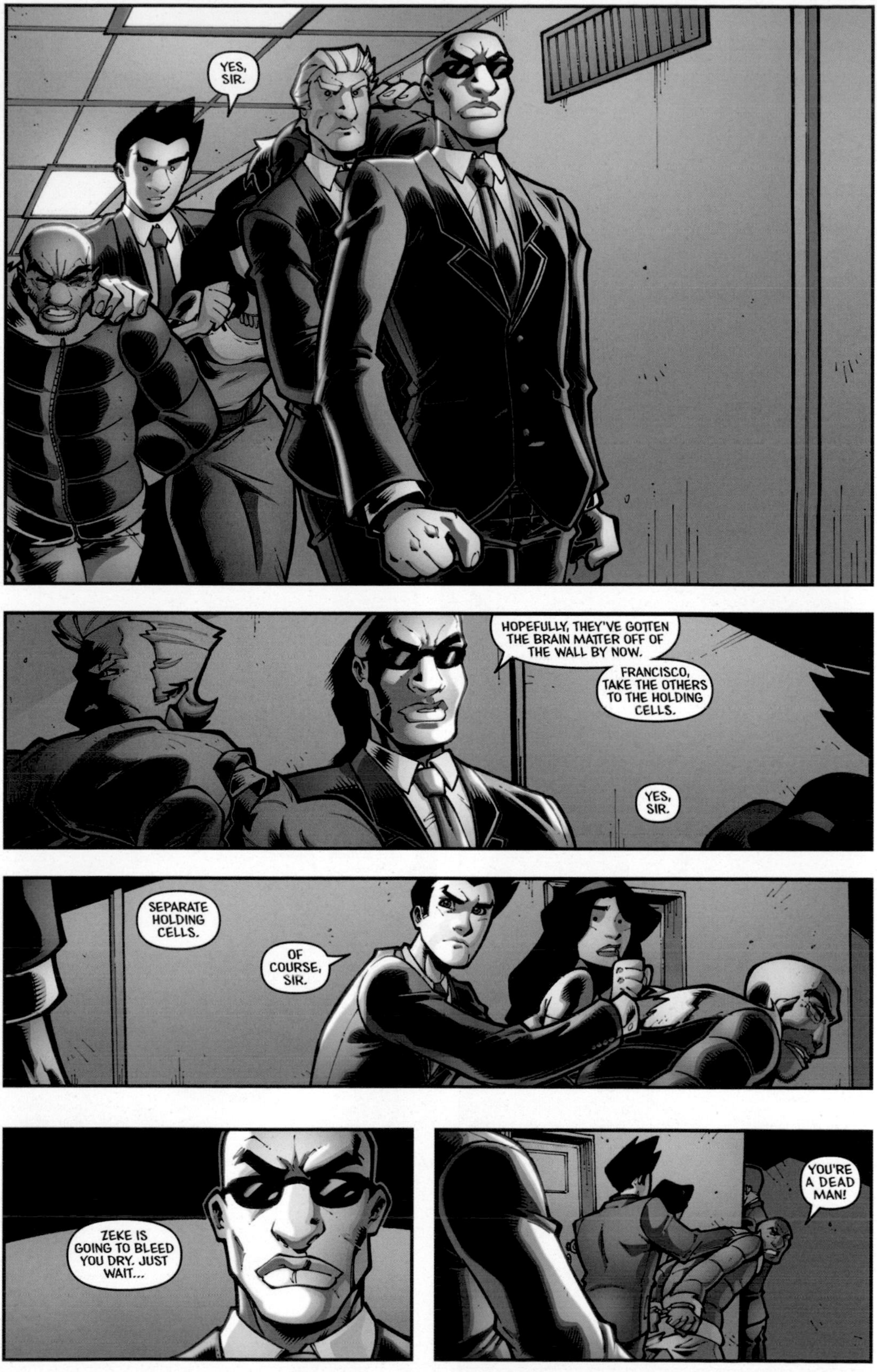
YES, SIR.
HOPEFULLY, THEY'VE GOTTEN THE BRAIN MATTER OFF OF THE WALL BY NOW.
FRANCISCO, TAKE THE OTHERS TO THE HOLDING CELLS.
YES, SIR.
SEPARATE HOLDING CELLS.
OF COURSE, SIR.
ZEKE IS GOING TO BLEED YOU DRY. JUST WAIT...
YOU'RE A DEAD MAN!

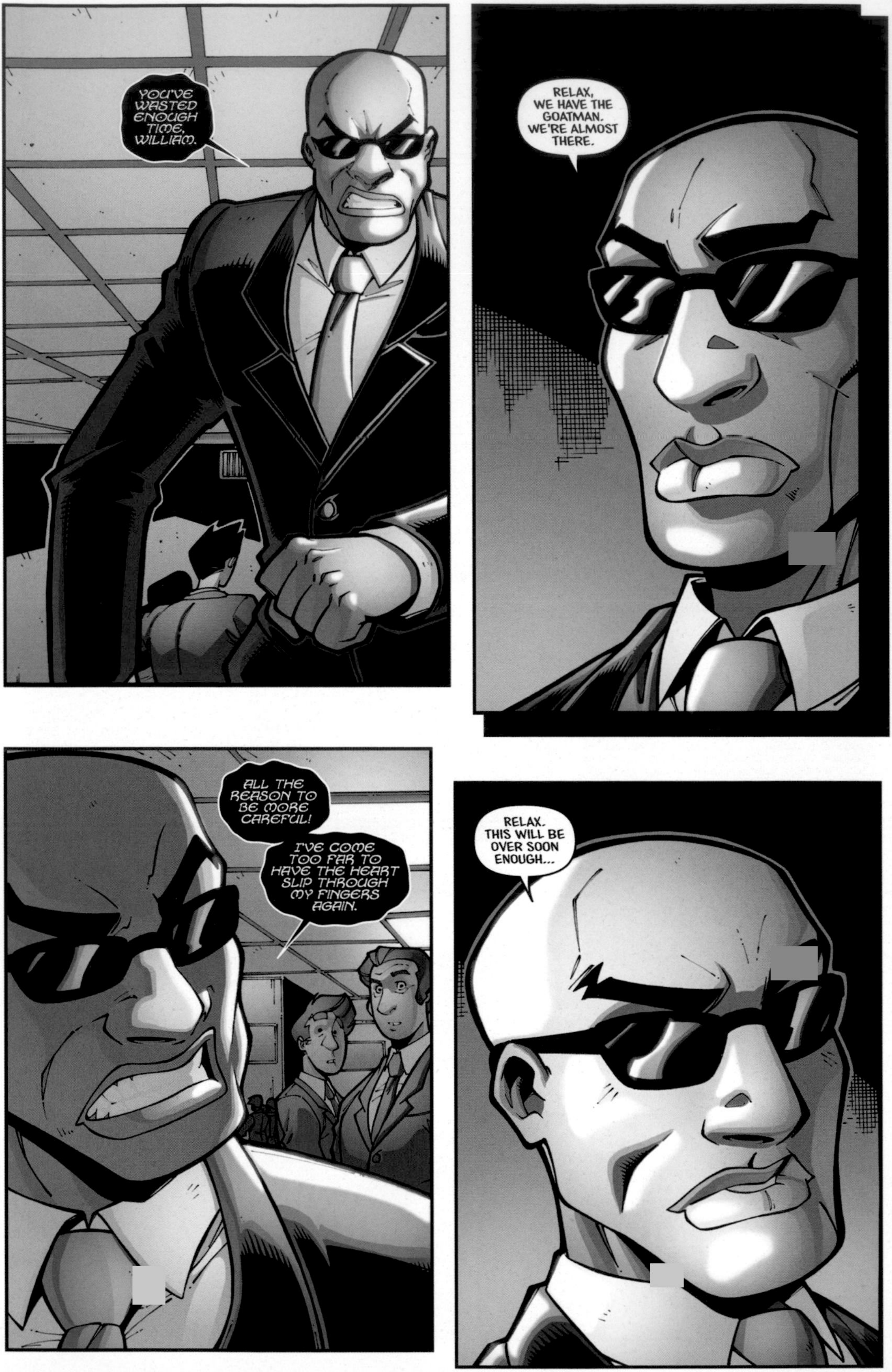
YOU'VE WASTED ENOUGH TIME, WILLIAM.
RELAX, WE HAVE THE GOATMAN. WE'RE ALMOST THERE.
ALL THE REASON TO BE MORE CAREFUL!
I'VE COME TOO FAR TO HAVE THE HEART SLIP THROUGH MY FINGERS AGAIN.
RELAX. THIS WILL BE OVER SOON ENOUGH...

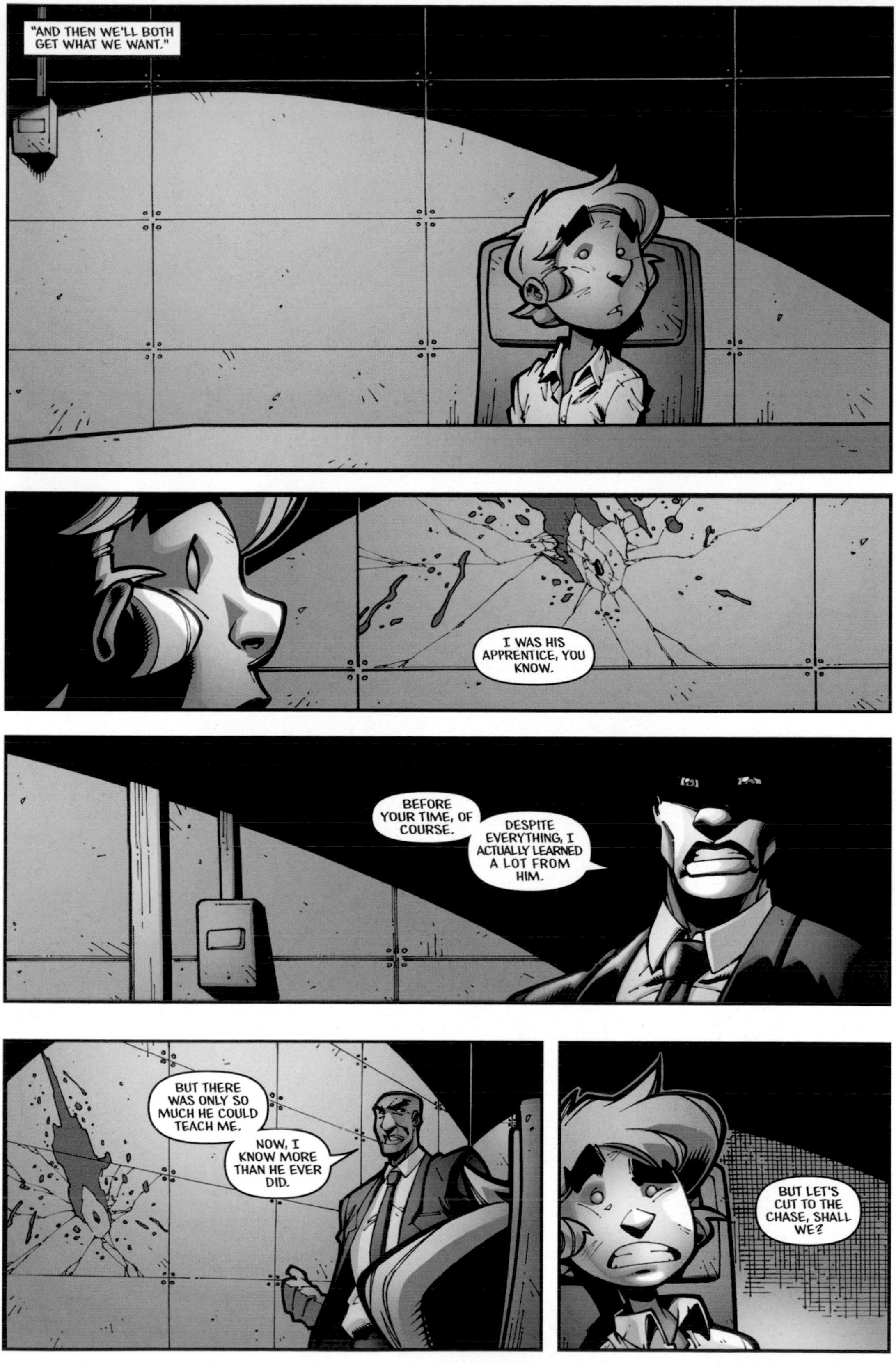
"AND THEN WE'LL BOTH GET WHAT WE WANT."
I WAS HIS APPRENTICE, YOU KNOW.
BEFORE YOUR TIME, OF COURSE.
DESPITE EVERYTHING, I ACTUALLY LEARNED A LOT FROM HIM.
BUT THERE WAS ONLY SO MUCH HE COULD TEACH ME.
NOW, I KNOW MORE THAN HE EVER DID.
BUT LET'S CUT TO THE CHASE, SHALL WE?

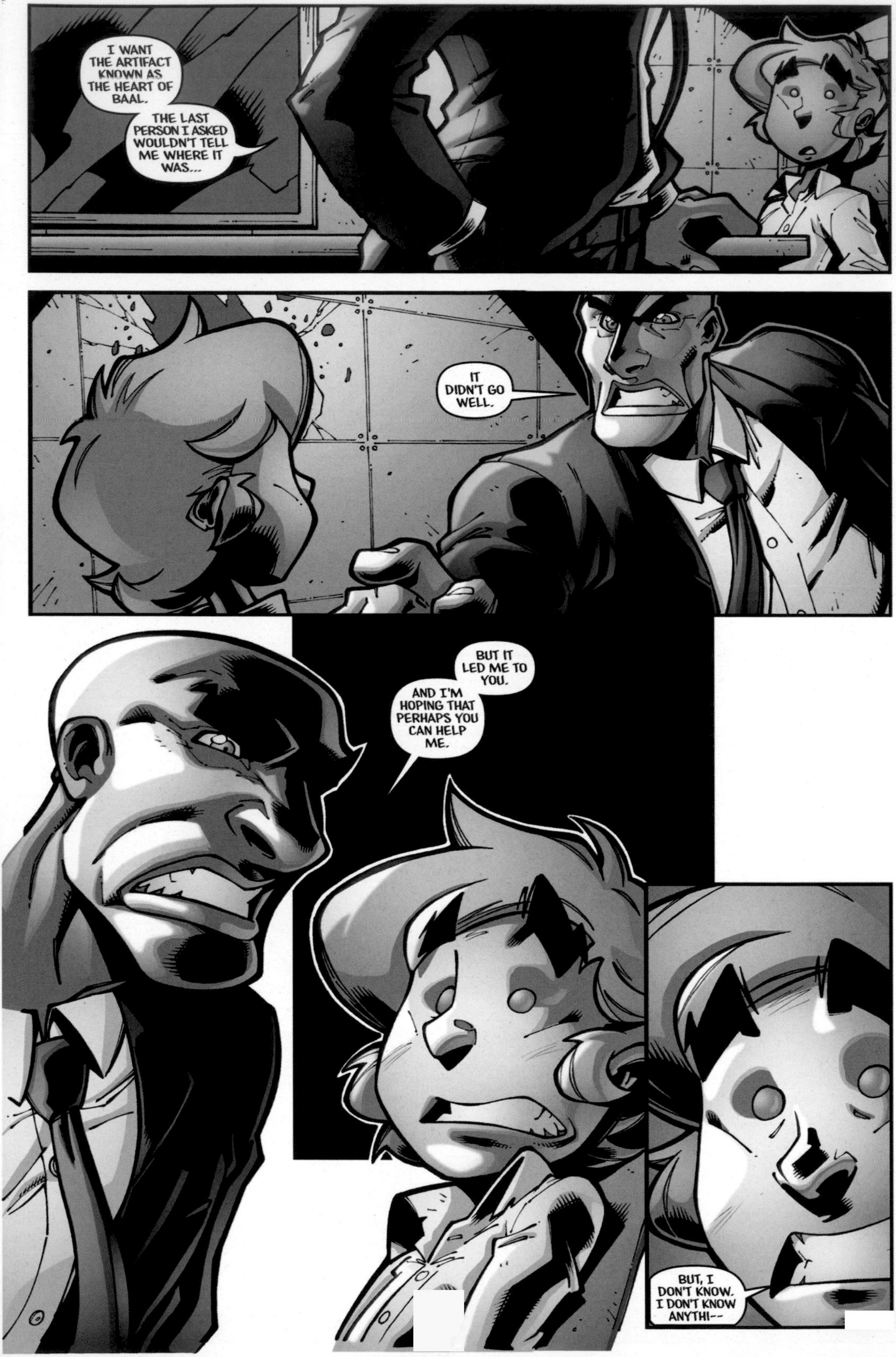
I WANT THE ARTIFACT KNOWN AS THE HEART OF BAAL.
THE LAST PERSON I ASKED WOULDN'T TELL ME WHERE IT WAS...
IT DIDN'T GO WELL.
BUT IT LED ME TO YOU.
AND I'M HOPING THAT PERHAPS YOU CAN HELP ME.
BUT, I DON'T KNOW. I DON'T KNOW ANYTHI--

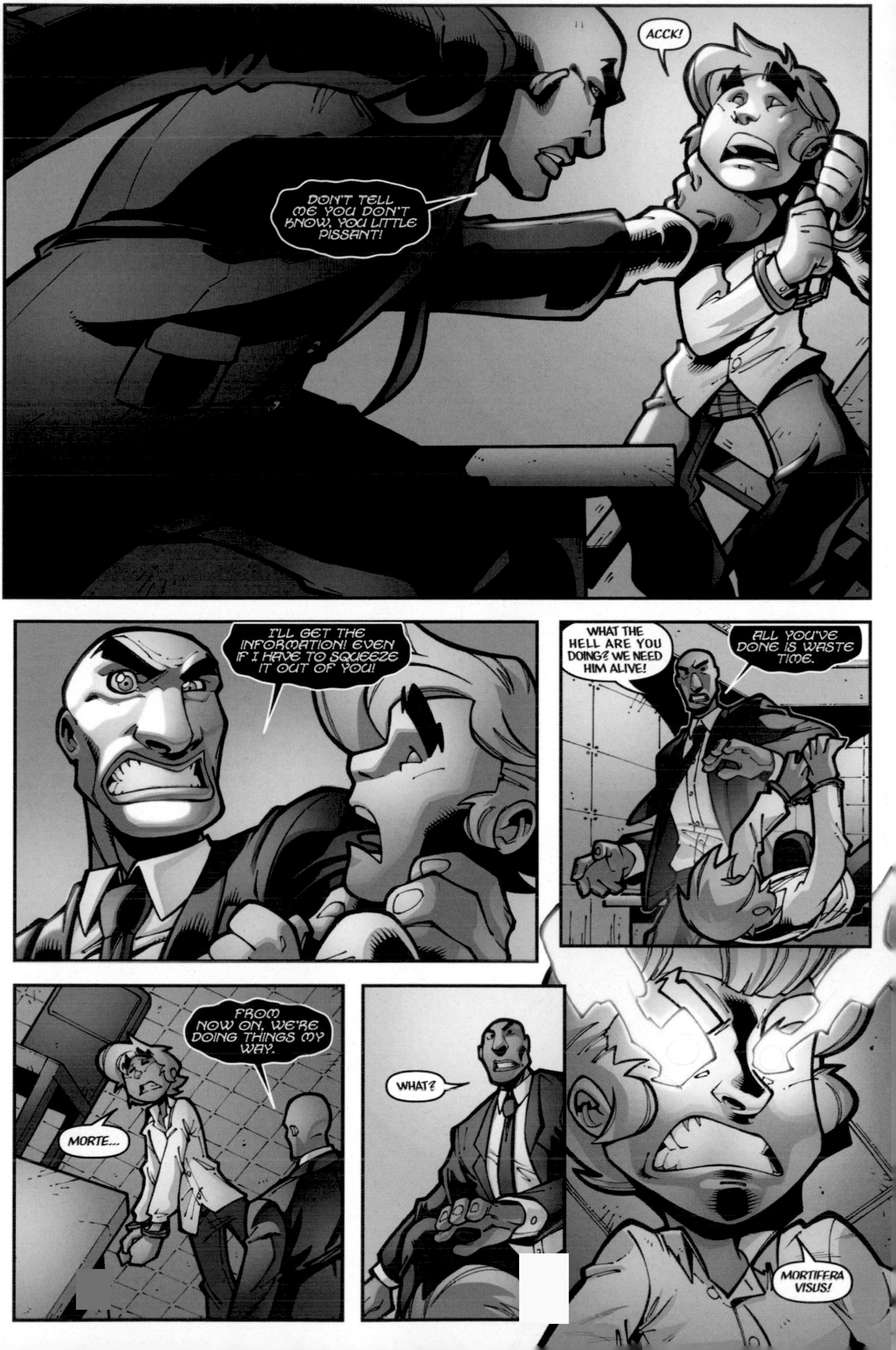
ACCK!
DON'T TELL ME YOU DON'T KNOW, YOU LITTLE PISSANT!
I'LL GET THE INFORMATION! EVEN IF I HAVE TO SQUEEZE IT OUT OF YOU!
WHAT THE HELL ARE YOU DOING? WE NEED HIM ALIVE!
ALL YOU'VE DONE IS WASTE TIME.
FROM NOW ON, WE'RE DOING THINGS MY WAY.
MORTE...
WHAT?
MORTIFERA VISUS!

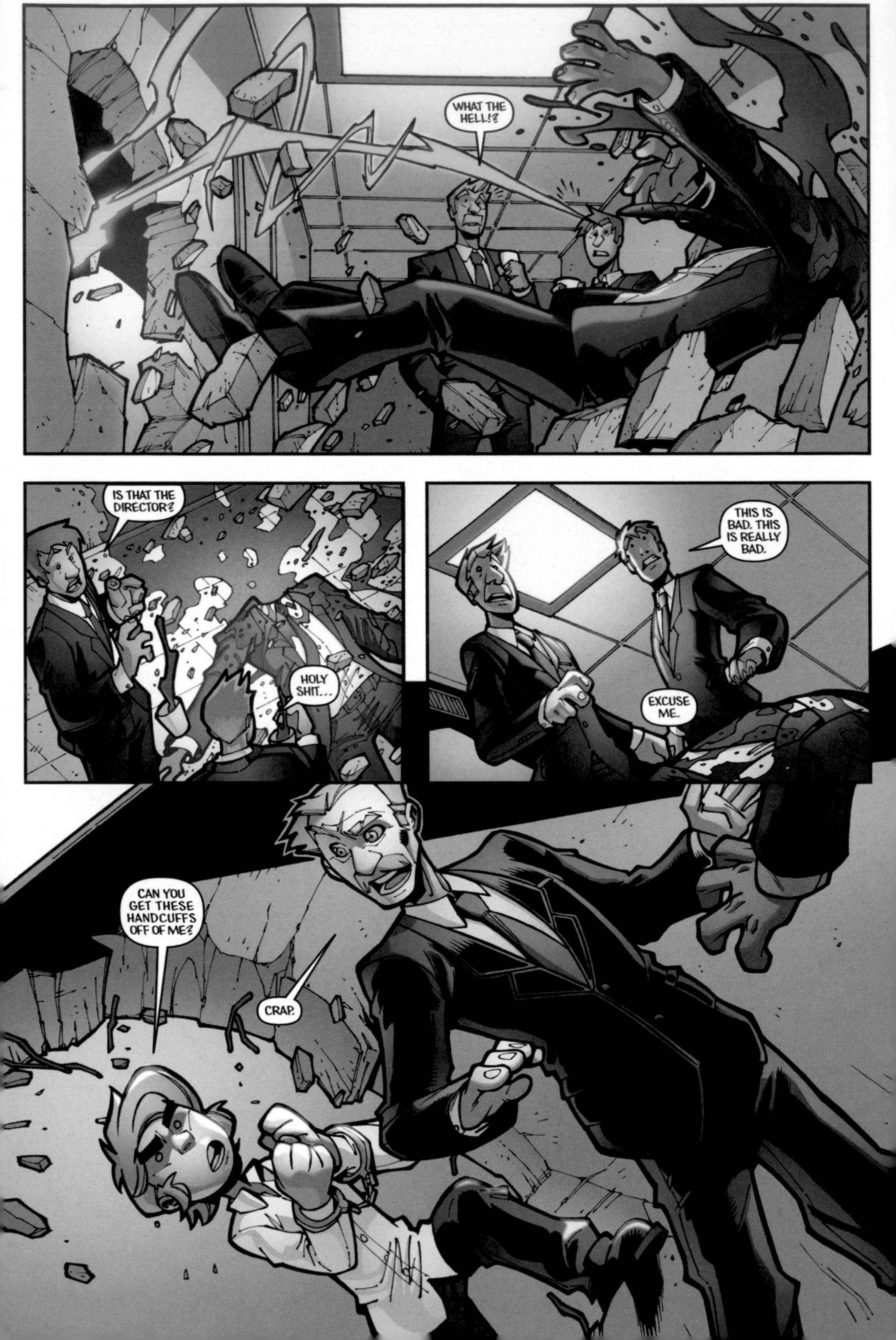
WHAT THE HELL!?
IS THAT THE DIRECTOR?
HOLY SHIT...
THIS IS BAD. THIS IS REALLY BAD.
EXCUSE ME.
CAN YOU GET THESE HANDCUFFS OFF OF ME?
CRAP.

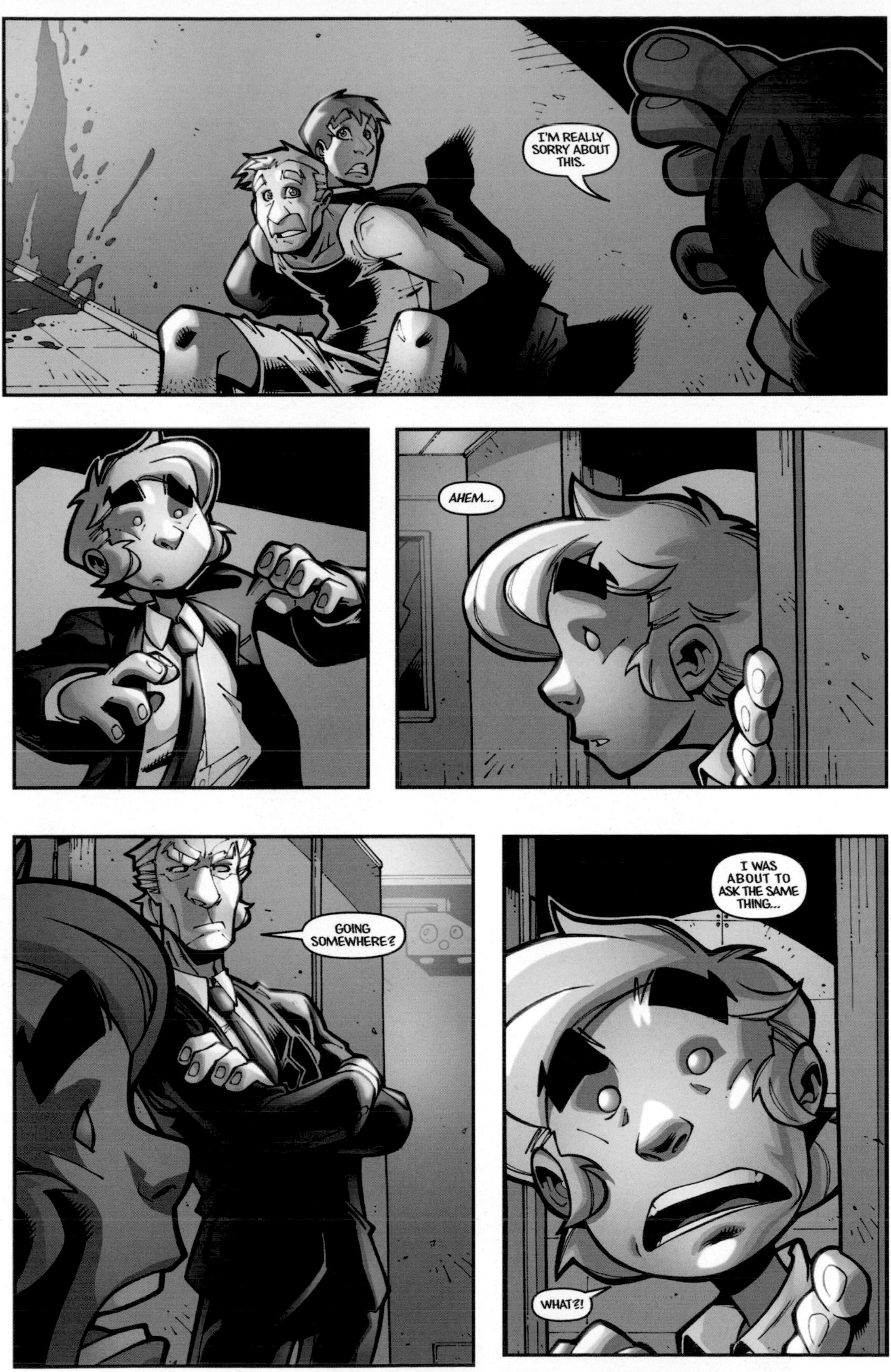
I'M REALLY SORRY ABOUT THIS.
AHEM...
GOING SOMEWHERE?
I WAS ABOUT TO ASK THE SAME THING...
WHAT?!

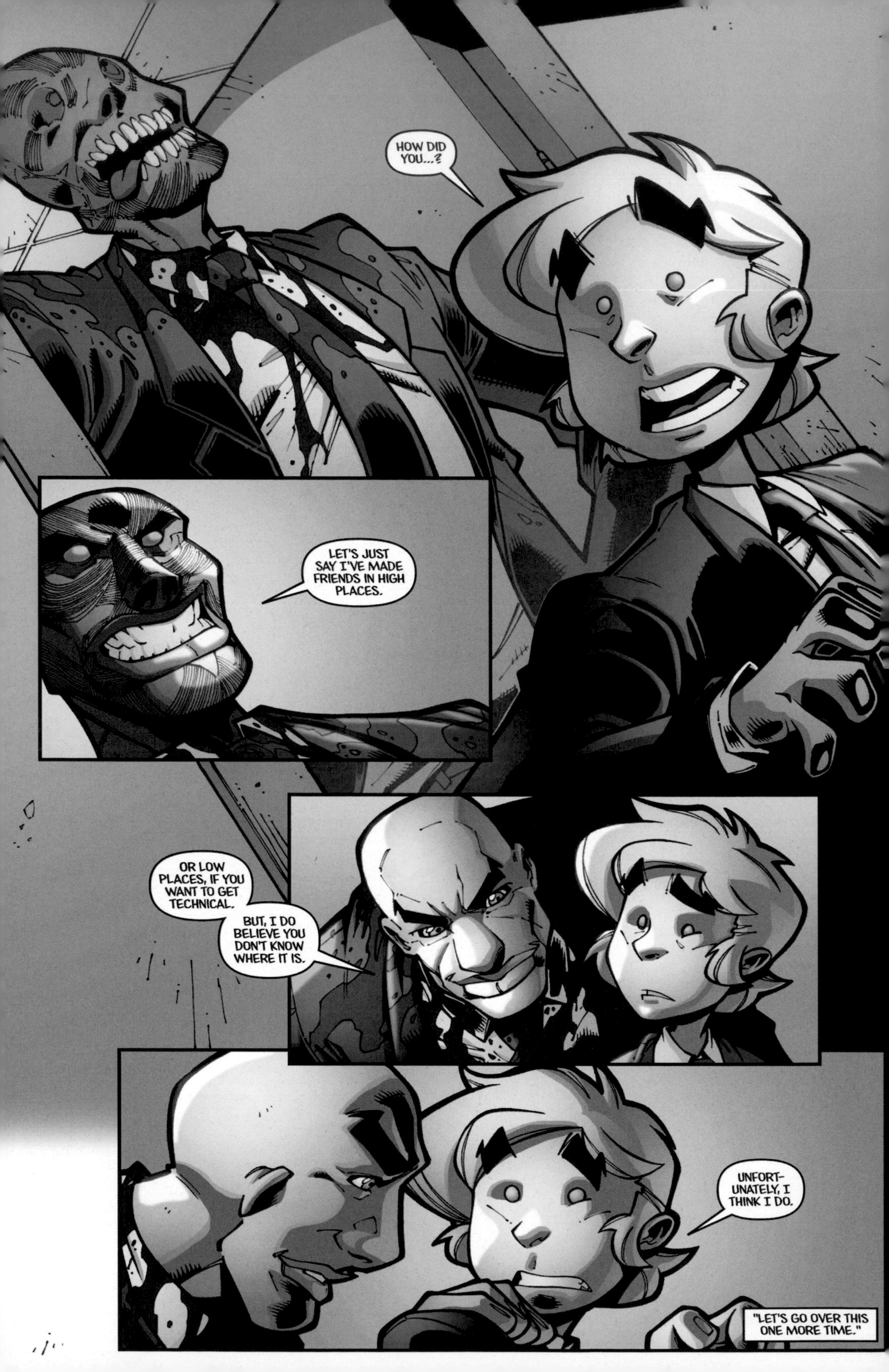
HOW DID YOU...?
LET'S JUST SAY I'VE MADE FRIENDS IN HIGH PLACES.
OR LOW PLACES, IF YOU WANT TO GET TECHNICAL.
BUT, I DO BELIEVE YOU DON'T KNOW WHERE IT IS.
UNFORT-UNATELY, I THINK I DO.
"LET'S GO OVER THIS ONE MORE TIME."

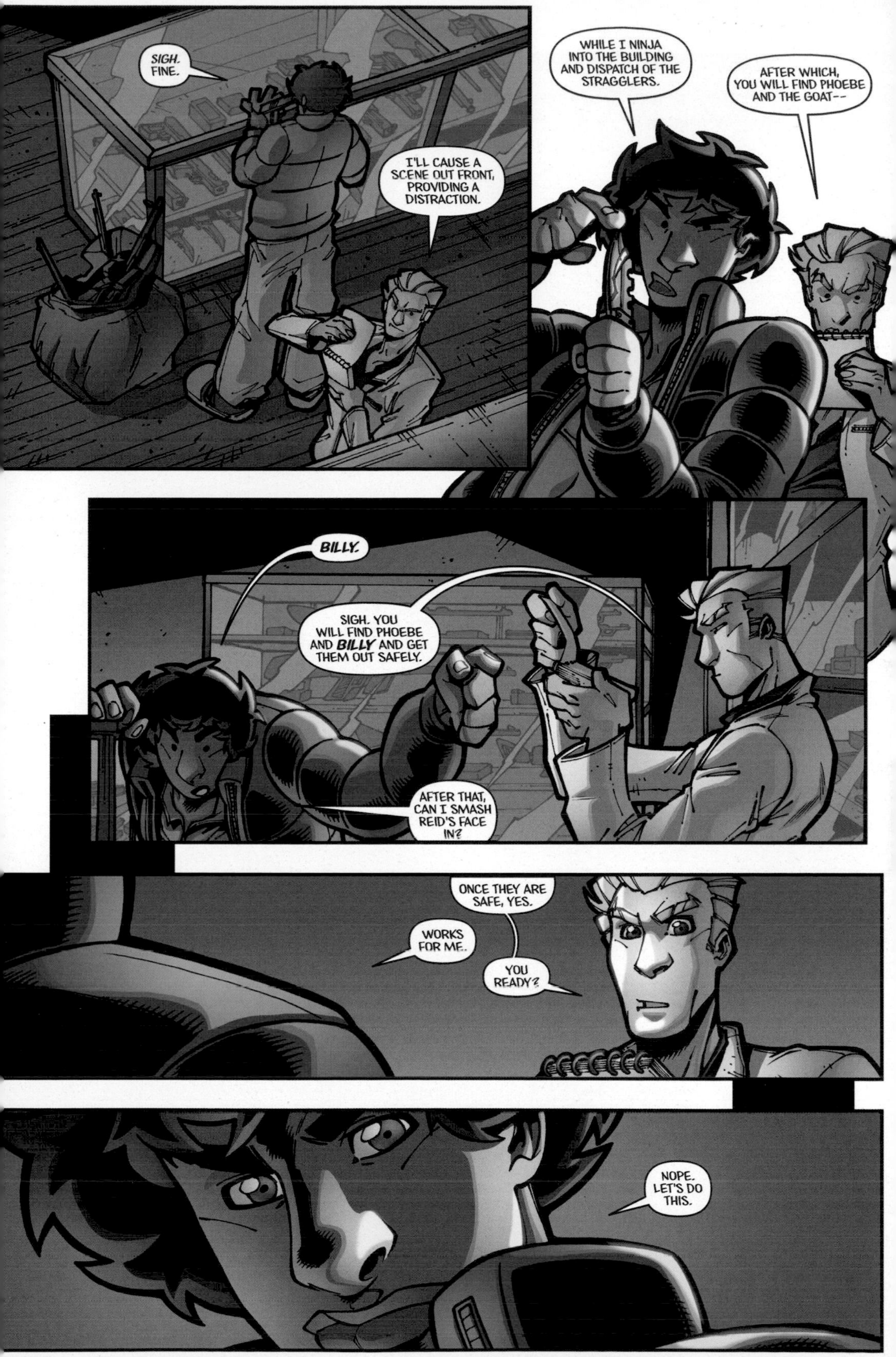
SIGH. FINE.
I'LL CAUSE A SCENE OUT FRONT, PROVIDING A DISTRACTION.
WHILE I NINJA INTO THE BUILDING AND DISPATCH OF THE STRAGGLERS.
AFTER WHICH, YOU WILL FIND PHOEBE AND THE GOAT--
BILLY.
SIGH. YOU WILL FIND PHOEBE AND BILLY AND GET THEM OUT SAFELY.
AFTER THAT, CAN I SMASH REID'S FACE IN?
ONCE THEY ARE SAFE, YES.
WORKS FOR ME.
YOU READY?
NOPE. LET'S DO THIS.

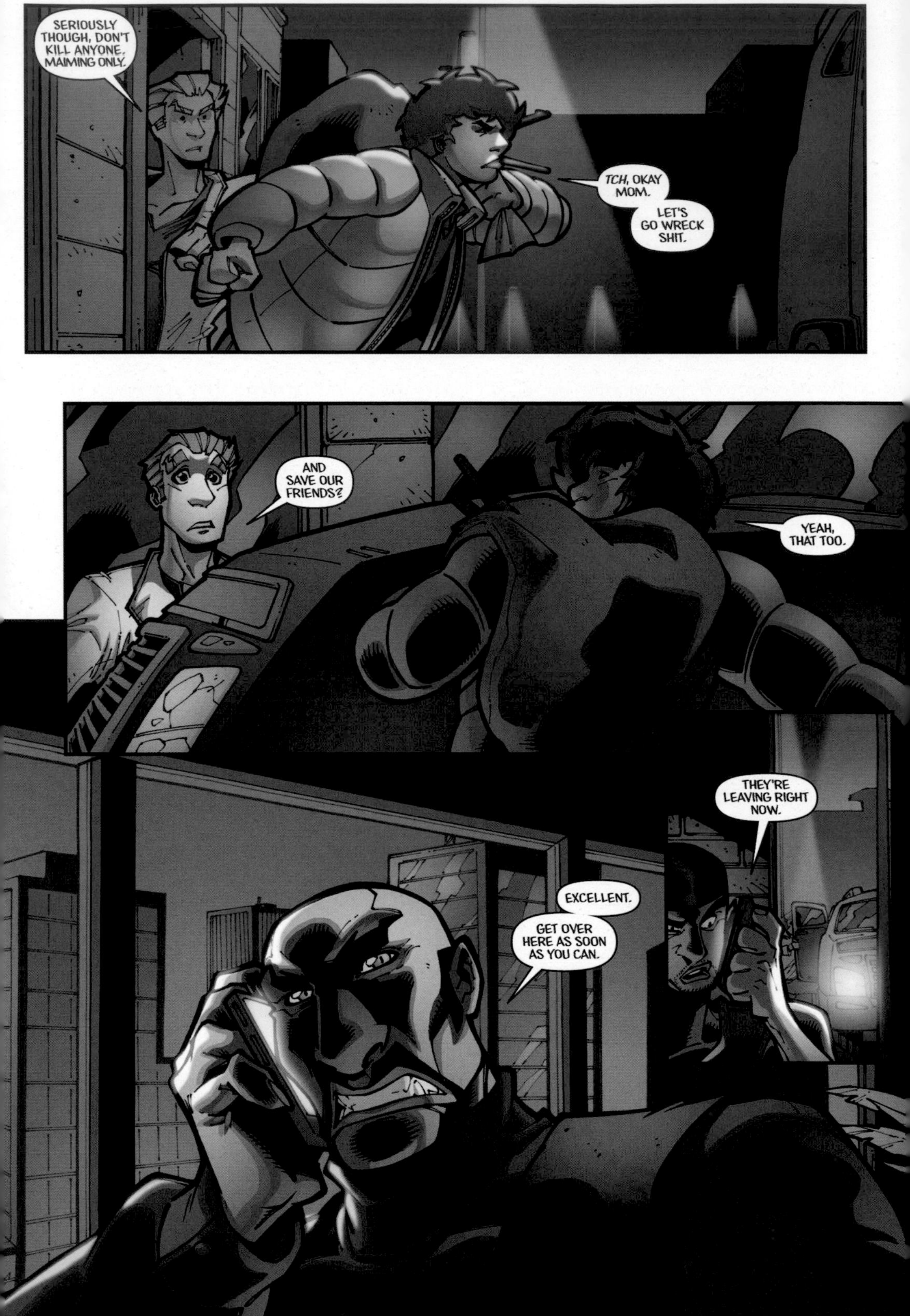
SERIOUSLY THOUGH, DON'T KILL ANYONE. MAIMING ONLY.
TCH, OKAY MOM.
LET'S GO WRECK SHIT.
AND SAVE OUR FRIENDS?
YEAH, THAT TOO.
THEY'RE LEAVING RIGHT NOW.
EXCELLENT.
GET OVER HERE AS SOON AS YOU CAN.

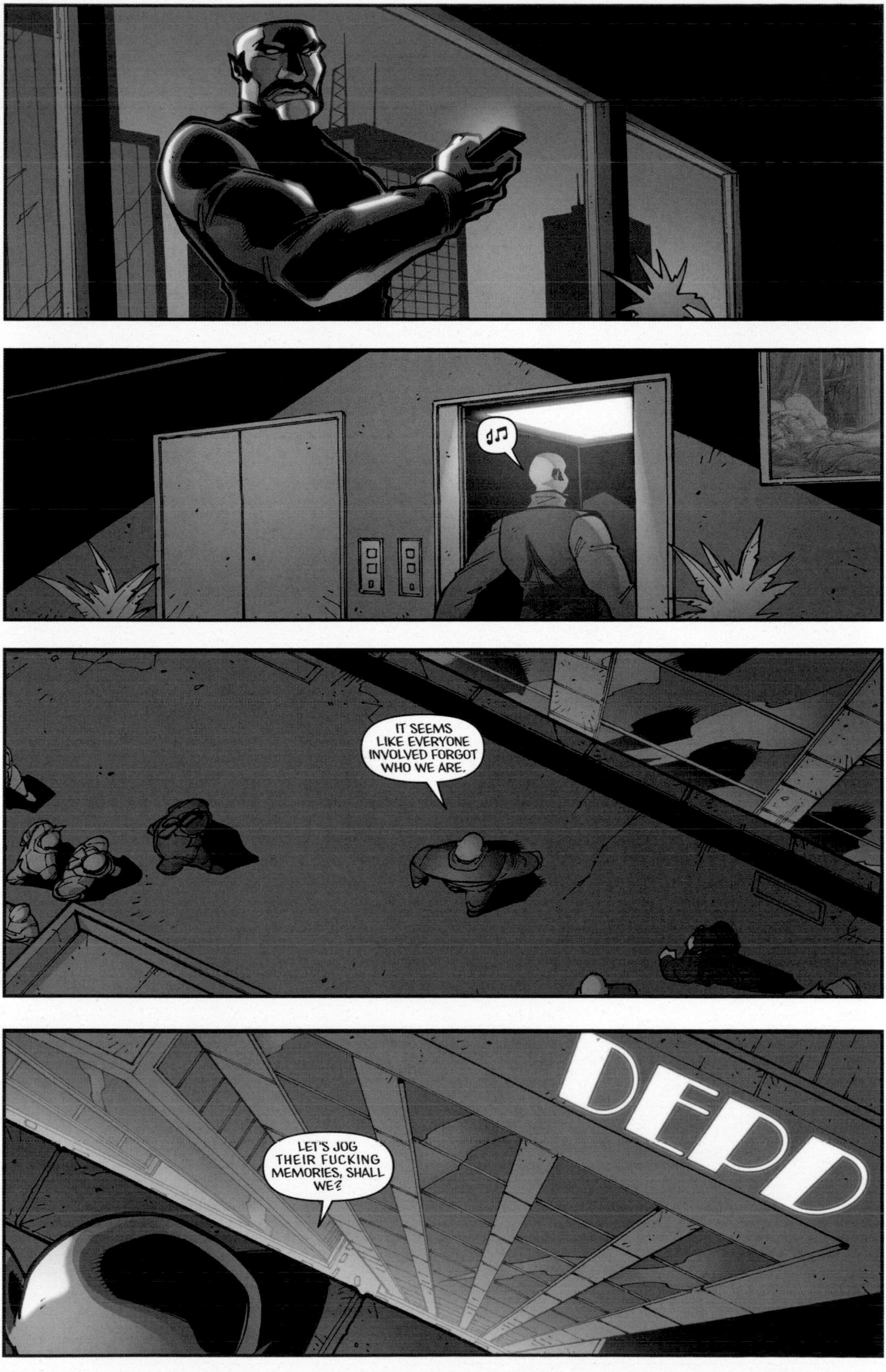

♫♪
IT SEEMS LIKE EVERYONE INVOLVED FORGOT WHO WE ARE.
DEPD
LET'S JOG THEIR FUCKING MEMORIES, SHALL WE?

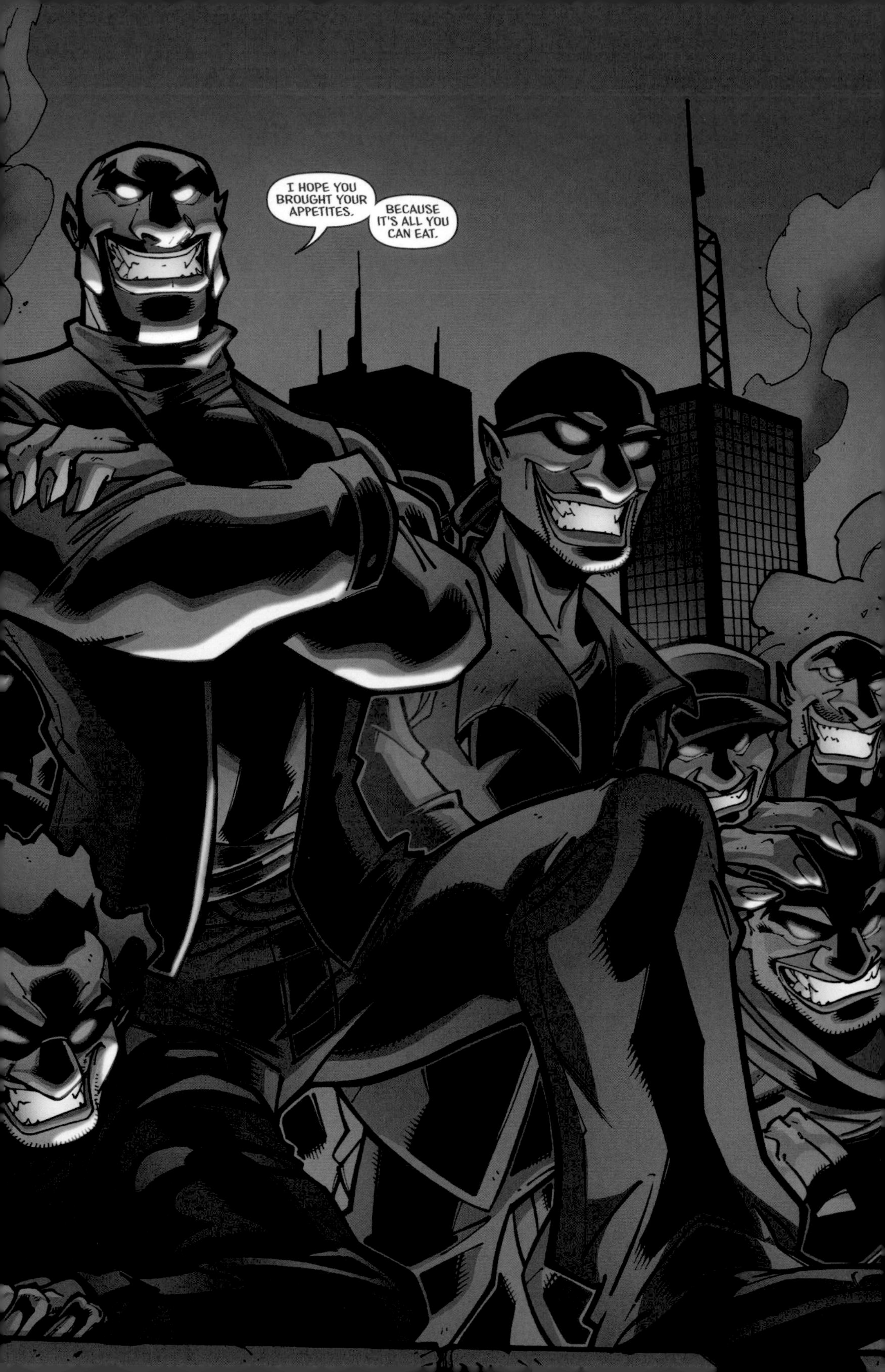
I HOPE YOU BROUGHT YOUR APPETITES.
BECAUSE IT'S ALL YOU CAN EAT.

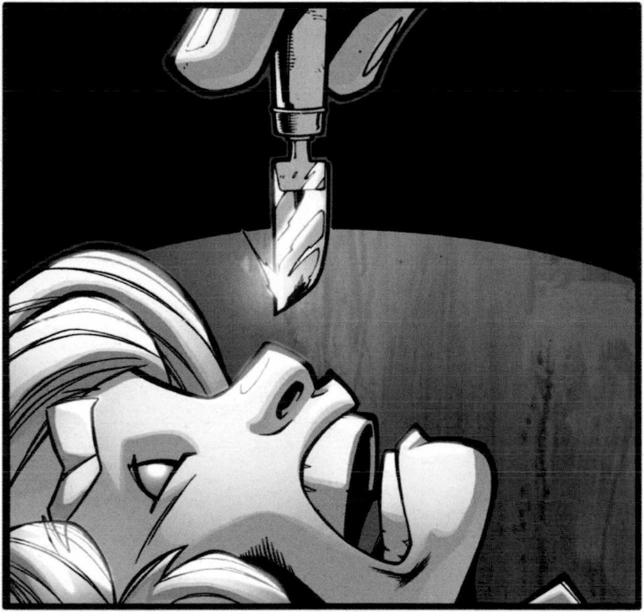

CHAPTER FOUR

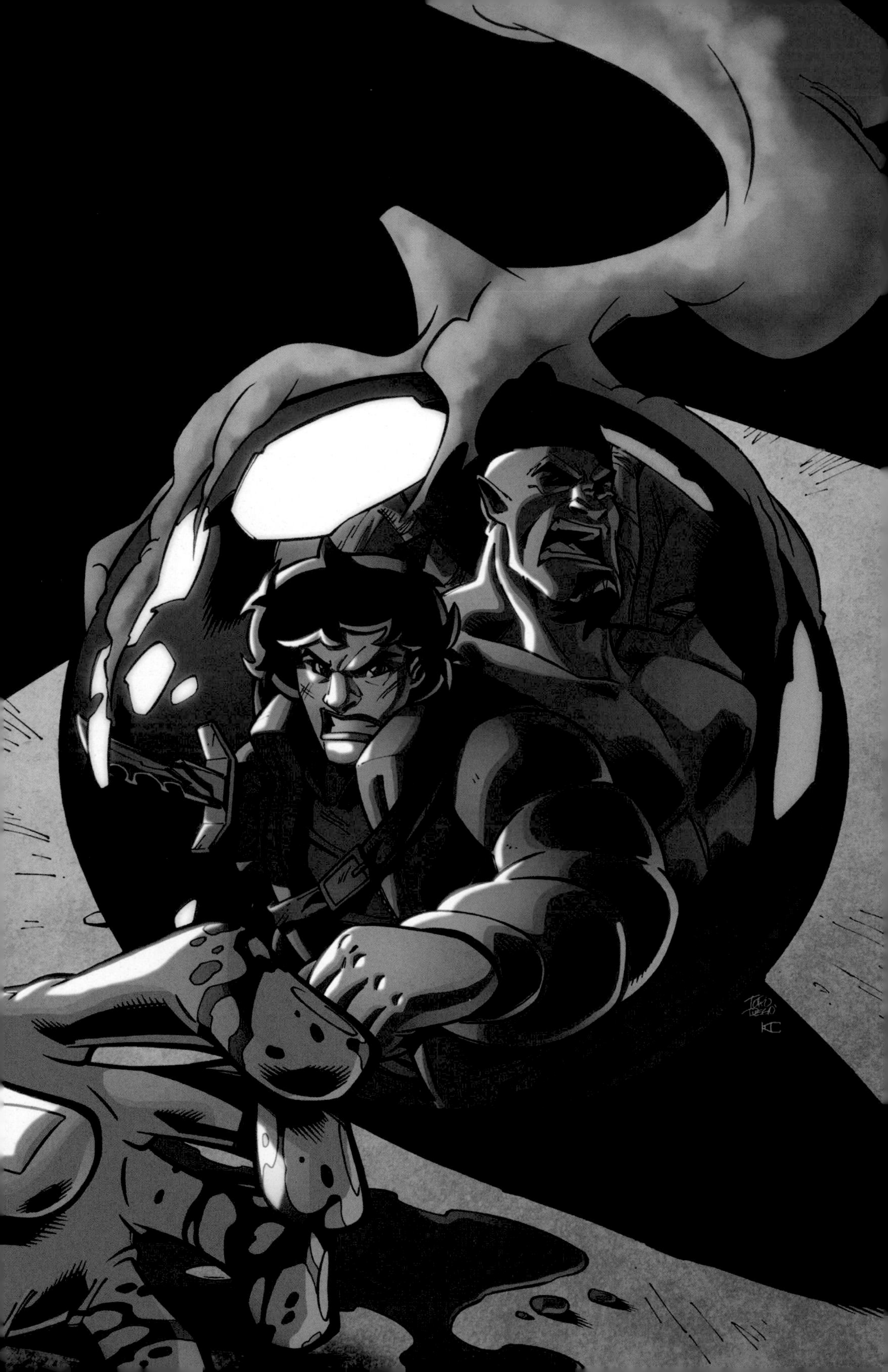

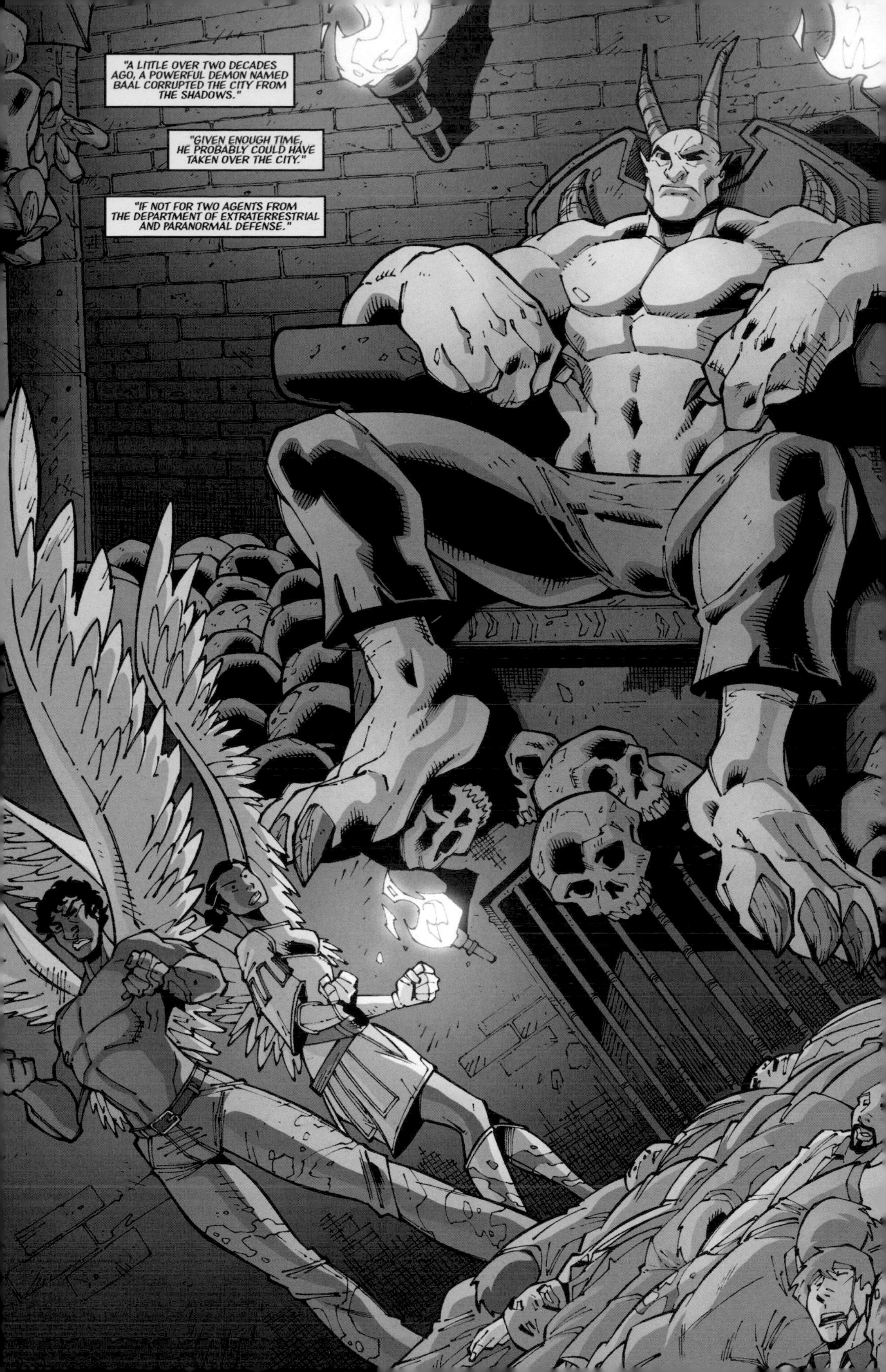
"A LITTLE OVER TWO DECADES AGO, A POWERFUL DEMON NAMED BAAL CORRUPTED THE CITY FROM THE SHADOWS."
"GIVEN ENOUGH TIME, HE PROBABLY COULD HAVE TAKEN OVER THE CITY."
"IF NOT FOR TWO AGENTS FROM THE DEPARTMENT OF EXTRATERRESTRIAL AND PARANORMAL DEFENSE."

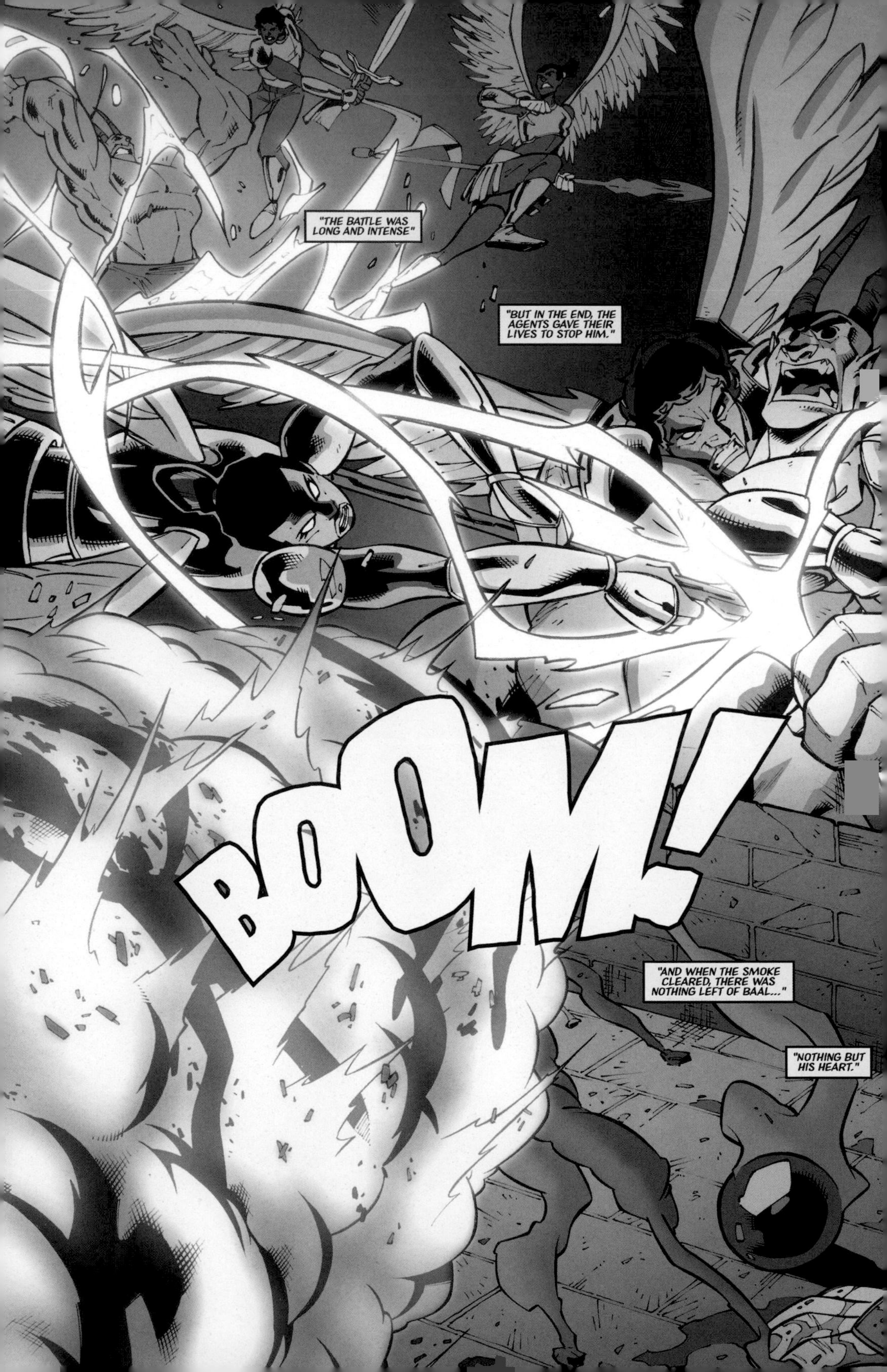
"THE BATTLE WAS LONG AND INTENSE"
"BUT IN THE END, THE AGENTS GAVE THEIR LIVES TO STOP HIM."
BOOM!
"AND WHEN THE SMOKE CLEARED, THERE WAS NOTHING LEFT OF BAAL..."
"NOTHING BUT HIS HEART."

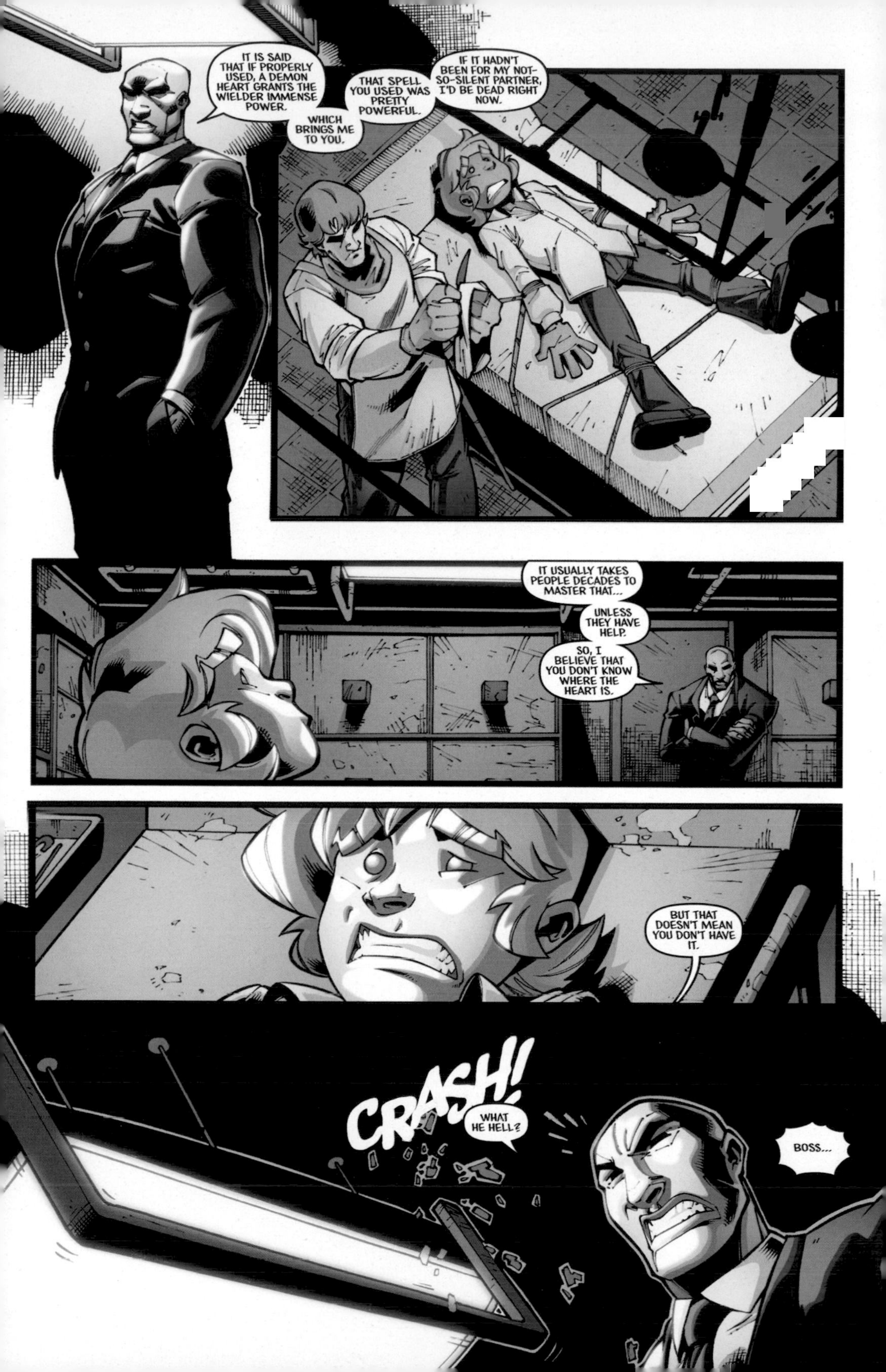
IT IS SAID THAT IF PROPERLY USED, A DEMON HEART GRANTS THE WIELDER IMMENSE POWER.
WHICH BRINGS ME TO YOU.
THAT SPELL YOU USED WAS PRETTY POWERFUL.
IF IT HADN'T BEEN FOR MY NOT-SO-SILENT PARTNER, I'D BE DEAD RIGHT NOW.
IT USUALLY TAKES PEOPLE DECADES TO MASTER THAT...
UNLESS THEY HAVE HELP.
SO, I BELIEVE THAT YOU DON'T KNOW WHERE THE HEART IS.
BUT THAT DOESN'T MEAN YOU DON'T HAVE IT.
CRASH!
WHAT HE HELL?
BOSS...

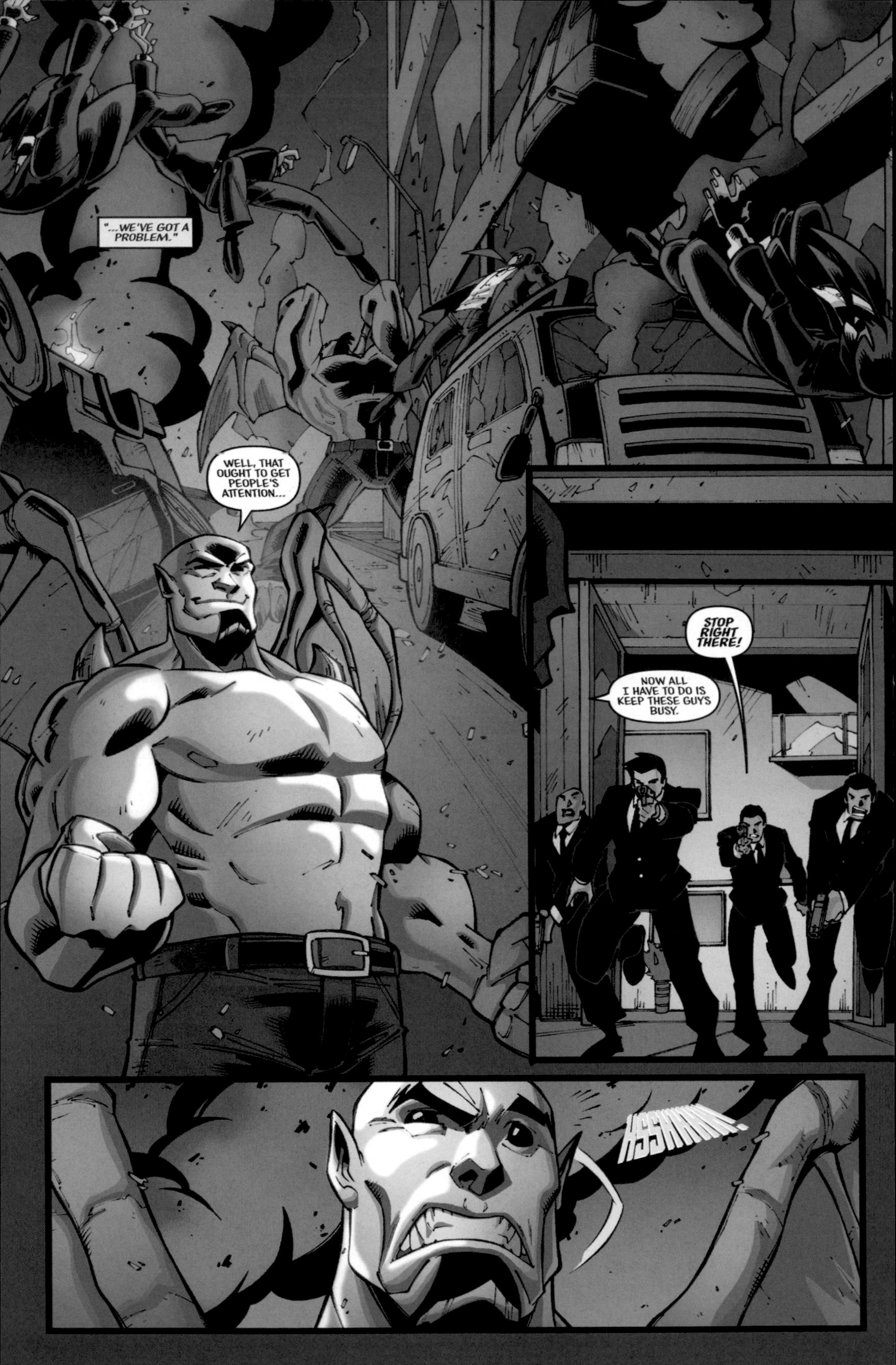
"...WE'VE GOT A PROBLEM."
WELL, THAT OUGHT TO GET PEOPLE'S ATTENTION...
STOP RIGHT THERE!
NOW ALL I HAVE TO DO IS KEEP THESE GUYS BUSY.
HSSHHHH.

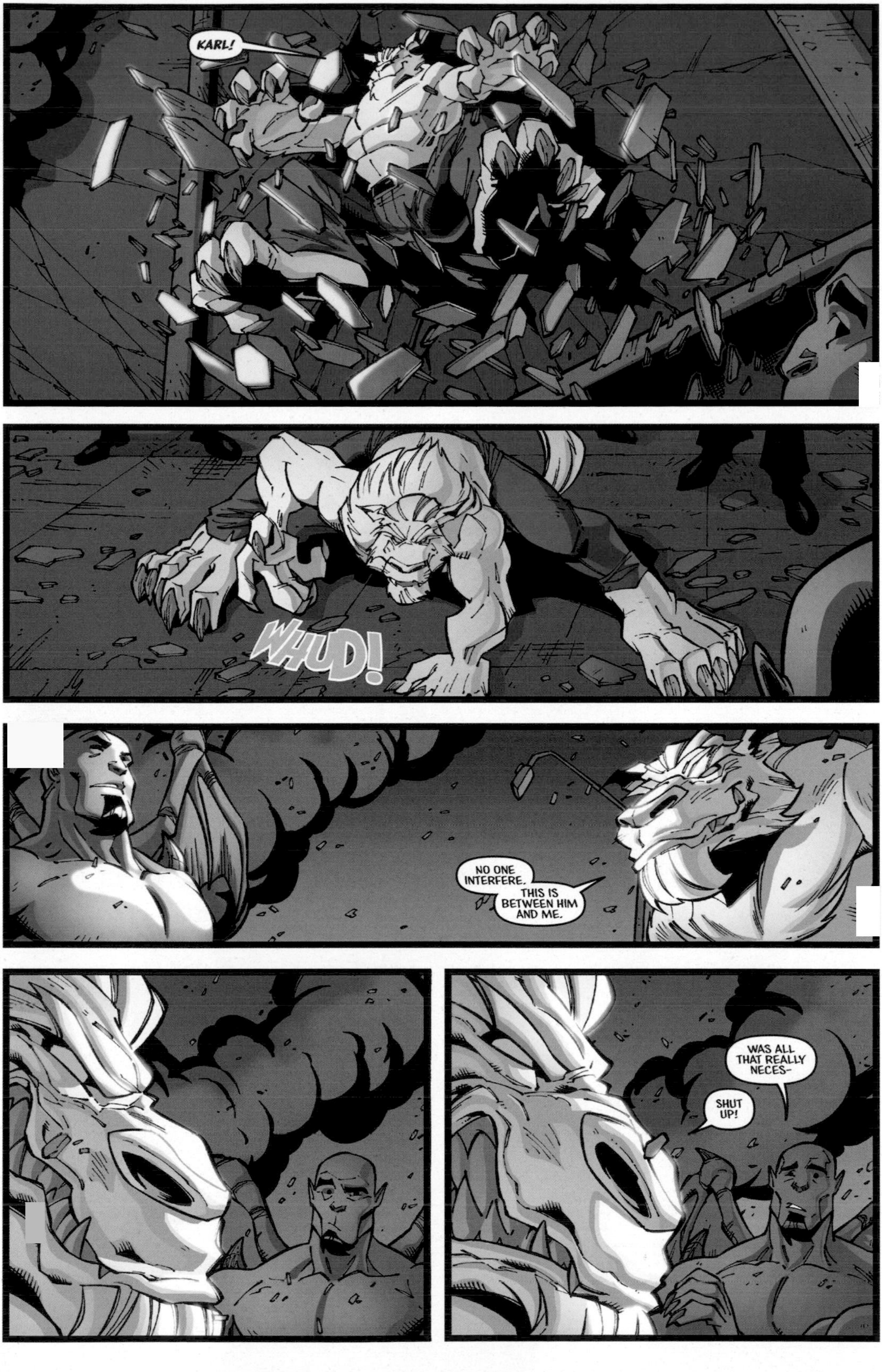

KARL!
WHUD!
NO ONE INTERFERE.
THIS IS BETWEEN HIM AND ME.
WAS ALL THAT REALLY NECES-
SHUT UP!

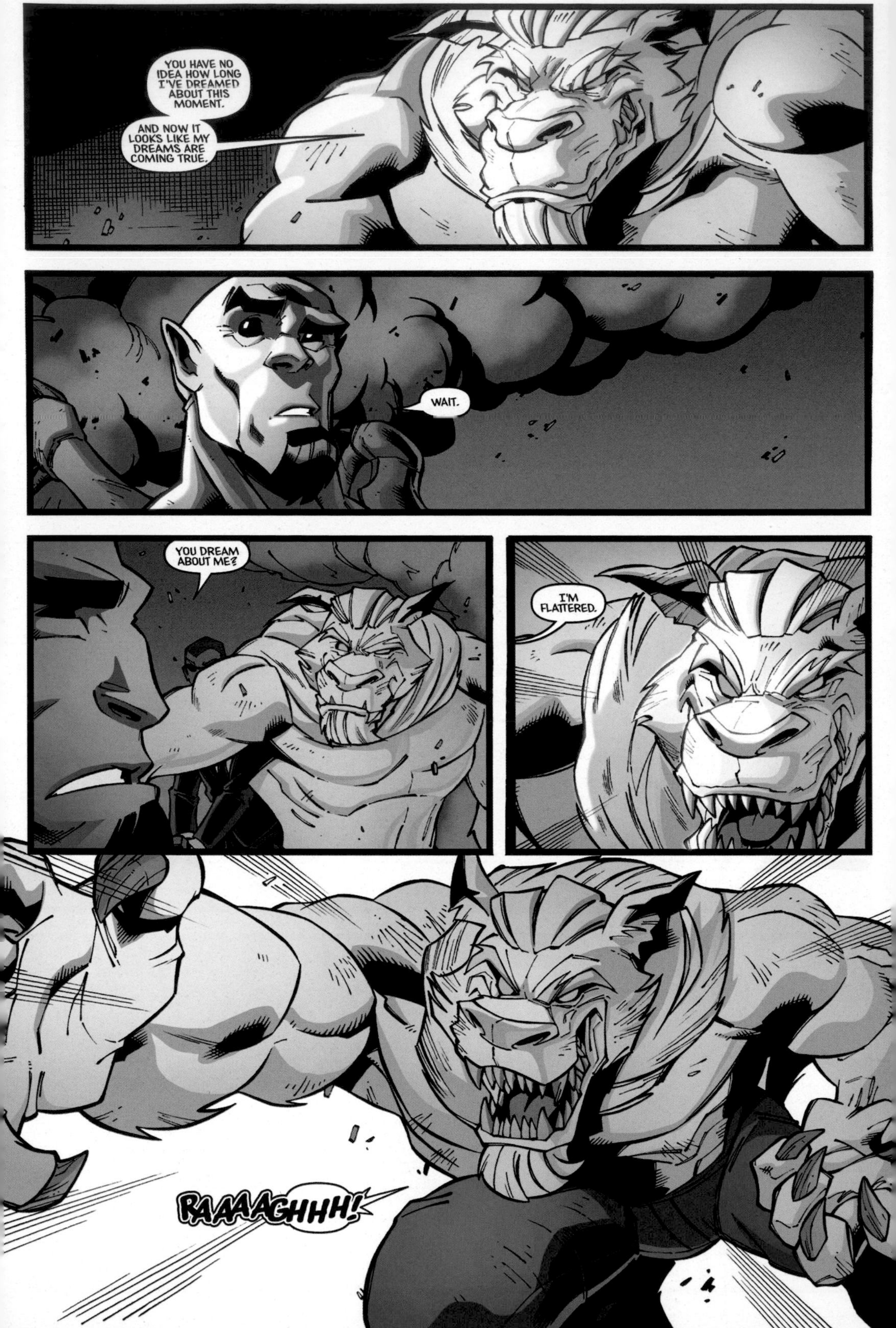
YOU HAVE NO IDEA HOW LONG I'VE DREAMED ABOUT THIS MOMENT.
AND NOW IT LOOKS LIKE MY DREAMS ARE COMING TRUE.
WAIT.
YOU DREAM ABOUT ME?
I'M FLATTERED.
RAAAAGHHH!

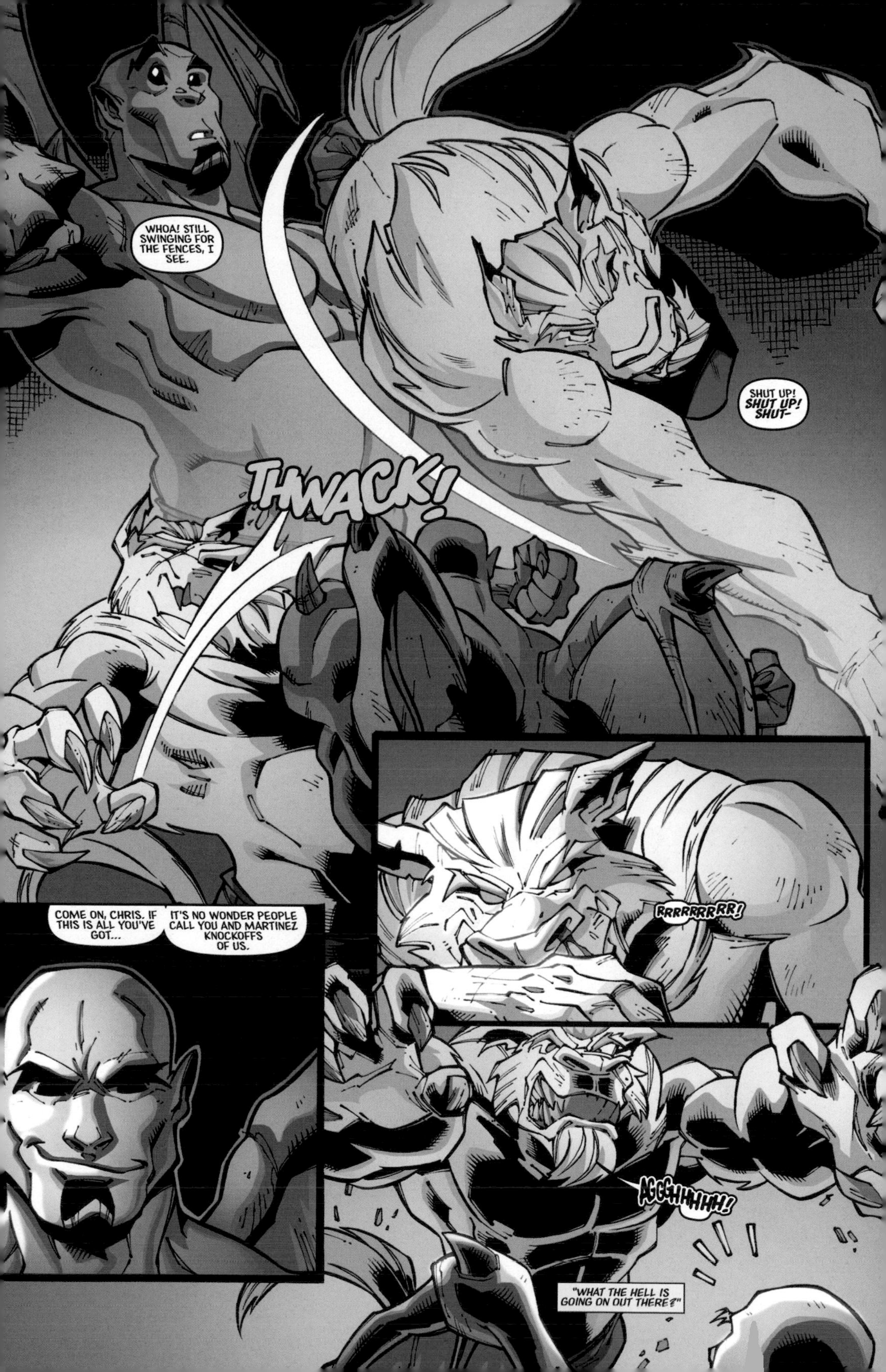
WHOA! STILL SWINGING FOR THE FENCES, I SEE.
SHUT UP! SHUT UP! SHUT-
THWACK!
COME ON, CHRIS. IF THIS IS ALL YOU'VE GOT...
IT'S NO WONDER PEOPLE CALL YOU AND MARTINEZ KNOCKOFFS OF US.
RRRRRRRRR!
AGGGHHHHH!
"WHAT THE HELL IS GOING ON OUT THERE?"

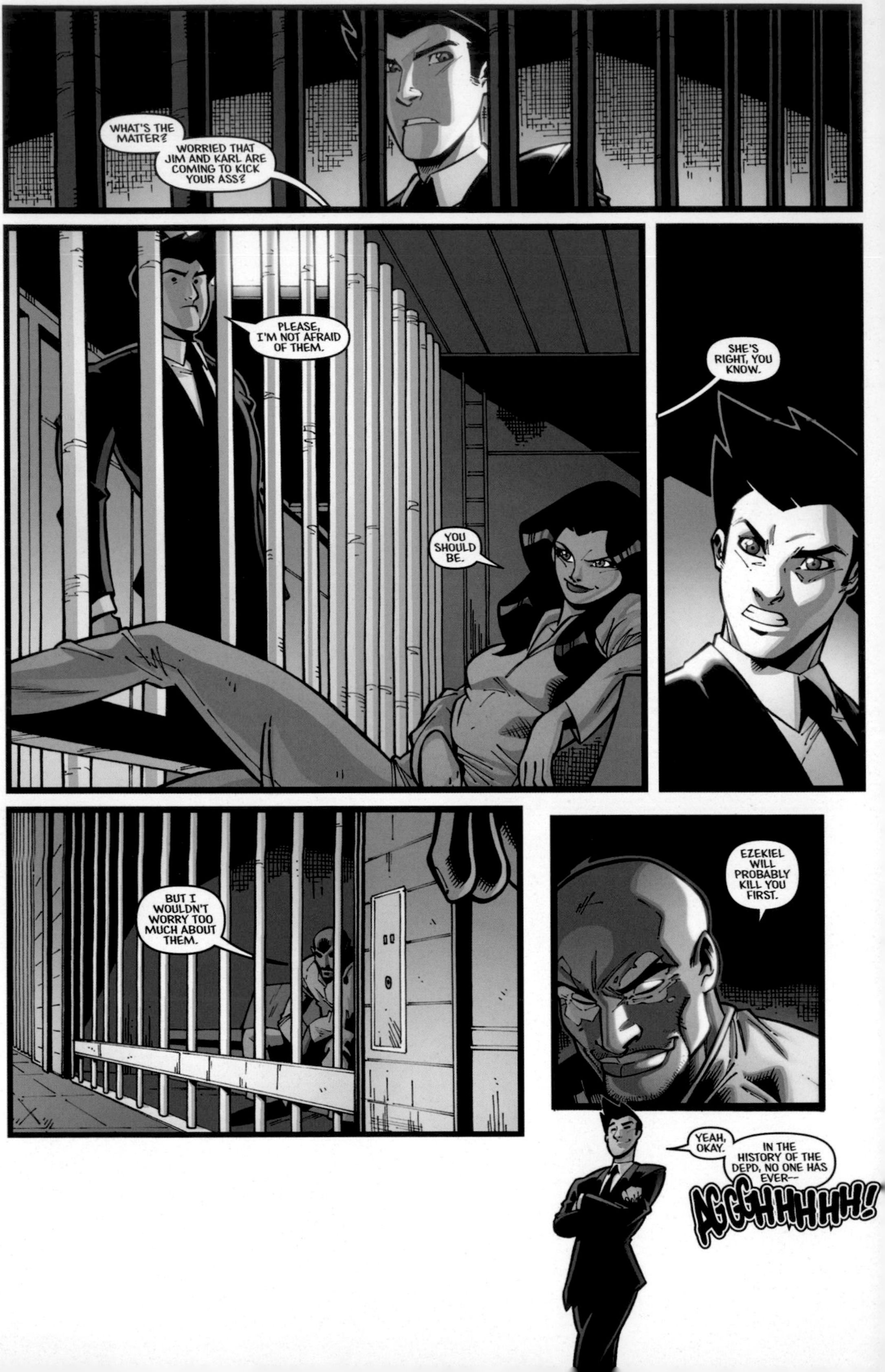
WHAT'S THE MATTER?
WORRIED THAT JIM AND KARL ARE COMING TO KICK YOUR ASS?
PLEASE, I'M NOT AFRAID OF THEM.
YOU SHOULD BE.
SHE'S RIGHT, YOU KNOW.
BUT I WOULDN'T WORRY TOO MUCH ABOUT THEM.
EZEKIEL WILL PROBABLY KILL YOU FIRST.
YEAH, OKAY.
IN THE HISTORY OF THE DEPD, NO ONE HAS EVER--
AGGGHHHHHH!

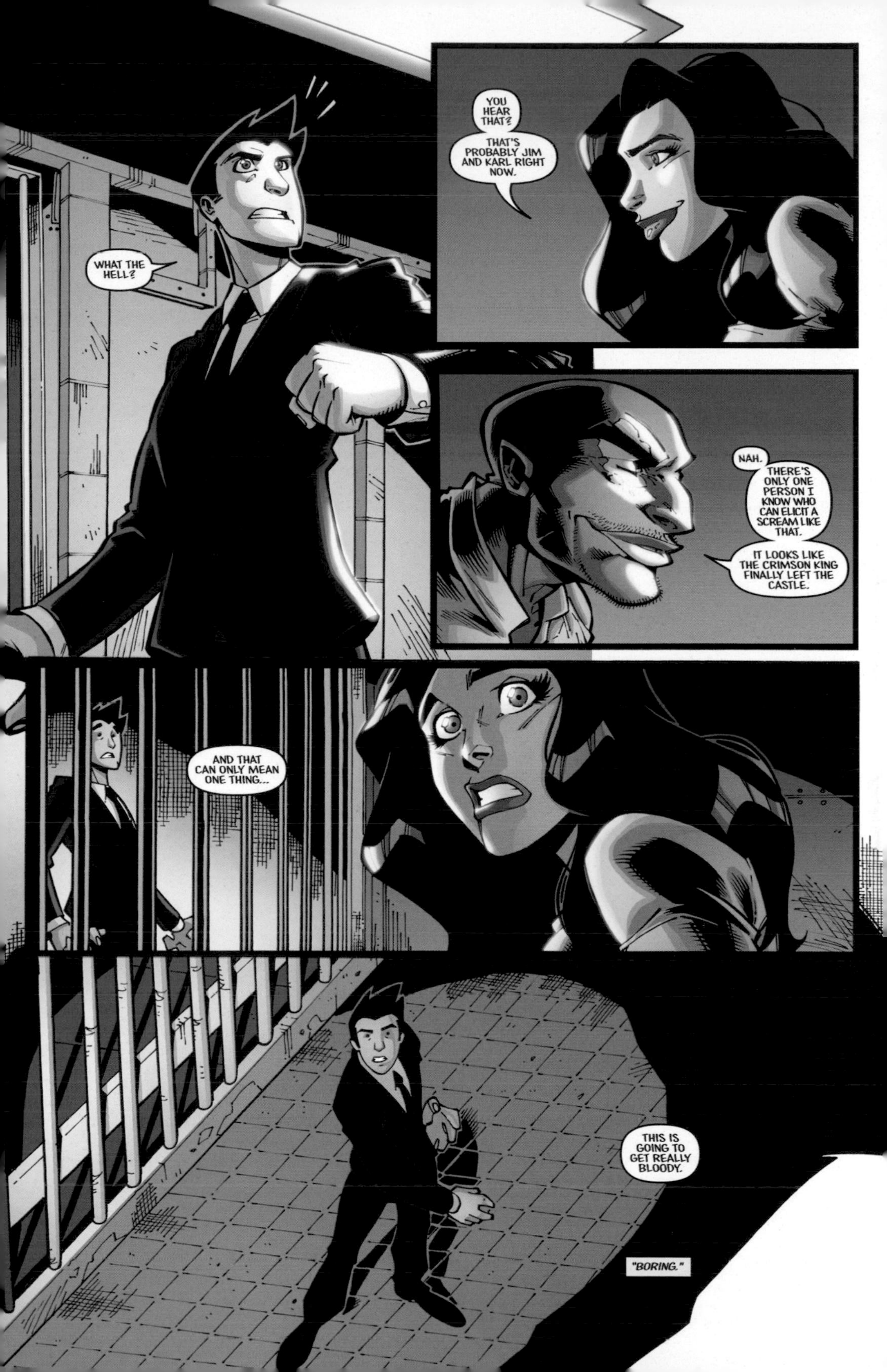
WHAT THE HELL?
YOU HEAR THAT?
THAT'S PROBABLY JIM AND KARL RIGHT NOW.
NAH.
THERE'S ONLY ONE PERSON I KNOW WHO CAN ELICIT A SCREAM LIKE THAT.
IT LOOKS LIKE THE CRIMSON KING FINALLY LEFT THE CASTLE.
AND THAT CAN ONLY MEAN ONE THING...
THIS IS GOING TO GET REALLY BLOODY.
"BORING."

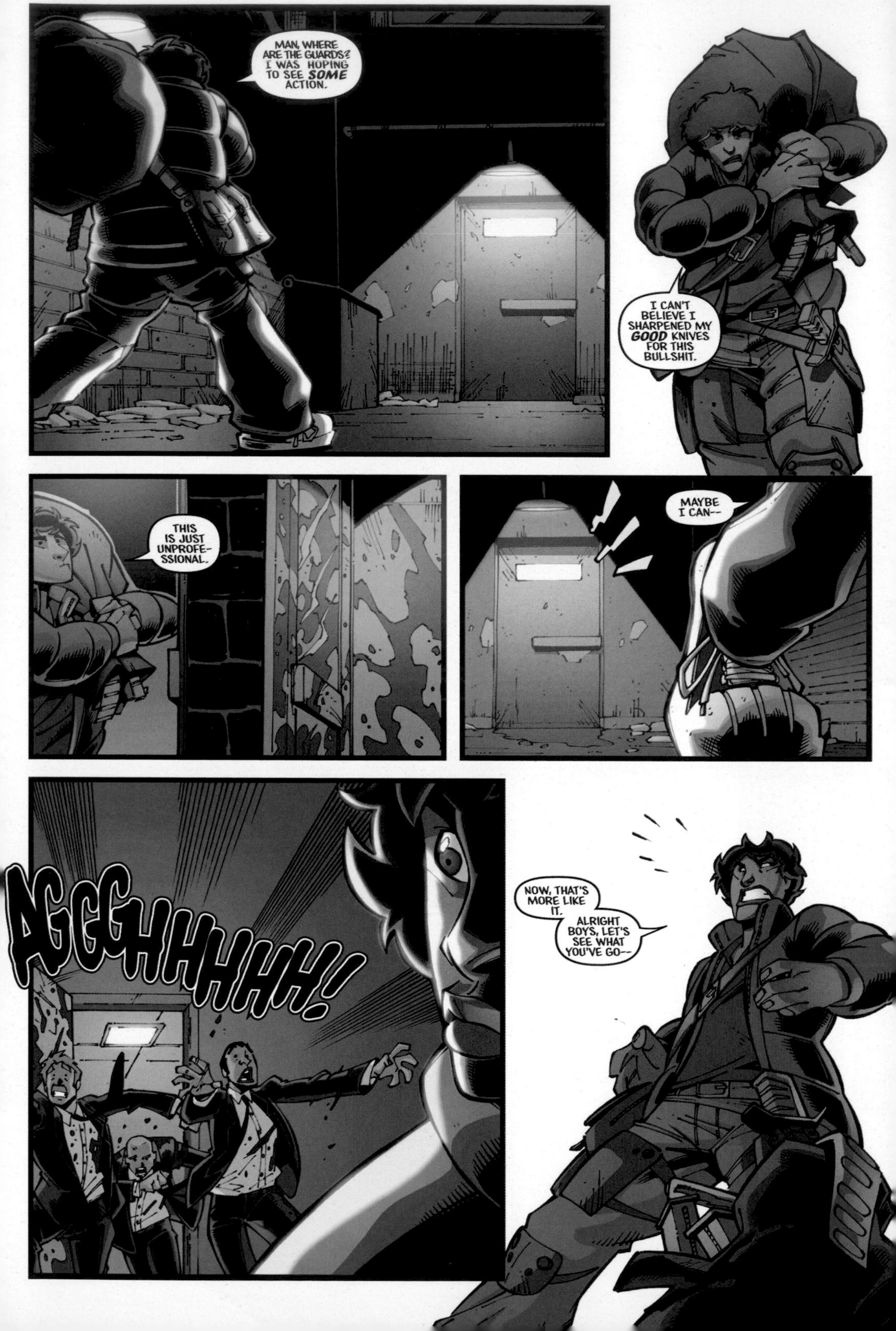
MAN, WHERE ARE THE GUARDS? I WAS HOPING TO SEE SOME ACTION.
I CAN'T BELIEVE I SHARPENED MY GOOD KNIVES FOR THIS BULLSHIT.
THIS IS JUST UNPROFESSIONAL.
MAYBE I CAN--
AGGGHHHHH!
NOW, THAT'S MORE LIKE IT.
ALRIGHT BOYS, LET'S SEE WHAT YOU'VE GO--

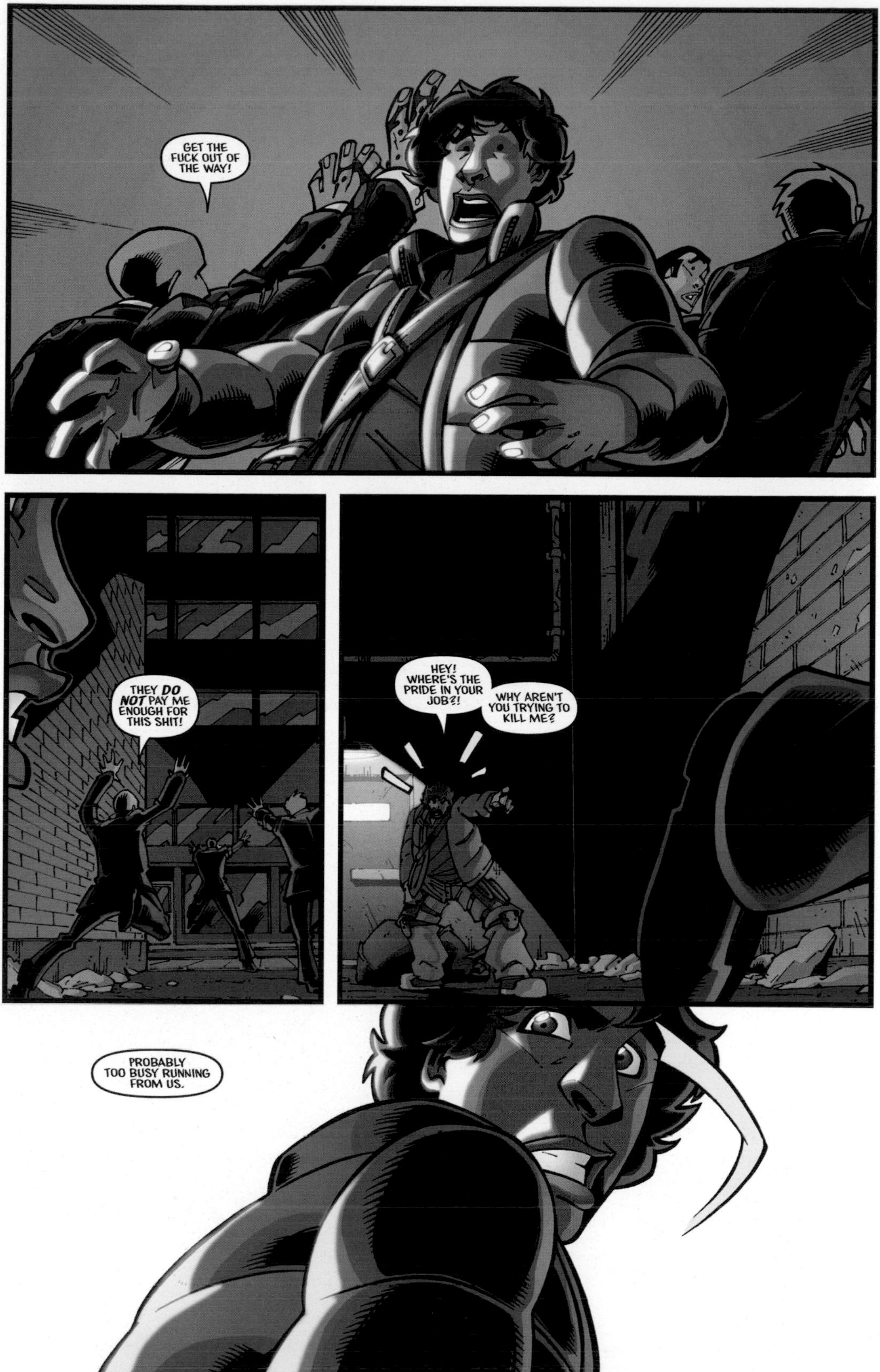
GET THE FUCK OUT OF THE WAY!
THEY DO NOT PAY ME ENOUGH FOR THIS SHIT!
HEY! WHERE'S THE PRIDE IN YOUR JOB?!
WHY AREN'T YOU TRYING TO KILL ME?
PROBABLY TOO BUSY RUNNING FROM US.

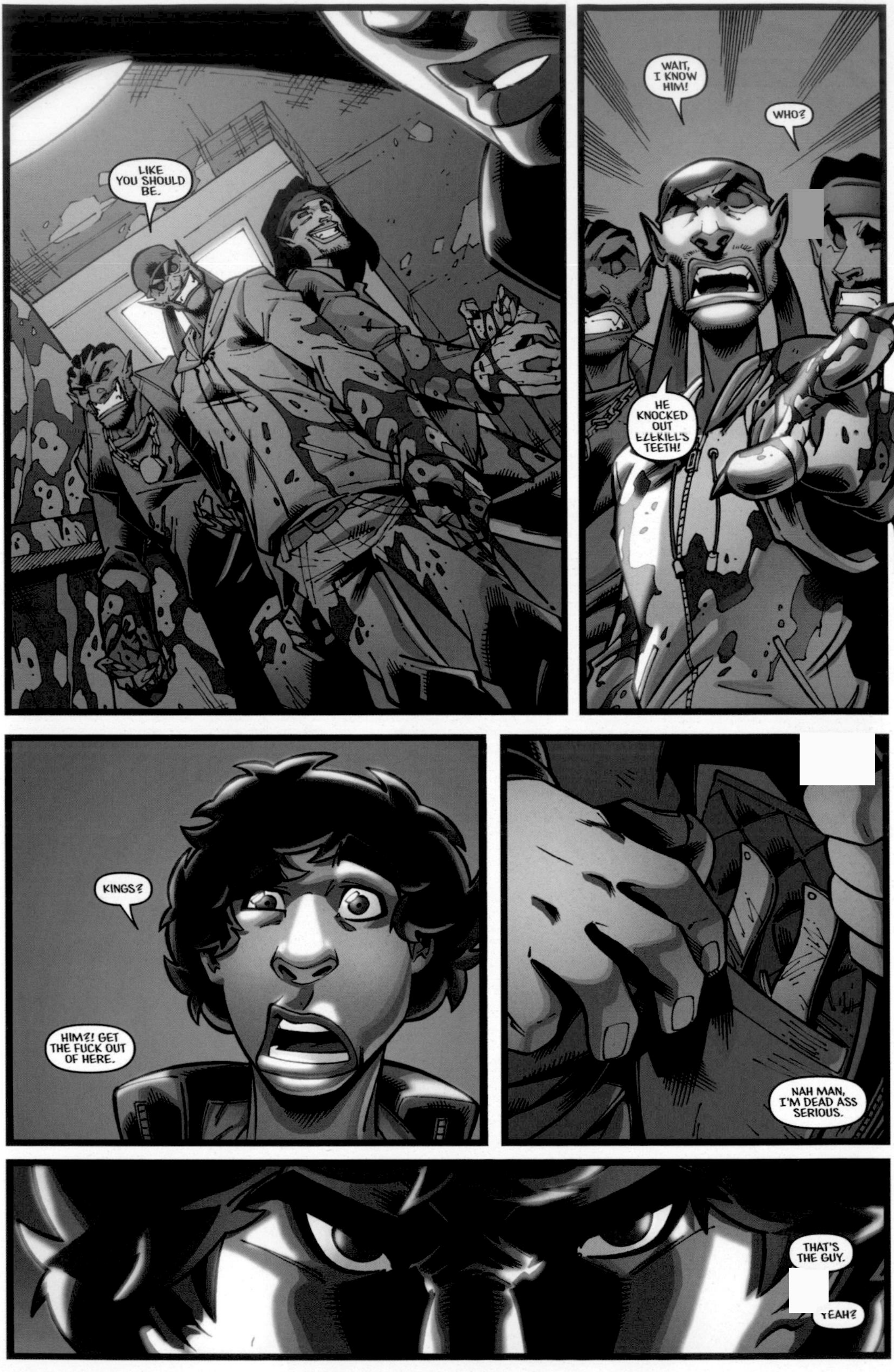
LIKE YOU SHOULD BE.
WAIT, I KNOW HIM!
WHO?
HE KNOCKED OUT EZEKIEL'S TEETH!
KINGS?
HIM?! GET THE FUCK OUT OF HERE.
NAH MAN, I'M DEAD ASS SERIOUS.
THAT'S THE GUY.
YEAH?

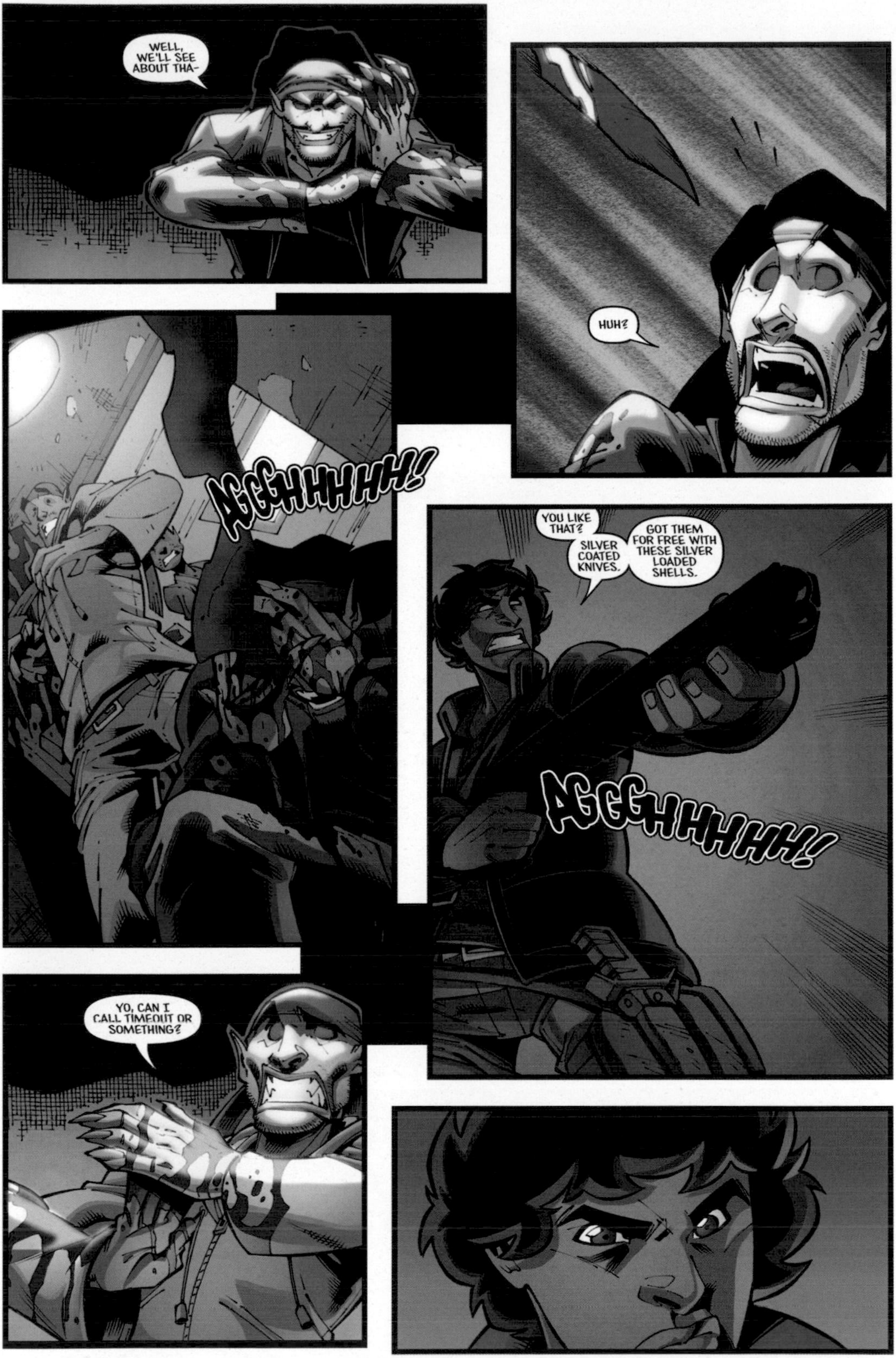
WELL, WE'LL SEE ABOUT THA-
HUH?
AGGHHHHH!
YOU LIKE THAT?
SILVER COATED KNIVES.
GOT THEM FOR FREE WITH THESE SILVER LOADED SHELLS.
AGGGHHHHHH!
YO, CAN I CALL TIMEOUT OR SOMETHING?

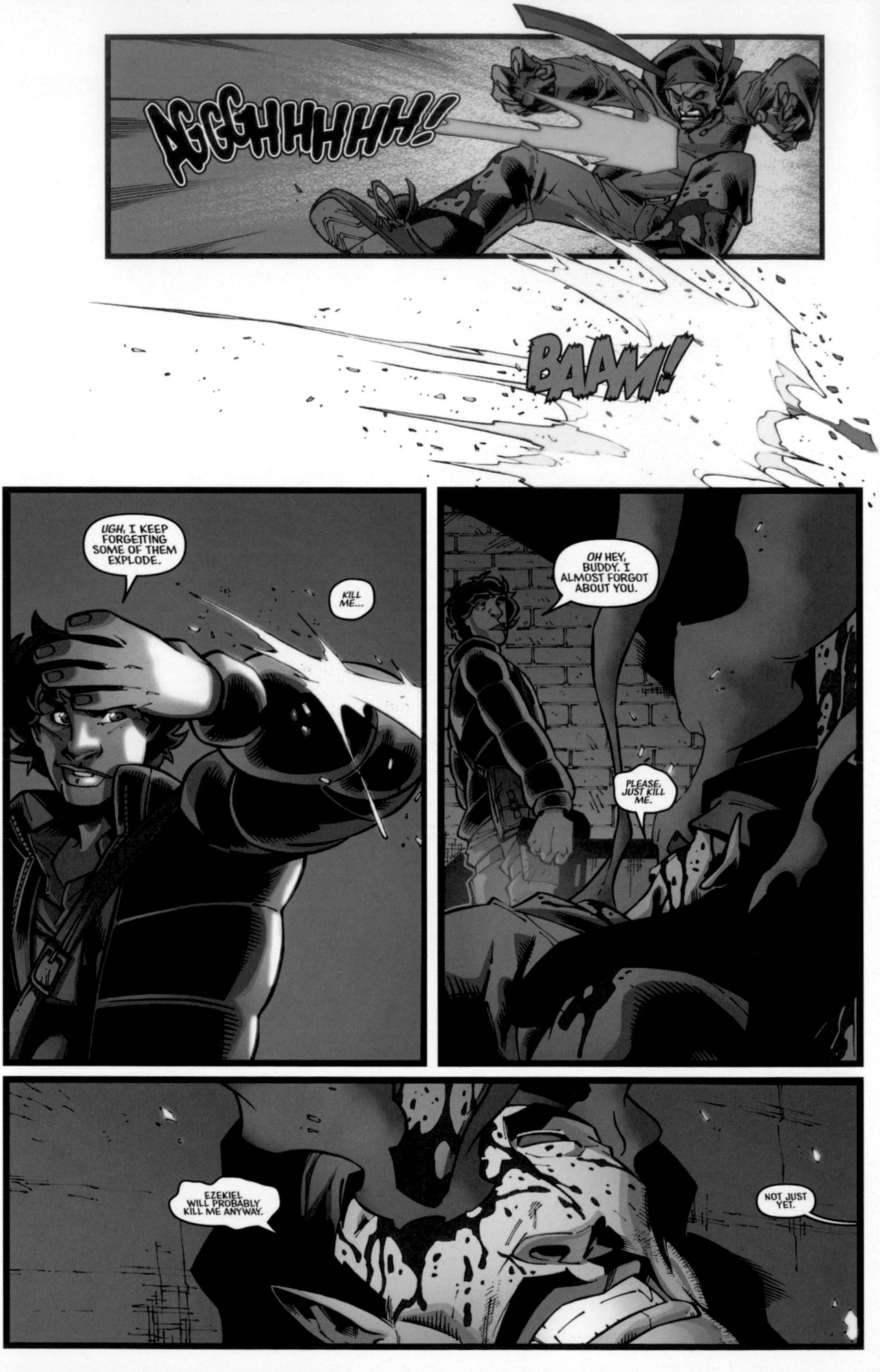
AGGGHHHHH!
BAAM!
UGH, I KEEP FORGETTING SOME OF THEM EXPLODE.
KILL ME...
OH HEY, BUDDY. I ALMOST FORGOT ABOUT YOU.
PLEASE, JUST KILL ME.
EZEKIEL WILL PROBABLY KILL ME ANYWAY.
NOT JUST YET.

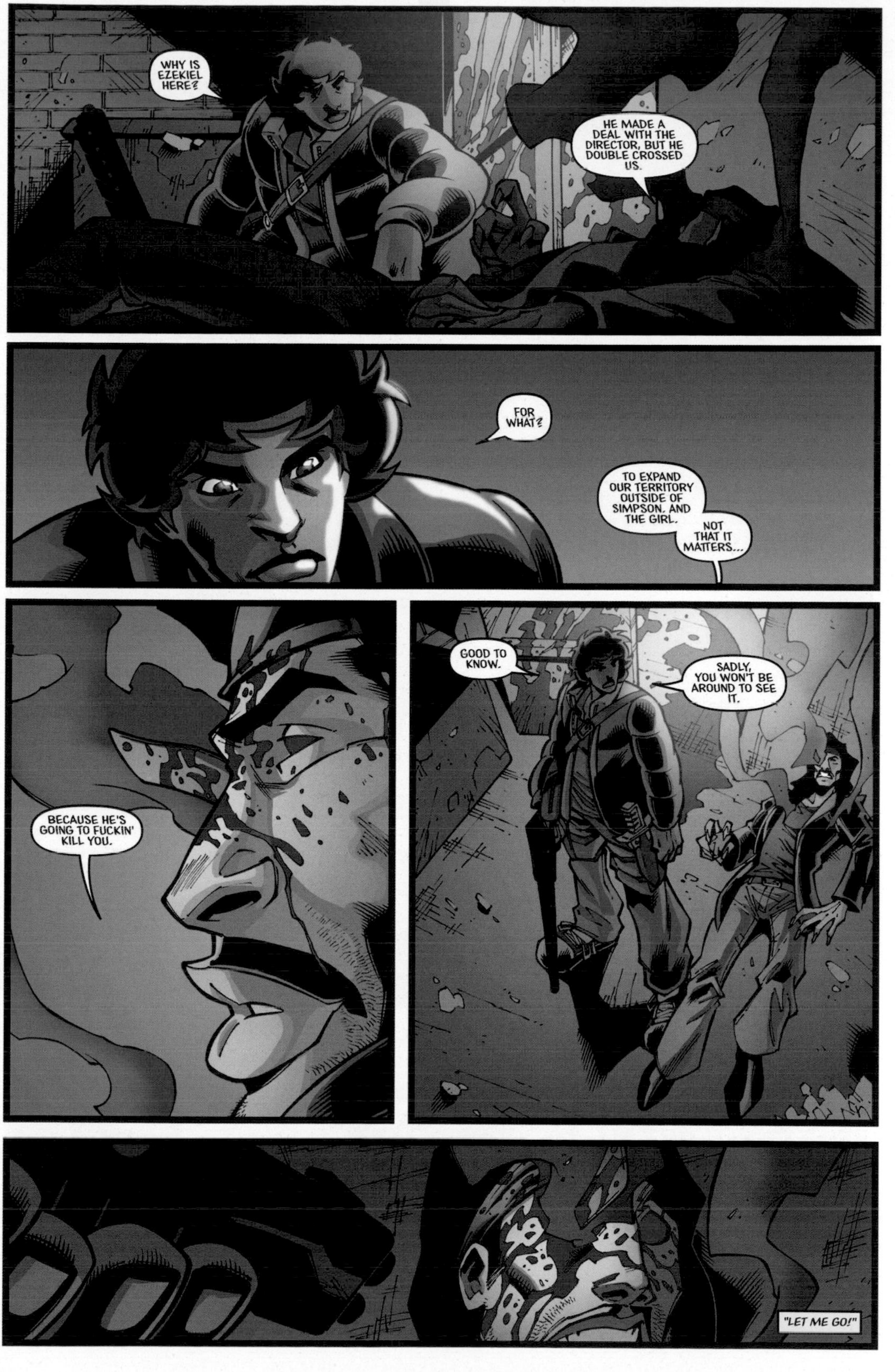
WHY IS EZEKIEL HERE?
HE MADE A DEAL WITH THE DIRECTOR, BUT HE DOUBLE CROSSED US.
FOR WHAT?
TO EXPAND OUR TERRITORY OUTSIDE OF SIMPSON, AND THE GIRL.
NOT THAT IT MATTERS...
BECAUSE HE'S GOING TO FUCKIN' KILL YOU.
GOOD TO KNOW.
SADLY, YOU WON'T BE AROUND TO SEE IT.
"LET ME GO!"

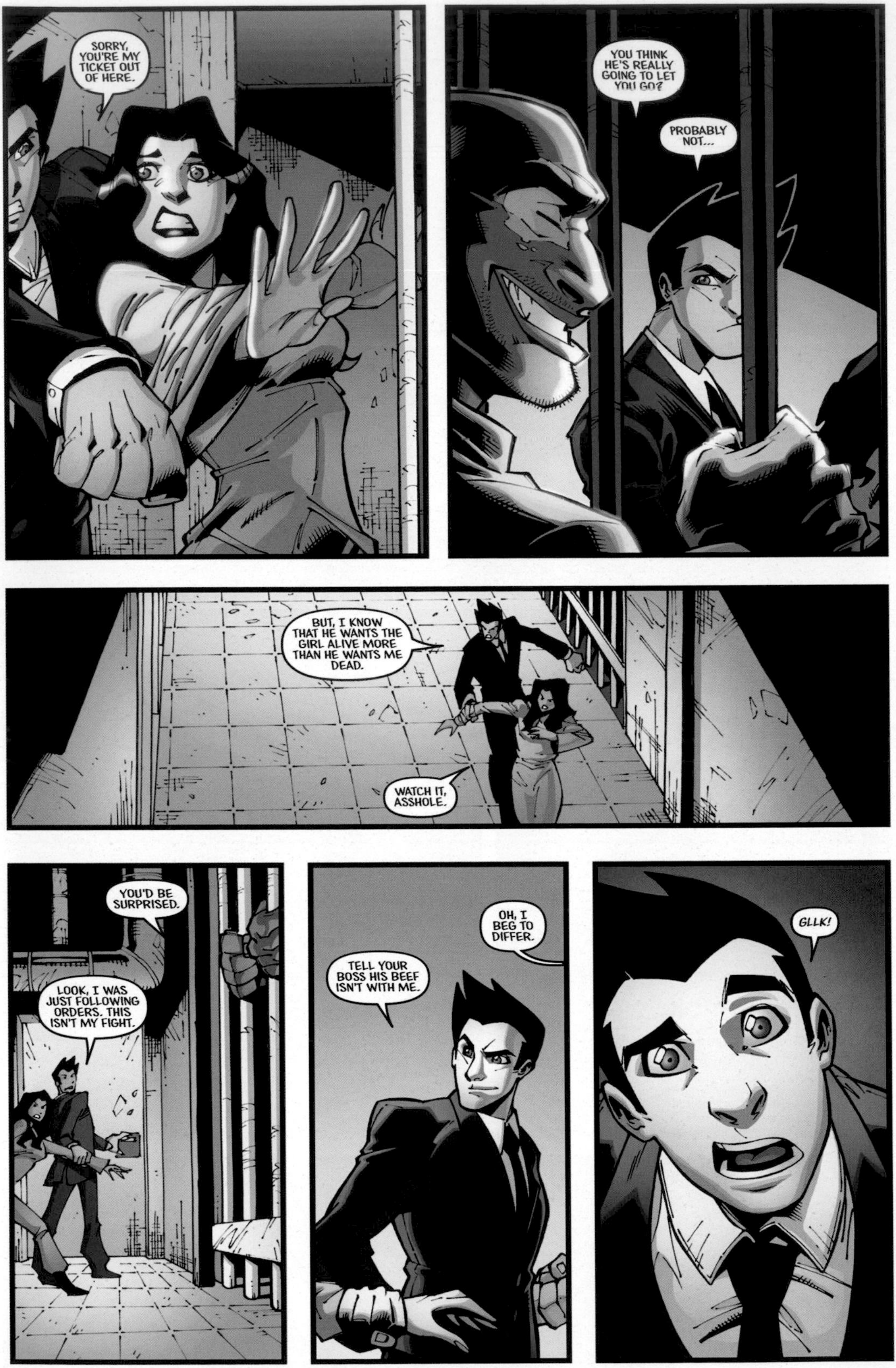
SORRY, YOU'RE MY TICKET OUT OF HERE.
YOU THINK HE'S REALLY GOING TO LET YOU GO?
PROBABLY NOT...
BUT, I KNOW THAT HE WANTS THE GIRL ALIVE MORE THAN HE WANTS ME DEAD.
WATCH IT, ASSHOLE.
YOU'D BE SURPRISED.
LOOK, I WAS JUST FOLLOWING ORDERS. THIS ISN'T MY FIGHT.
TELL YOUR BOSS HIS BEEF ISN'T WITH ME.
OH, I BEG TO DIFFER.
GLLK!

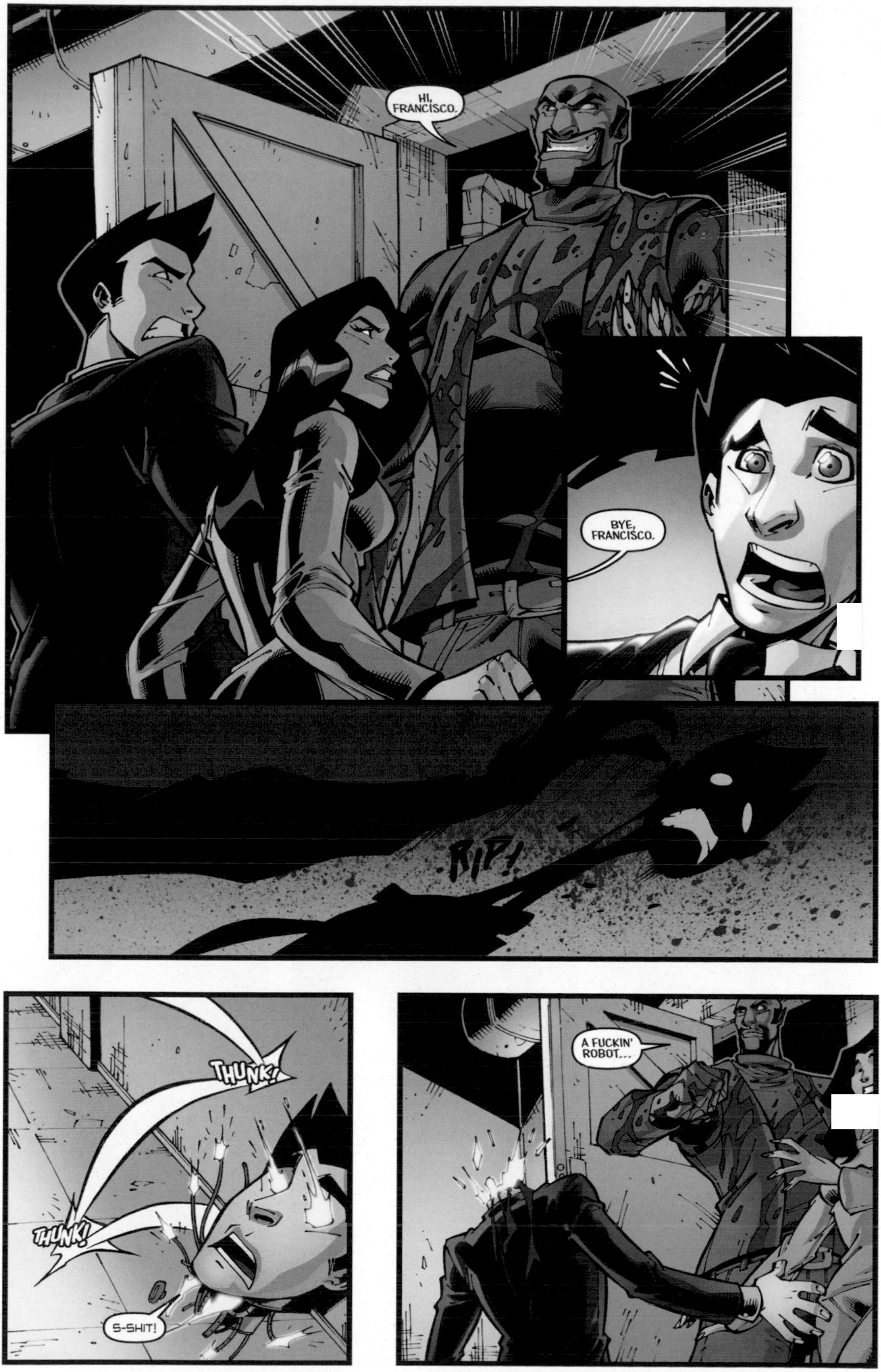
HI, FRANCISCO.
BYE, FRANCISCO.
RIP!
THUNK!
THUNK!
S-SHIT!
A FUCKIN' ROBOT...

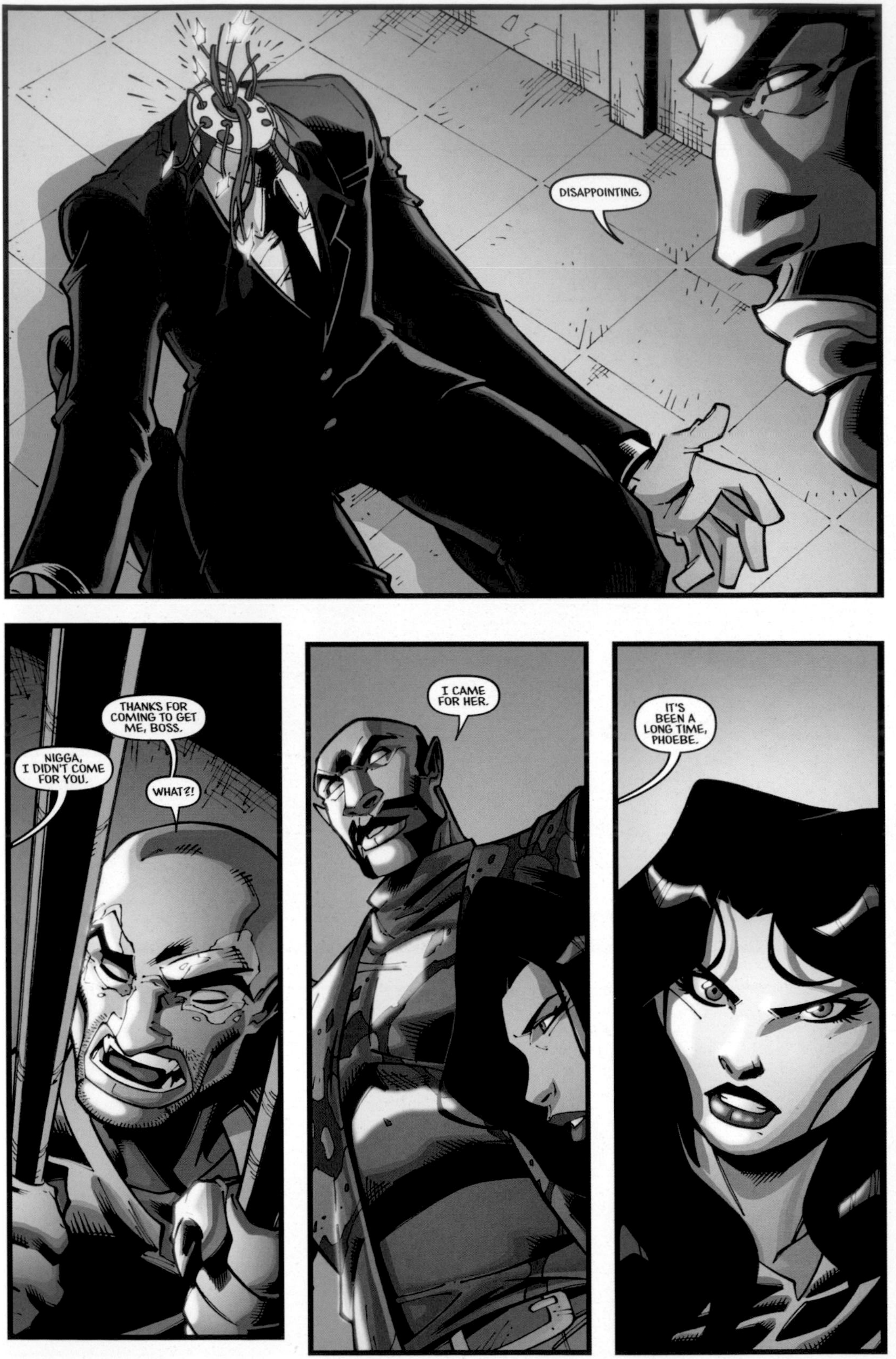
DISAPPOINTING.
THANKS FOR COMING TO GET ME, BOSS.
NIGGA, I DIDN'T COME FOR YOU.
WHAT?!
I CAME FOR HER.
IT'S BEEN A LONG TIME, PHOEBE.

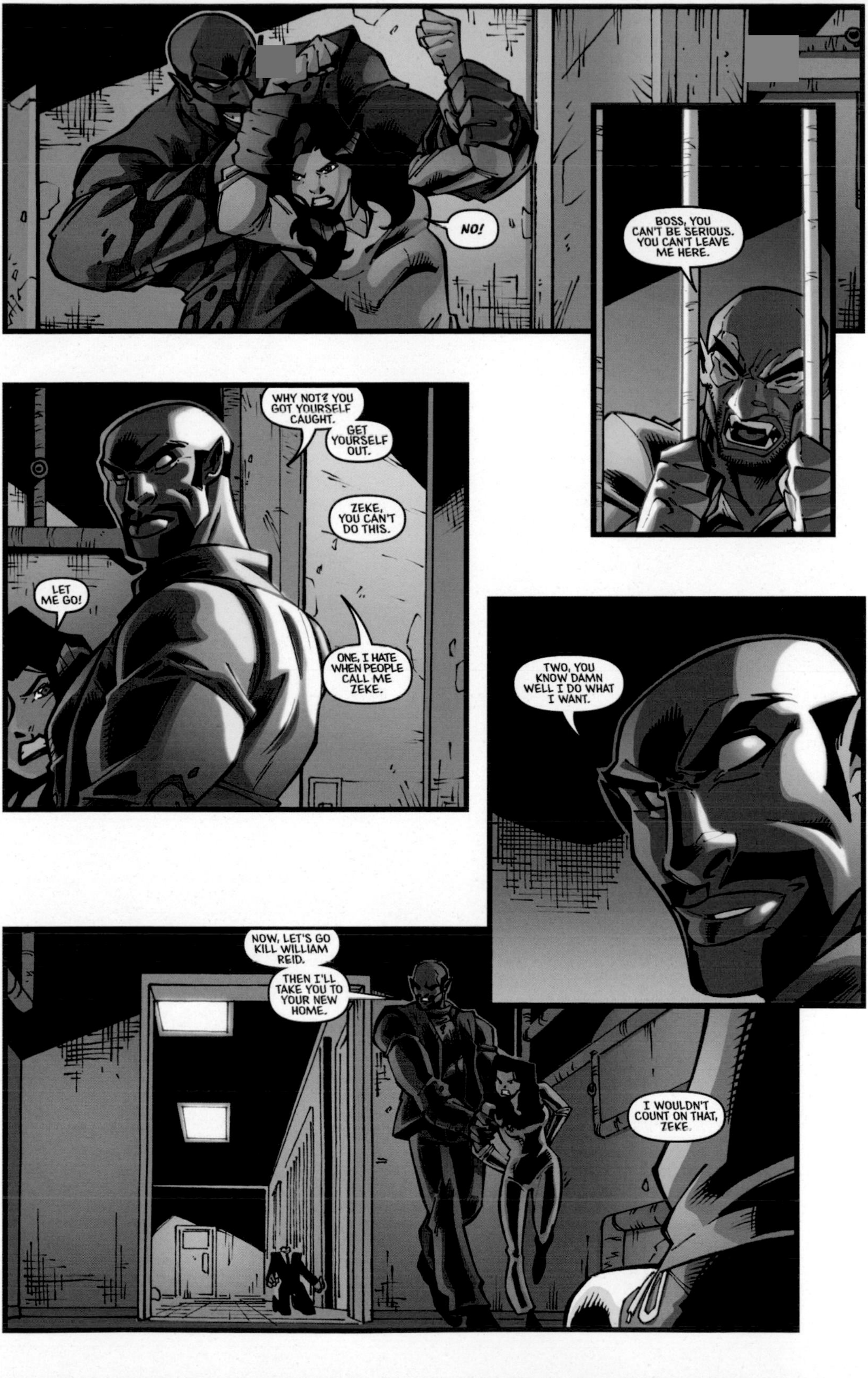
NO!
BOSS, YOU CAN'T BE SERIOUS. YOU CAN'T LEAVE ME HERE.
WHY NOT? YOU GOT YOURSELF CAUGHT.
GET YOURSELF OUT.
ZEKE, YOU CAN'T DO THIS.
LET ME GO!
ONE, I HATE WHEN PEOPLE CALL ME ZEKE.
TWO, YOU KNOW DAMN WELL I DO WHAT I WANT.
NOW, LET'S GO KILL WILLIAM REID.
THEN I'LL TAKE YOU TO YOUR NEW HOME.
I WOULDN'T COUNT ON THAT, ZEKE.

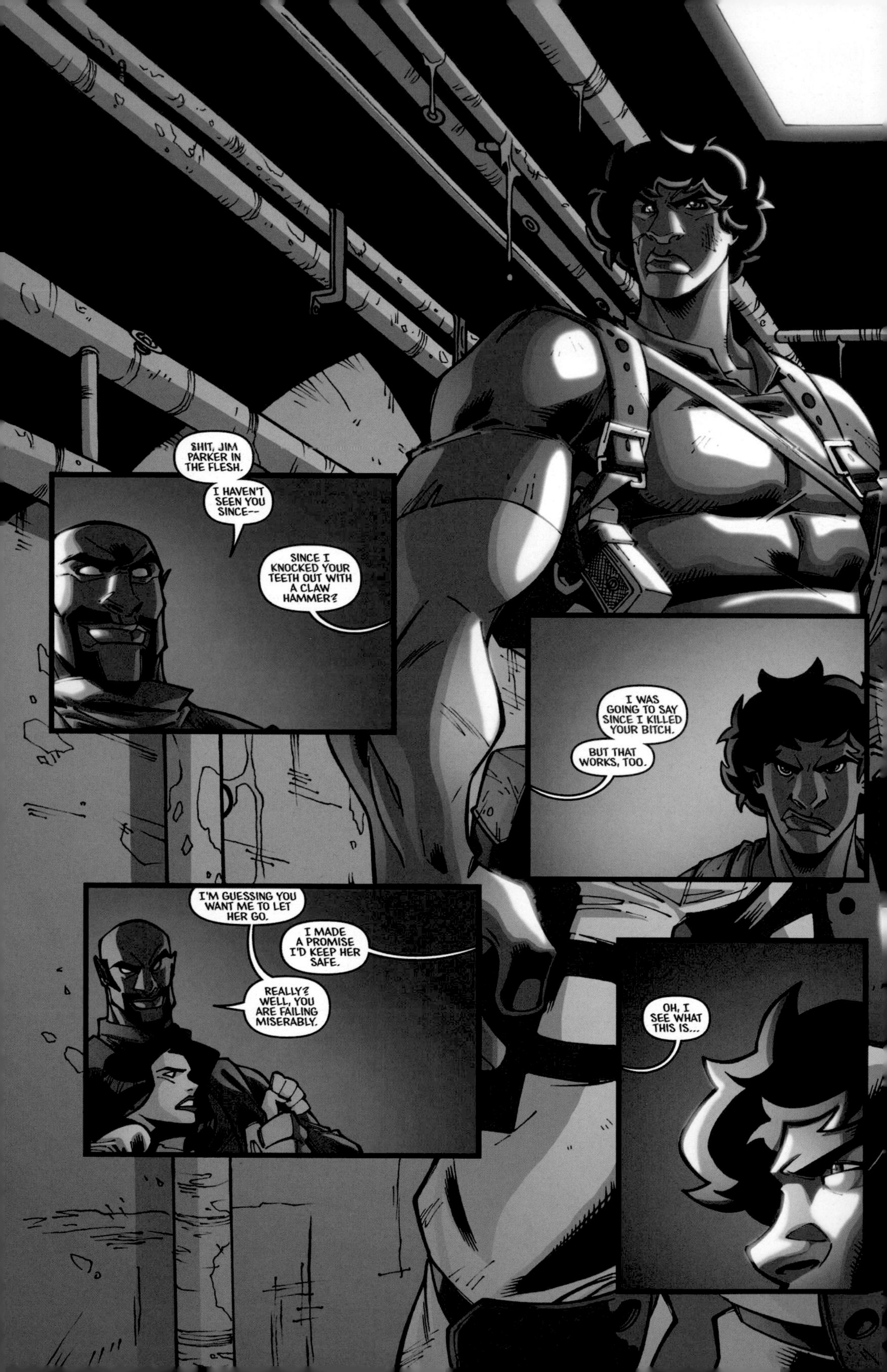
SHIT, JIM PARKER IN THE FLESH.
I HAVEN'T SEEN YOU SINCE--
SINCE I KNOCKED YOUR TEETH OUT WITH A CLAW HAMMER?
I WAS GOING TO SAY SINCE I KILLED YOUR BITCH.
BUT THAT WORKS, TOO.
I'M GUESSING YOU WANT ME TO LET HER GO.
I MADE A PROMISE I'D KEEP HER SAFE.
REALLY? WELL, YOU ARE FAILING MISERABLY.
OH, I SEE WHAT THIS IS...

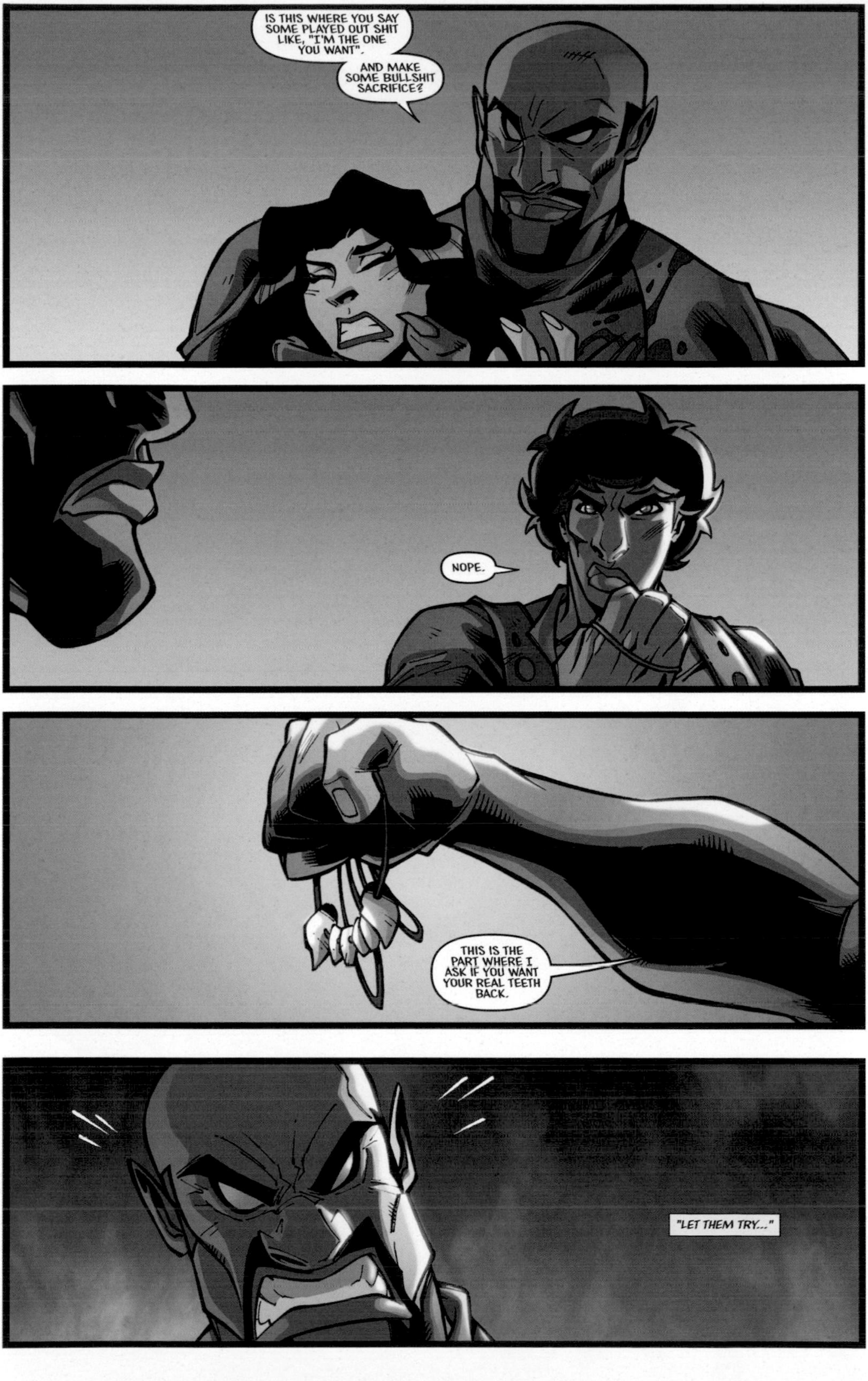
IS THIS WHERE YOU SAY SOME PLAYED OUT SHIT LIKE, "I'M THE ONE YOU WANT".
AND MAKE SOME BULLSHIT SACRIFICE?
NOPE.
THIS IS THE PART WHERE I ASK IF YOU WANT YOUR REAL TEETH BACK.
"LET THEM TRY..."

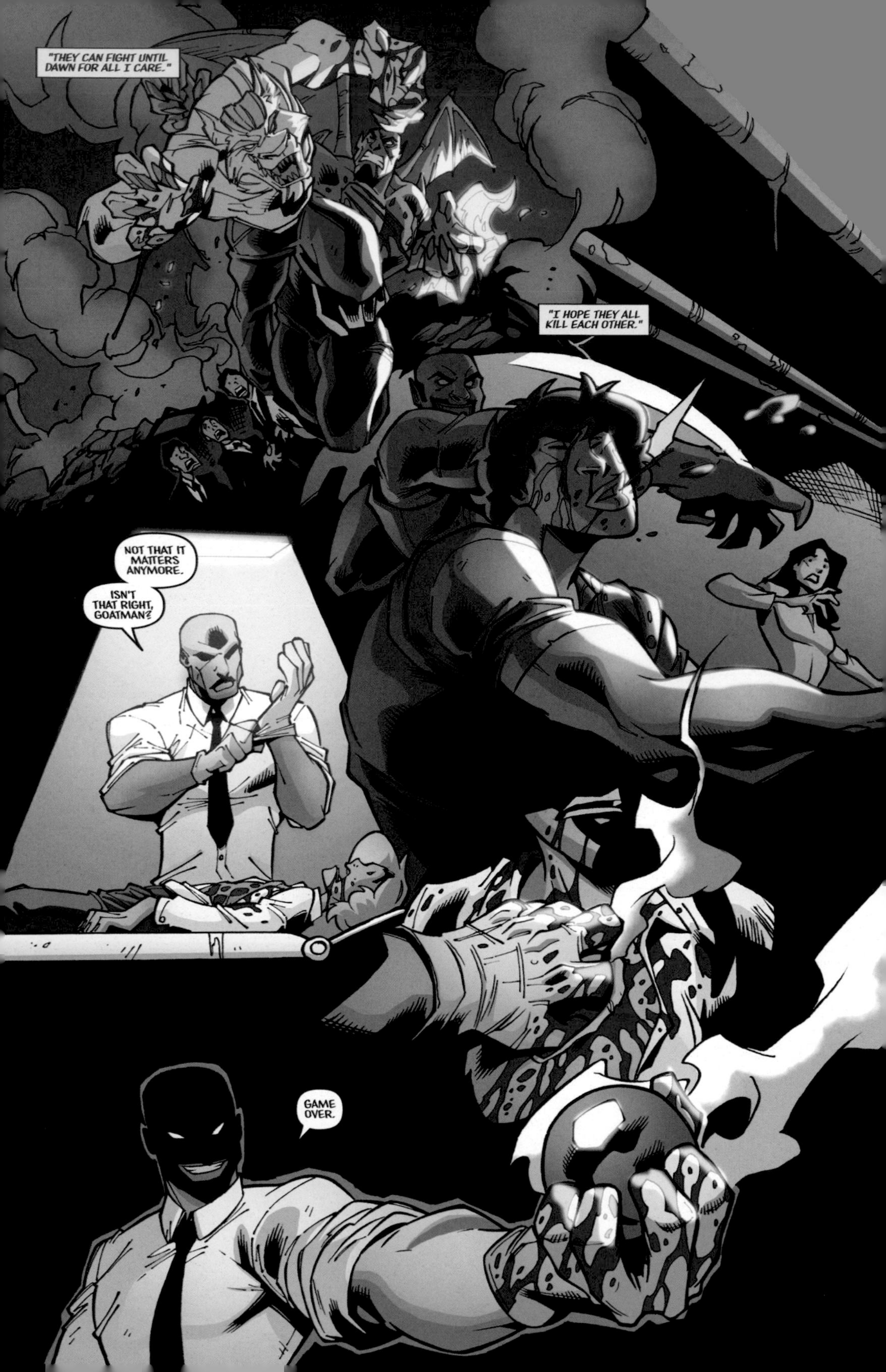
"THEY CAN FIGHT UNTIL DAWN FOR ALL I CARE."
"I HOPE THEY ALL KILL EACH OTHER."
NOT THAT IT MATTERS ANYMORE.
ISN'T THAT RIGHT, GOATMAN?
GAME OVER.

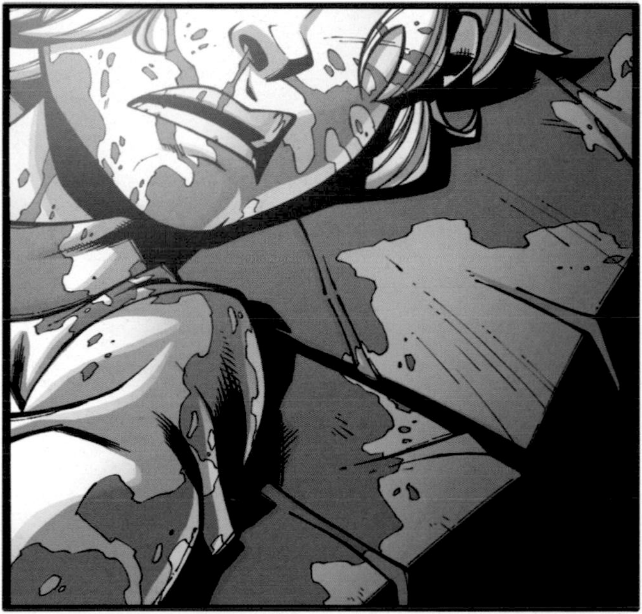

CHAPTER FIVE

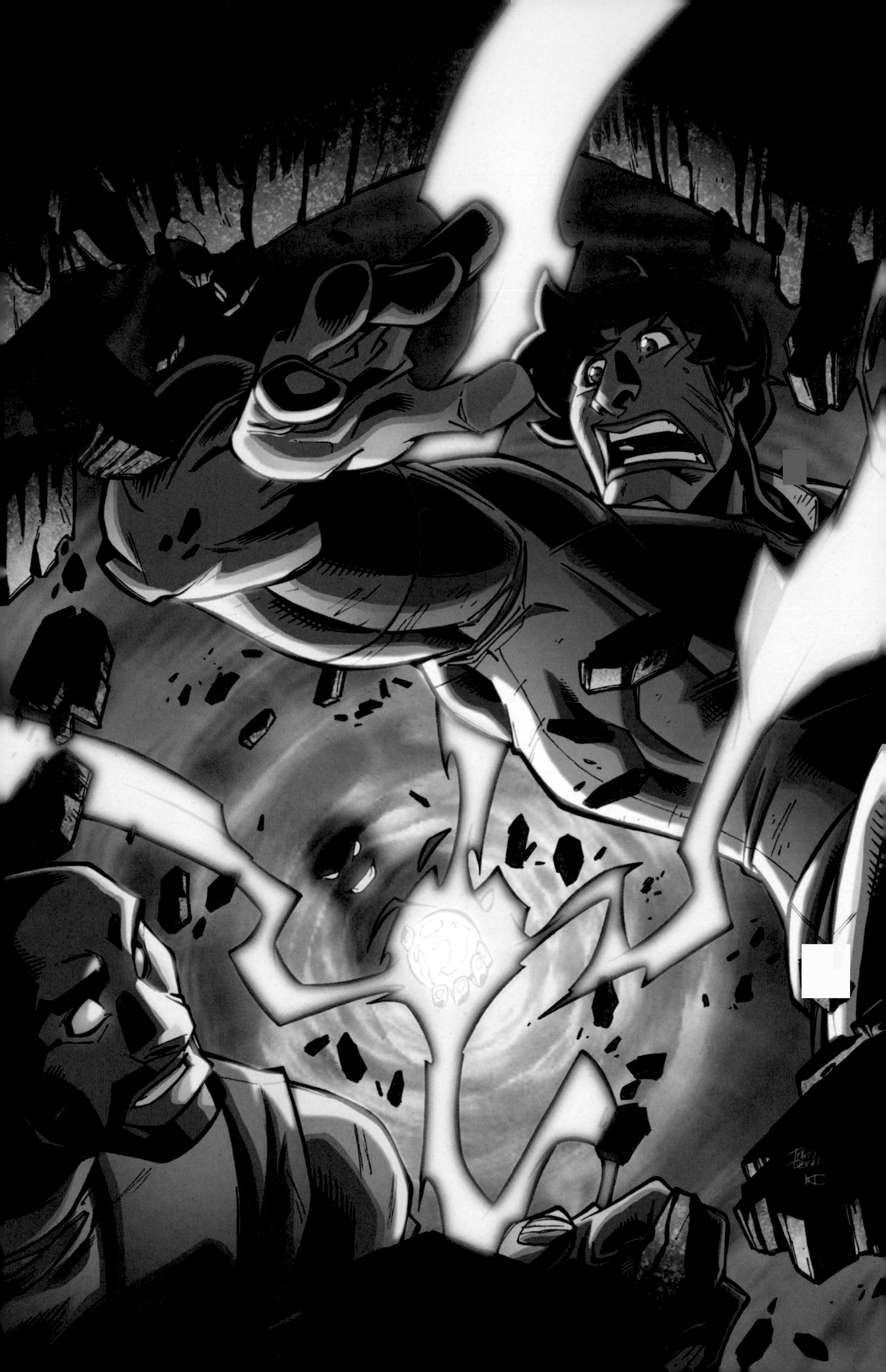

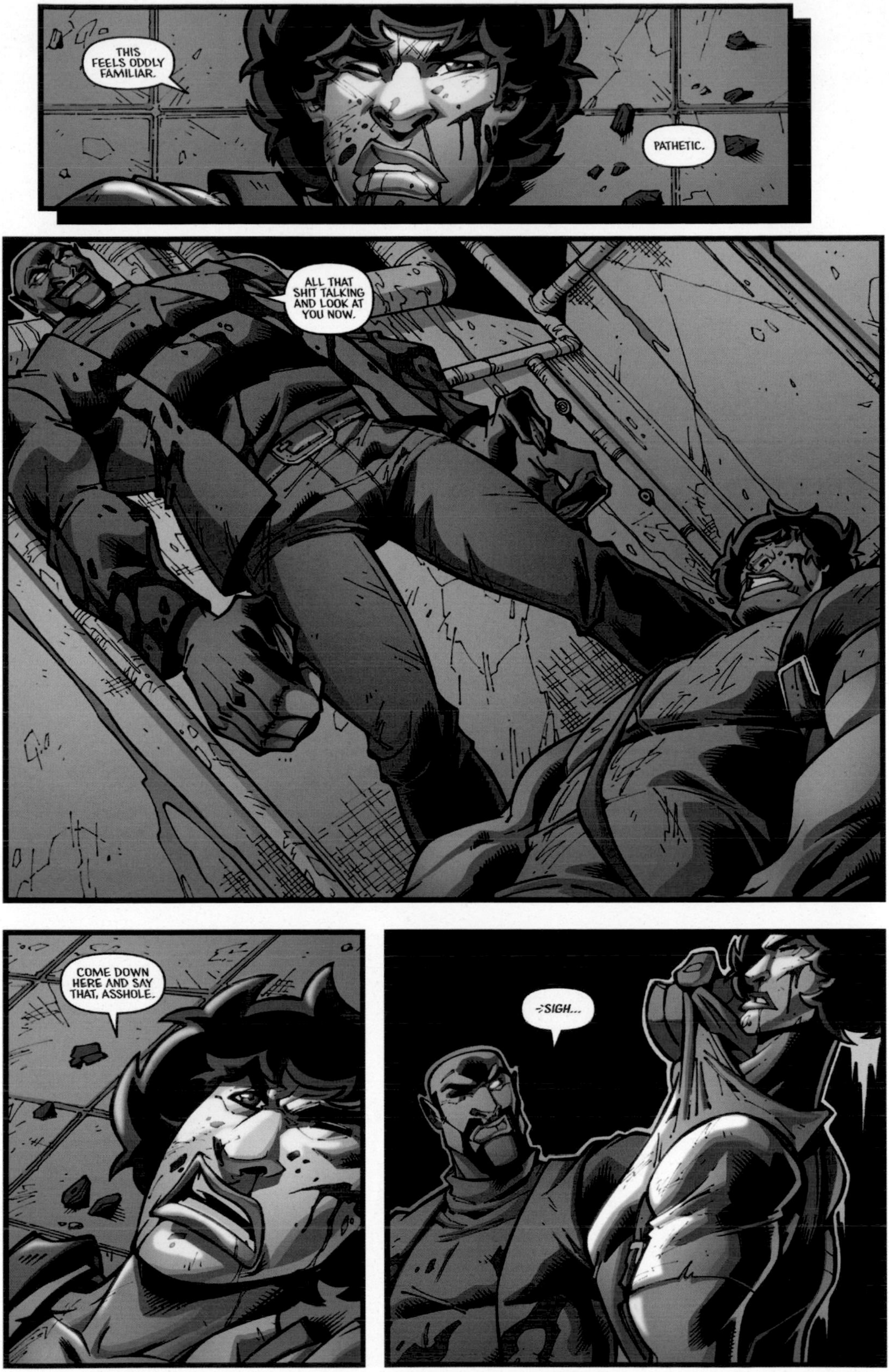
THIS FEELS ODDLY FAMILIAR.
PATHETIC.
ALL THAT SHIT TALKING AND LOOK AT YOU NOW.
COME DOWN HERE AND SAY THAT, ASSHOLE.
-SIGH...

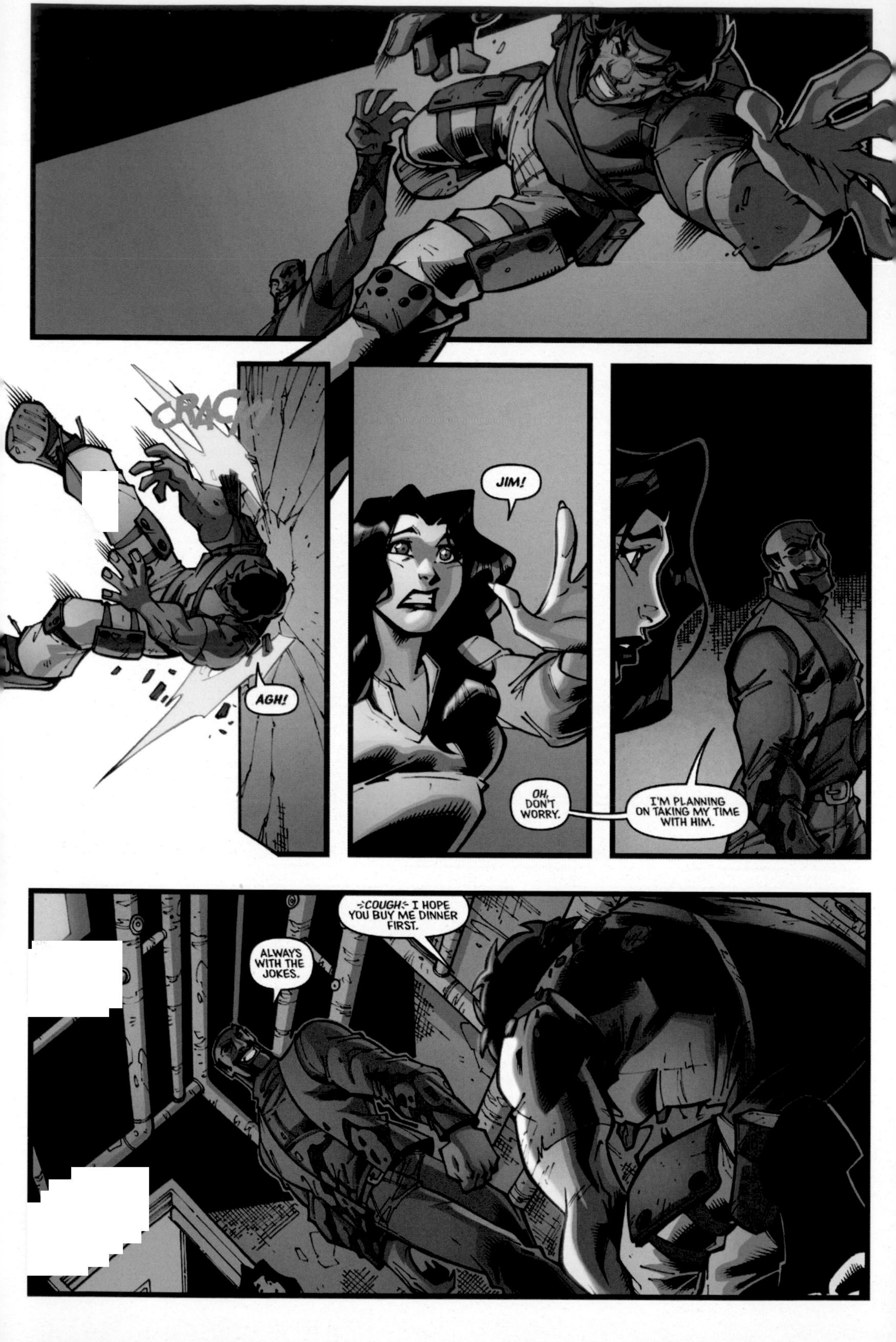
CRACK!
AGH!
JIM!
OH, DON'T WORRY.
I'M PLANNING ON TAKING MY TIME WITH HIM.
ALWAYS WITH THE JOKES.
-COUGH- I HOPE YOU BUY ME DINNER FIRST.

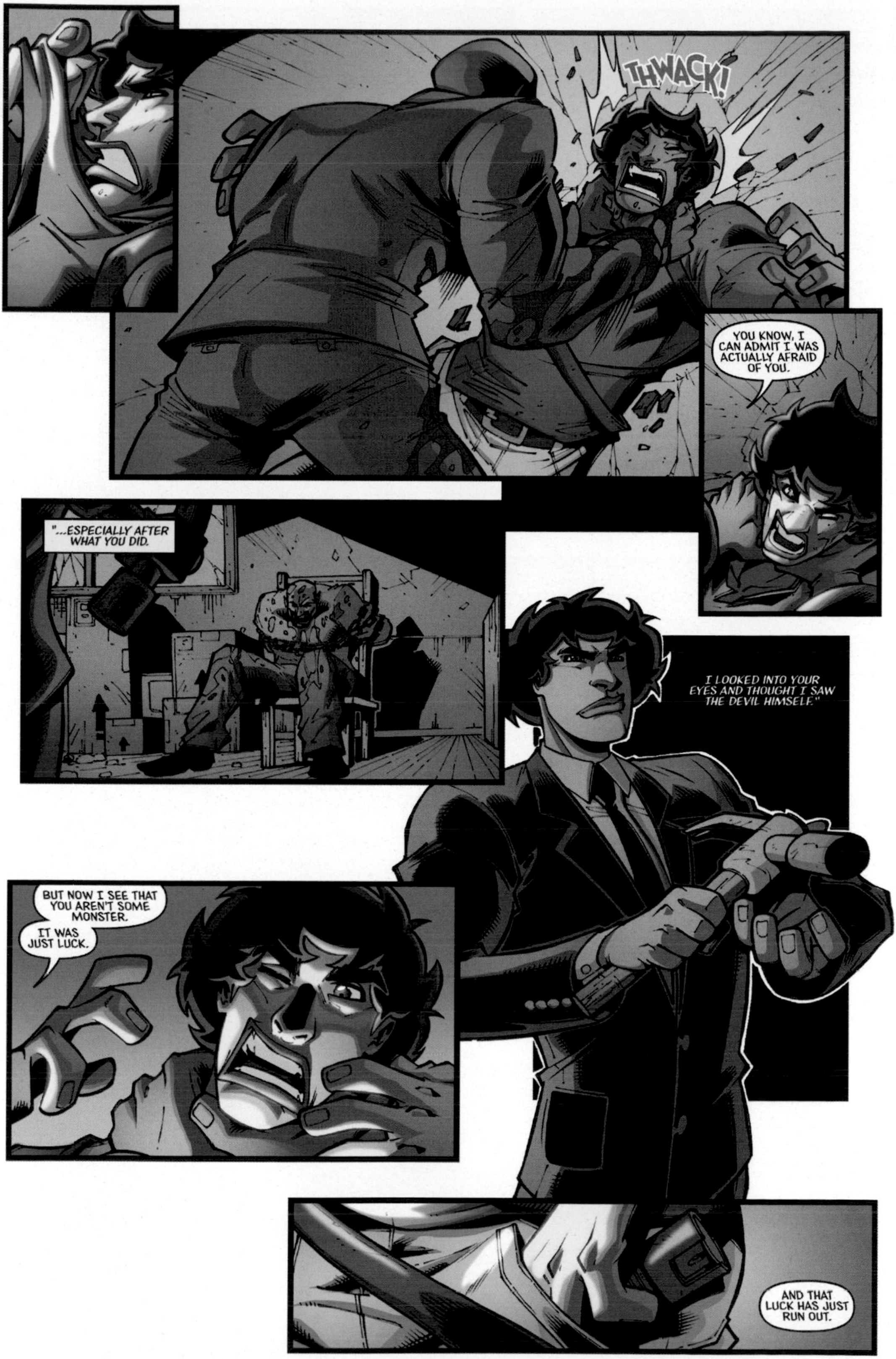
THWACK!
YOU KNOW, I CAN ADMIT I WAS ACTUALLY AFRAID OF YOU.
"...ESPECIALLY AFTER WHAT YOU DID.
I LOOKED INTO YOUR EYES AND THOUGHT I SAW THE DEVIL HIMSELF."
BUT NOW I SEE THAT YOU AREN'T SOME MONSTER.
IT WAS JUST LUCK.
AND THAT LUCK HAS JUST RUN OUT.

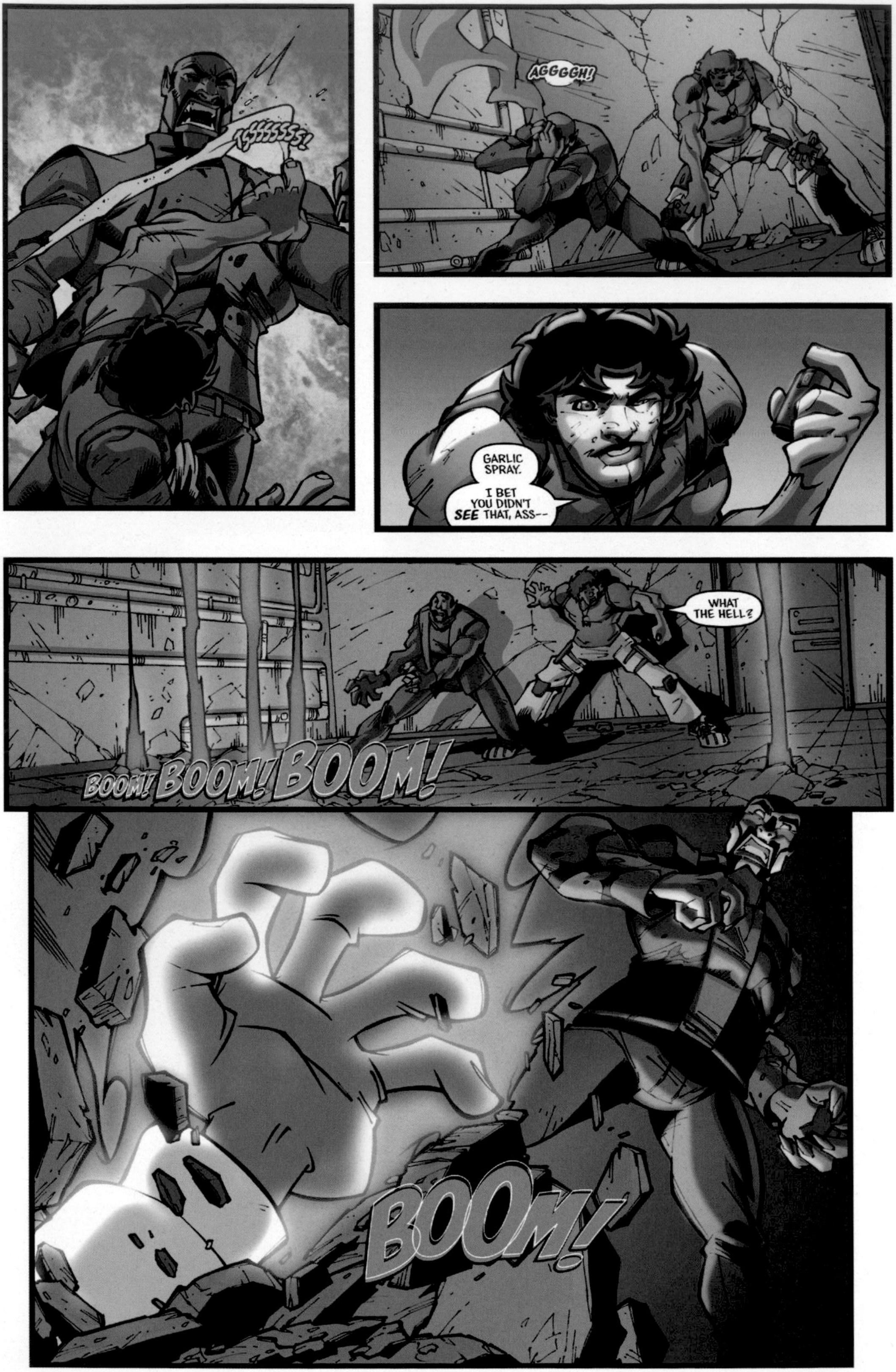
TSSSSSSS!
AGGGGH!
GARLIC SPRAY.
I BET YOU DIDN'T SEE THAT, ASS--
WHAT THE HELL?
BOOM! BOOM! BOOM!
BOOM!

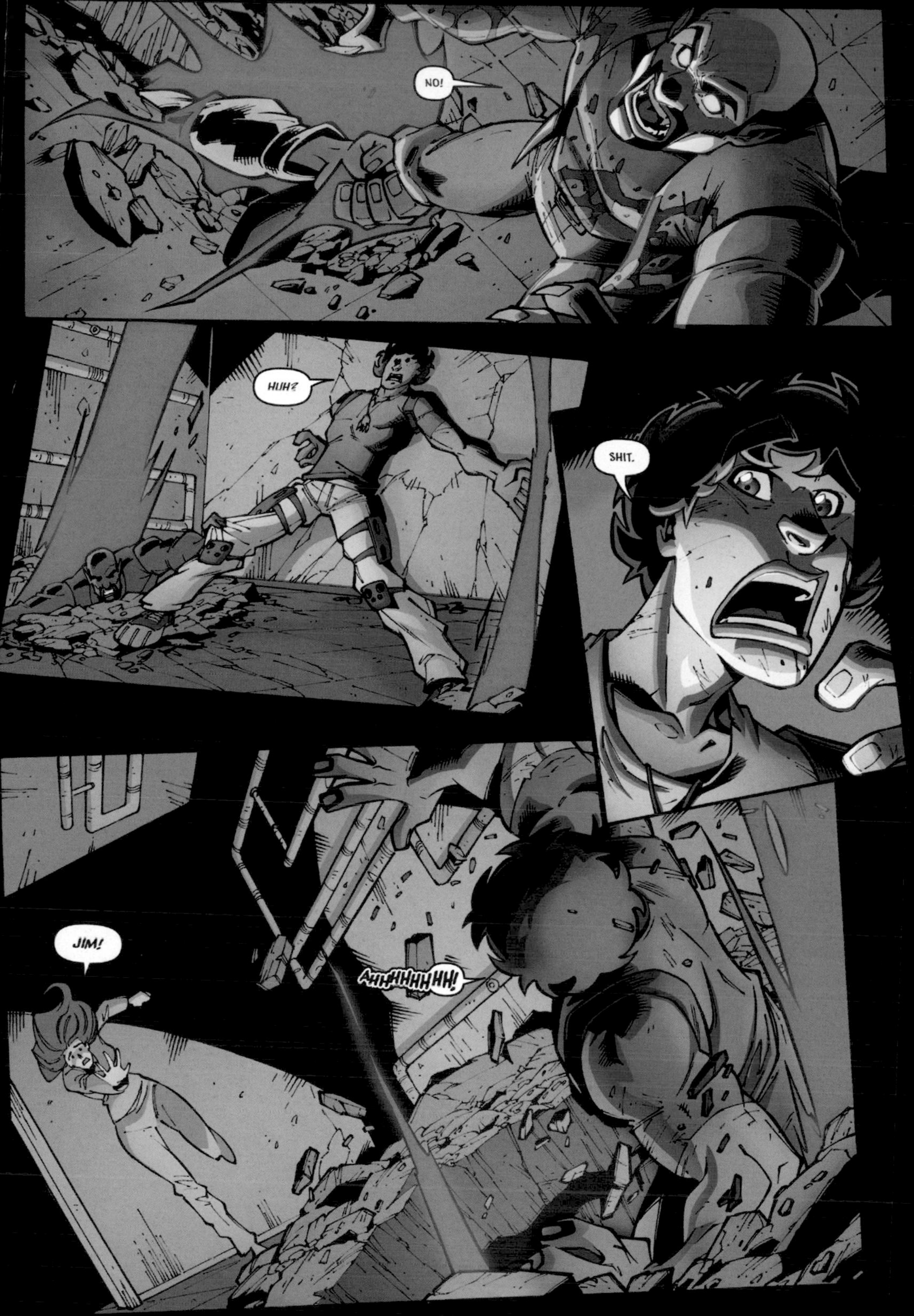
NO!
HUH?
SHIT.
JIM!
AHHHHHHHH!

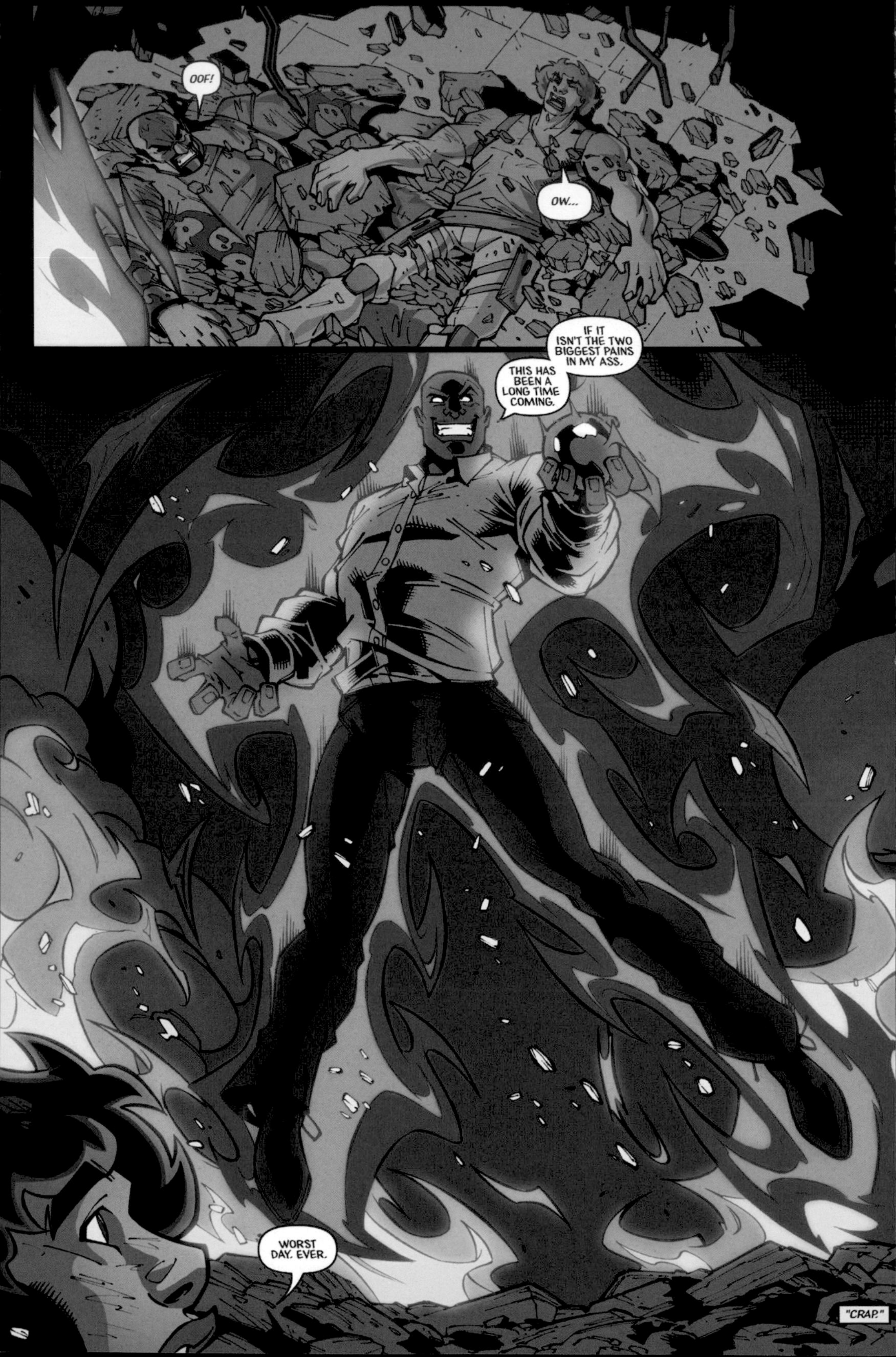

OOF!
OW...
IF IT ISN'T THE TWO BIGGEST PAINS IN MY ASS.
THIS HAS BEEN A LONG TIME COMING.
WORST DAY. EVER.
"CRAP."

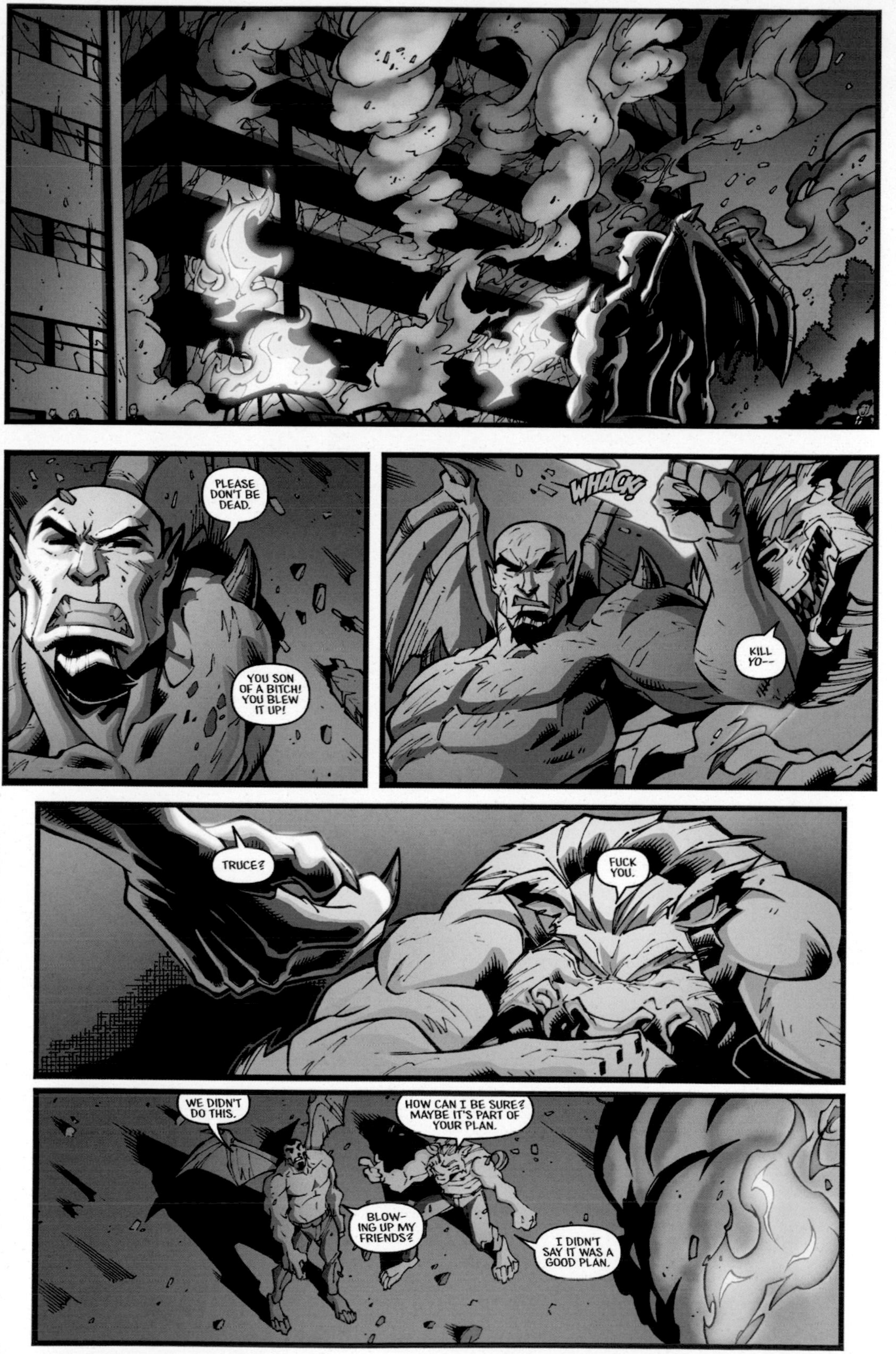
PLEASE DON'T BE DEAD.
YOU SON OF A BITCH! YOU BLEW IT UP!
WHACK!
KILL YO--
TRUCE?
FUCK YOU.
WE DIDN'T DO THIS.
HOW CAN I BE SURE? MAYBE IT'S PART OF YOUR PLAN.
BLOW-ING UP MY FRIENDS?
I DIDN'T SAY IT WAS A GOOD PLAN.

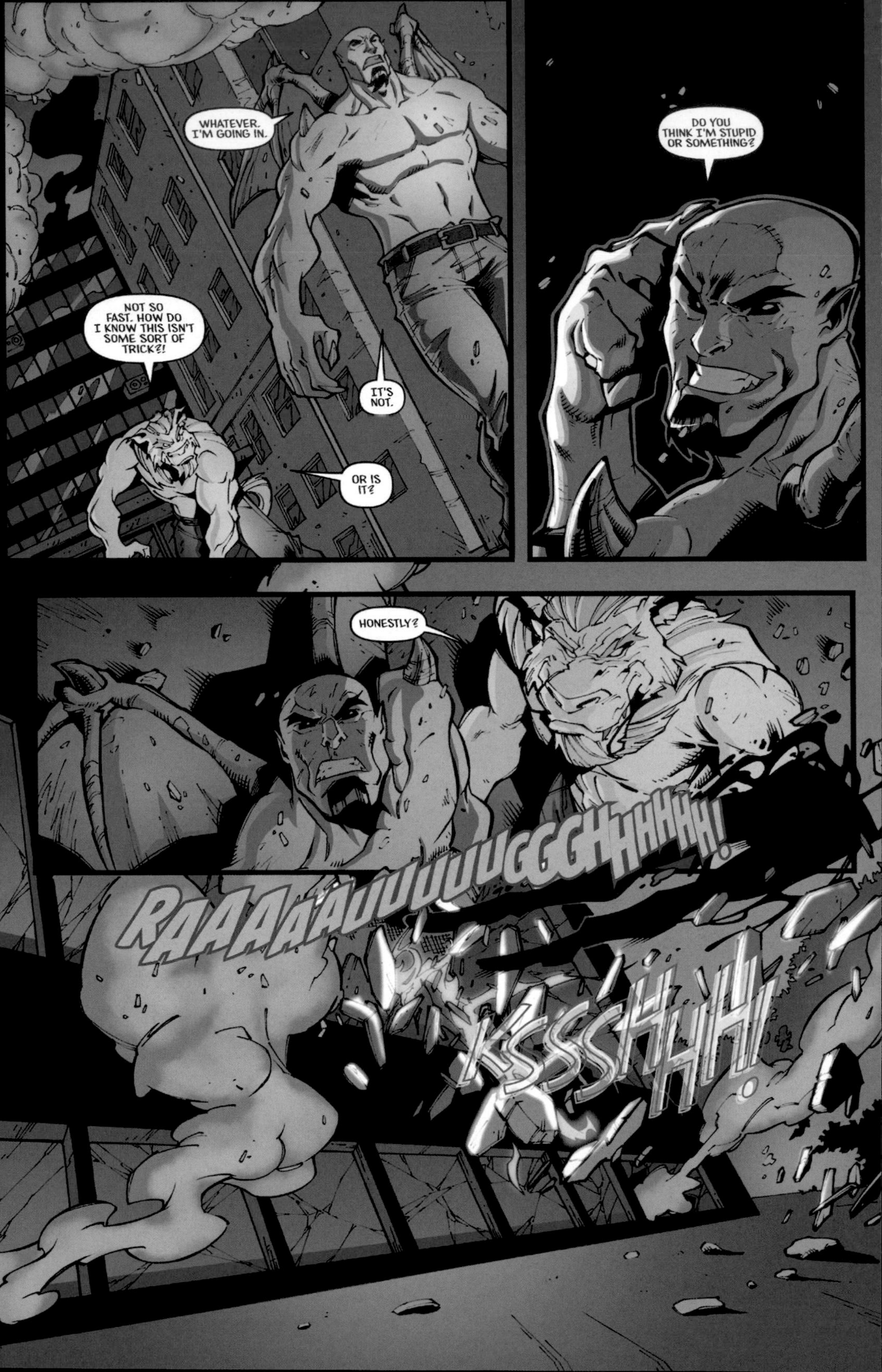
WHATEVER. I'M GOING IN.
NOT SO FAST. HOW DO I KNOW THIS ISN'T SOME SORT OF TRICK?!
IT'S NOT.
OR IS IT?
DO YOU THINK I'M STUPID OR SOMETHING?
HONESTLY?
RAAAAAUUUUUUGGGHHHHH!
KSSSHHH!

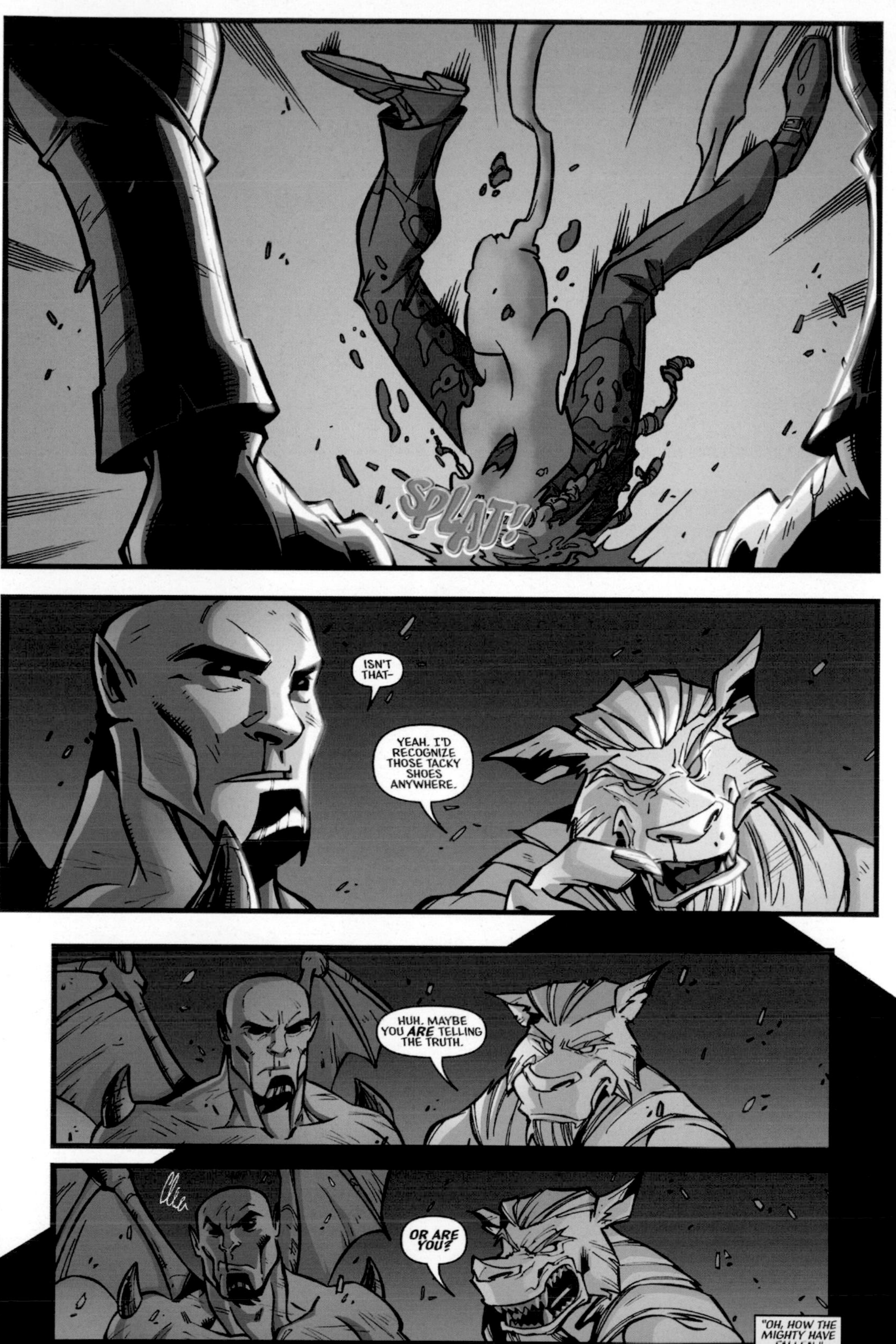
SPLAT!
ISN'T THAT-
YEAH. I'D RECOGNIZE THOSE TACKY SHOES ANYWHERE.
HUH. MAYBE YOU ARE TELLING THE TRUTH.
OR ARE YOU?
"OH, HOW THE MIGHTY HAVE FALLEN."

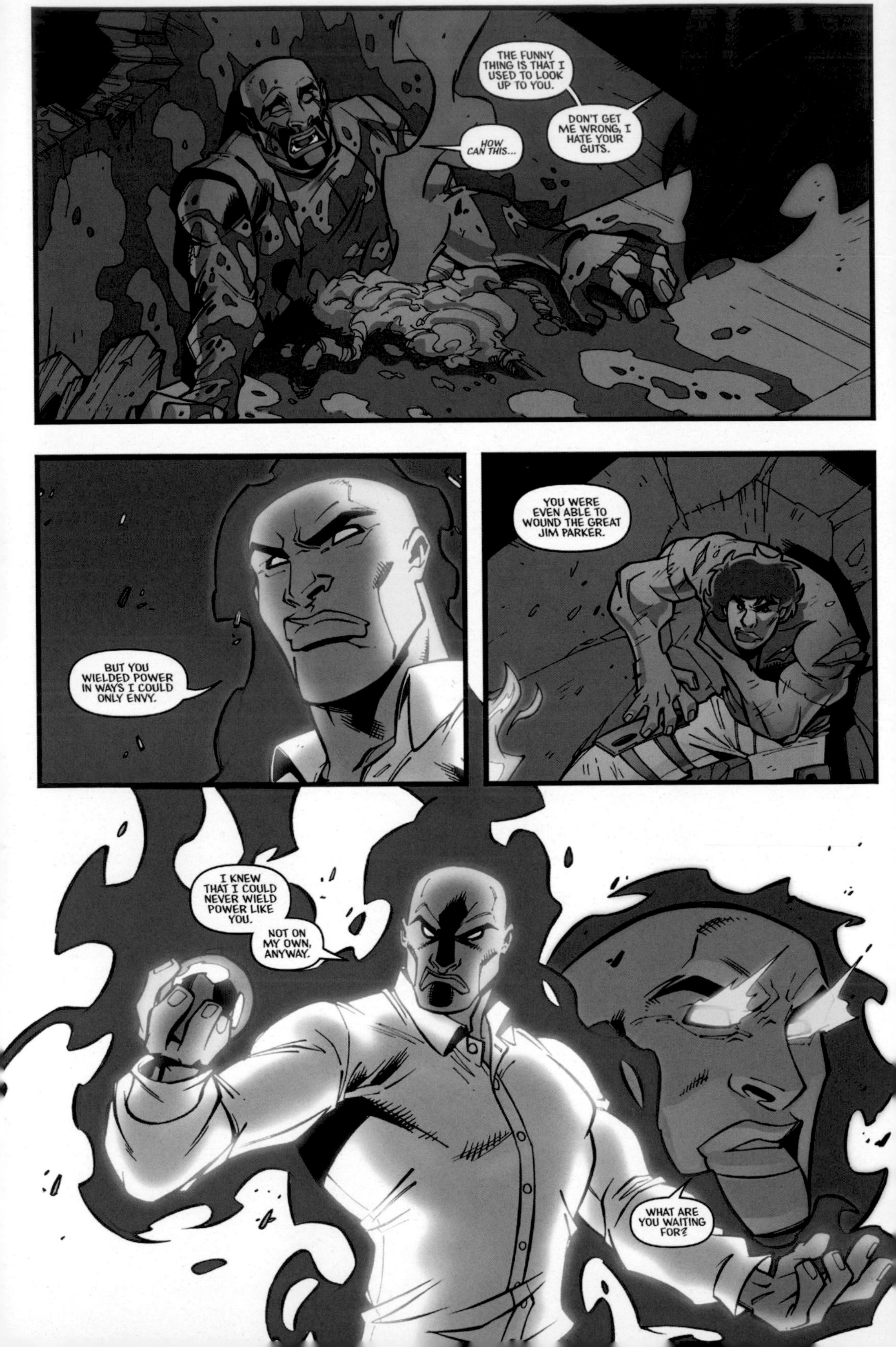
THE FUNNY THING IS THAT I USED TO LOOK UP TO YOU.
DON'T GET ME WRONG, I HATE YOUR GUTS.
HOW CAN THIS...
BUT YOU WIELDED POWER IN WAYS I COULD ONLY ENVY.
YOU WERE EVEN ABLE TO WOUND THE GREAT JIM PARKER.
I KNEW THAT I COULD NEVER WIELD POWER LIKE YOU.
NOT ON MY OWN, ANYWAY.
WHAT ARE YOU WAITING FOR?

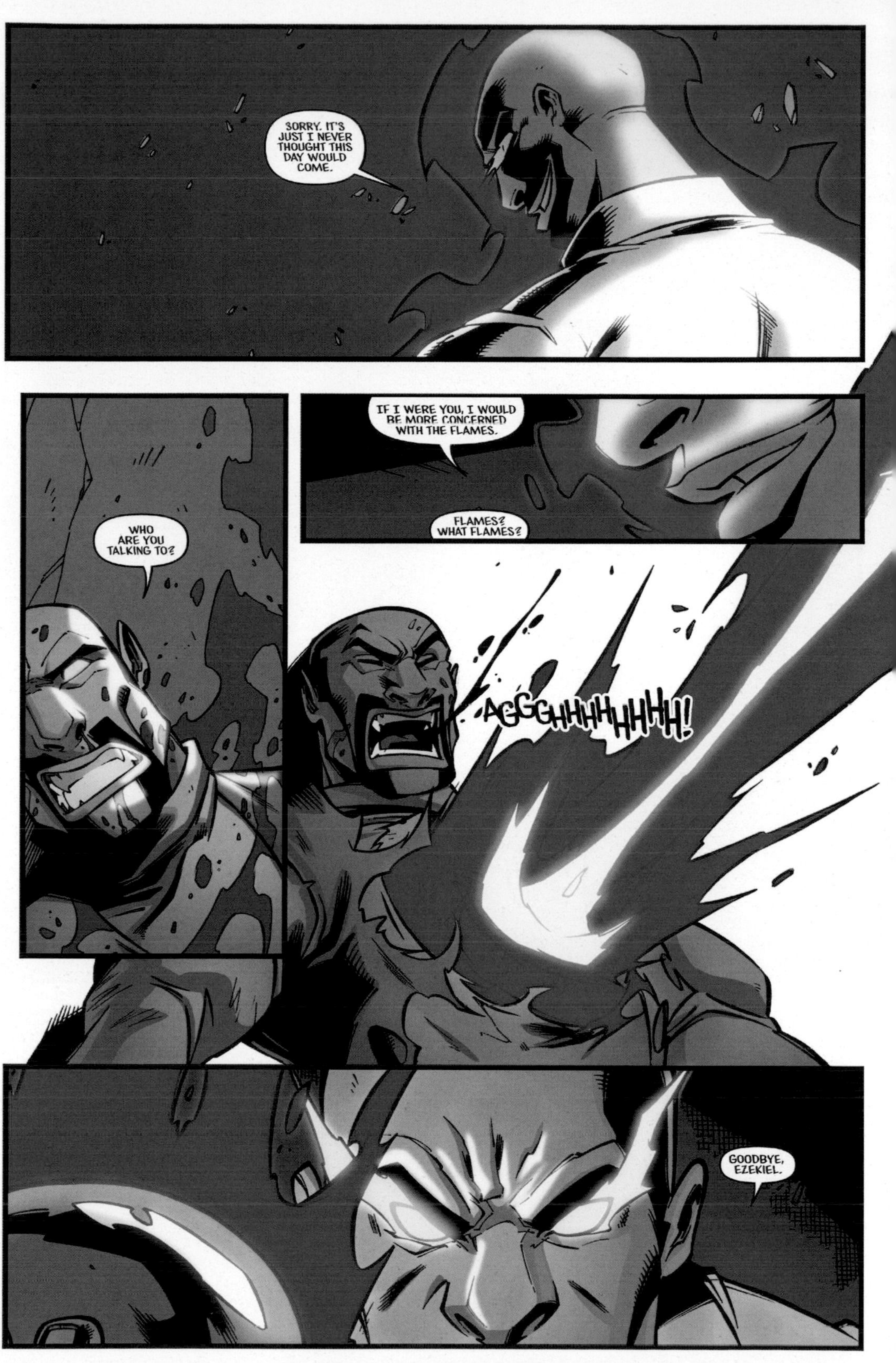
SORRY. IT'S JUST I NEVER THOUGHT THIS DAY WOULD COME.
IF I WERE YOU, I WOULD BE MORE CONCERNED WITH THE FLAMES.
FLAMES? WHAT FLAMES?
WHO ARE YOU TALKING TO?
AGGGHHHHHHHHH!
GOODBYE, EZEKIEL.

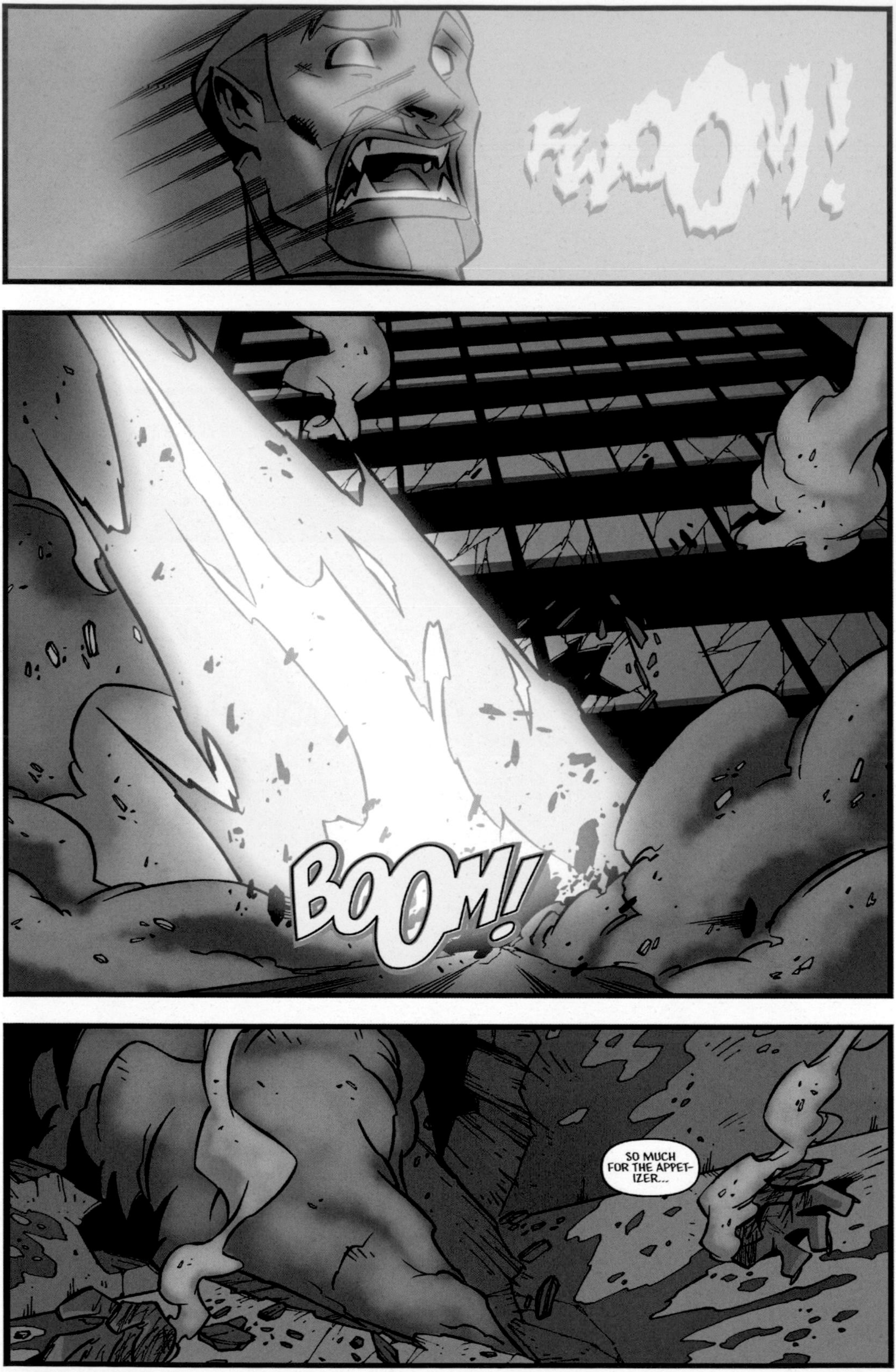
FWOOM!
BOOM!
SO MUCH FOR THE APPET-IZER...

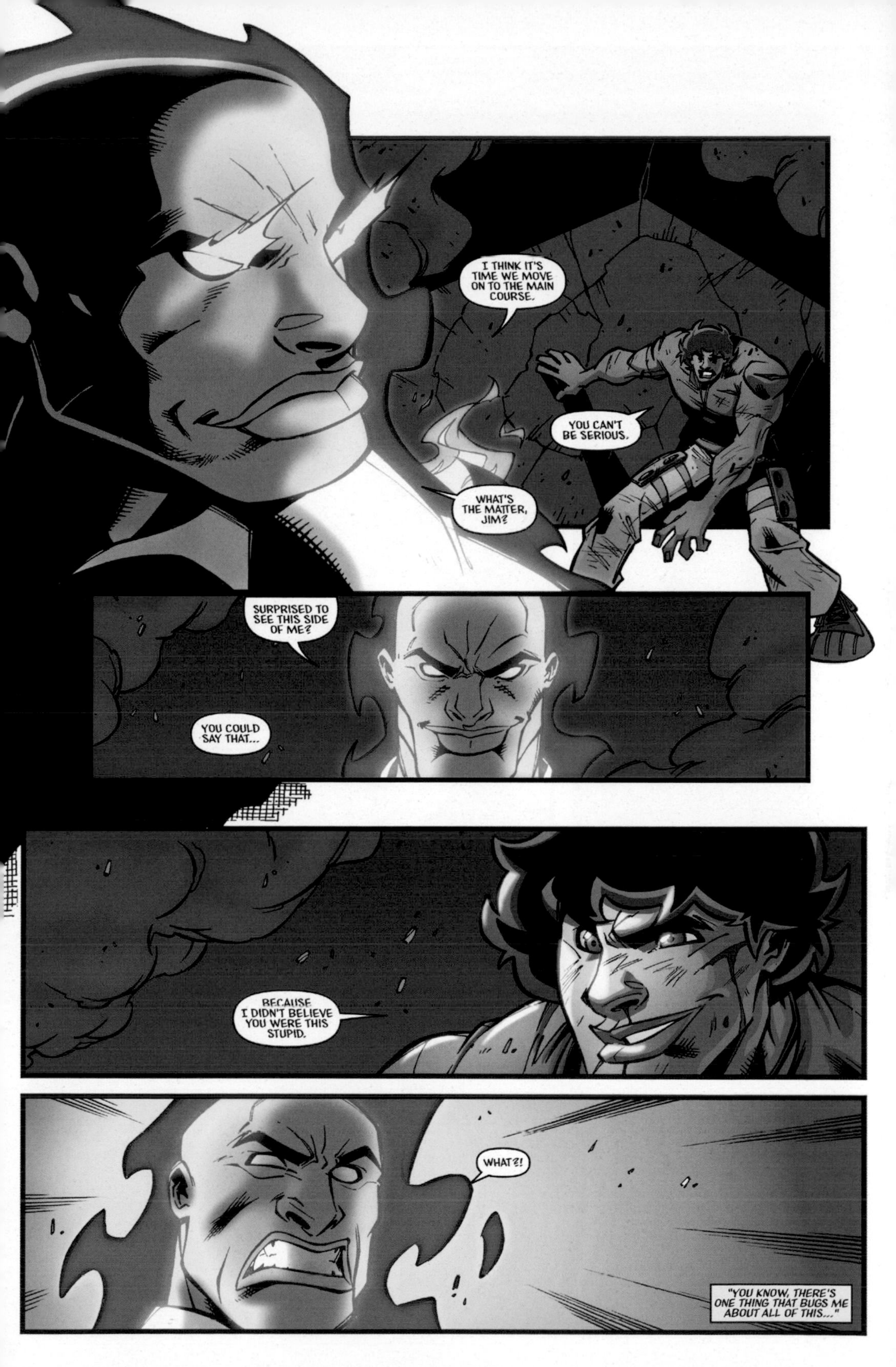
I THINK IT'S TIME WE MOVE ON TO THE MAIN COURSE.
YOU CAN'T BE SERIOUS.
WHAT'S THE MATTER, JIM?
SURPRISED TO SEE THIS SIDE OF ME?
YOU COULD SAY THAT...
BECAUSE I DIDN'T BELIEVE YOU WERE THIS STUPID.
WHAT?!
"YOU KNOW, THERE'S ONE THING THAT BUGS ME ABOUT ALL OF THIS..."

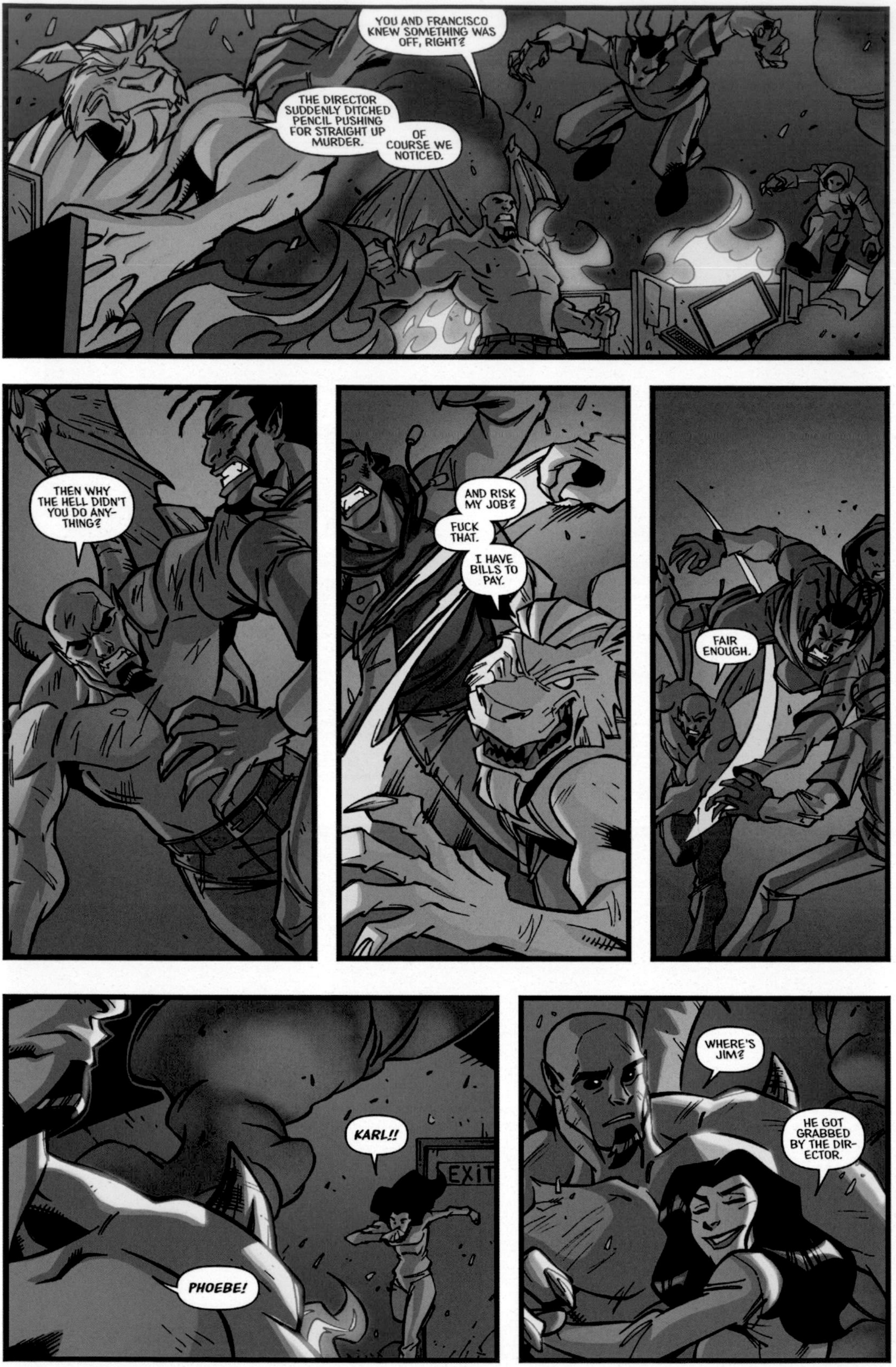
YOU AND FRANCISCO KNEW SOMETHING WAS OFF, RIGHT?
THE DIRECTOR SUDDENLY DITCHED PENCIL PUSHING FOR STRAIGHT UP MURDER.
OF COURSE WE NOTICED.
THEN WHY THE HELL DIDN'T YOU DO ANY-THING?
AND RISK MY JOB?
FUCK THAT.
I HAVE BILLS TO PAY.
FAIR ENOUGH.
KARL!!
EXIT
PHOEBE!
WHERE'S JIM?
HE GOT GRABBED BY THE DIR-ECTOR.

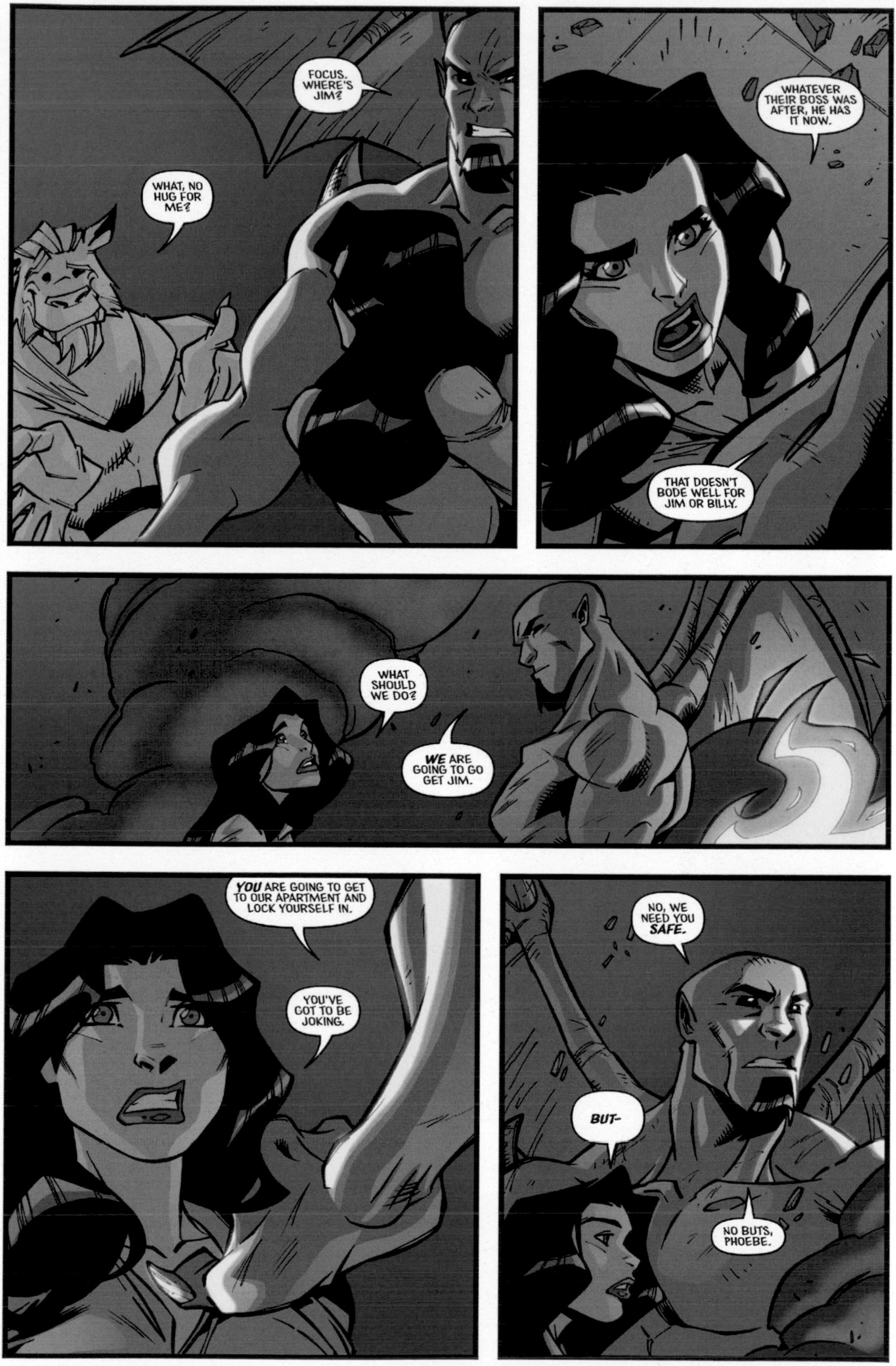
FOCUS. WHERE'S JIM?
WHAT, NO HUG FOR ME?
WHATEVER THEIR BOSS WAS AFTER, HE HAS IT NOW.
THAT DOESN'T BODE WELL FOR JIM OR BILLY.
WHAT SHOULD WE DO?
WE ARE GOING TO GO GET JIM.
YOU ARE GOING TO GET TO OUR APARTMENT AND LOCK YOURSELF IN.
YOU'VE GOT TO BE JOKING.
NO, WE NEED YOU SAFE.
BUT-
NO BUTS, PHOEBE.

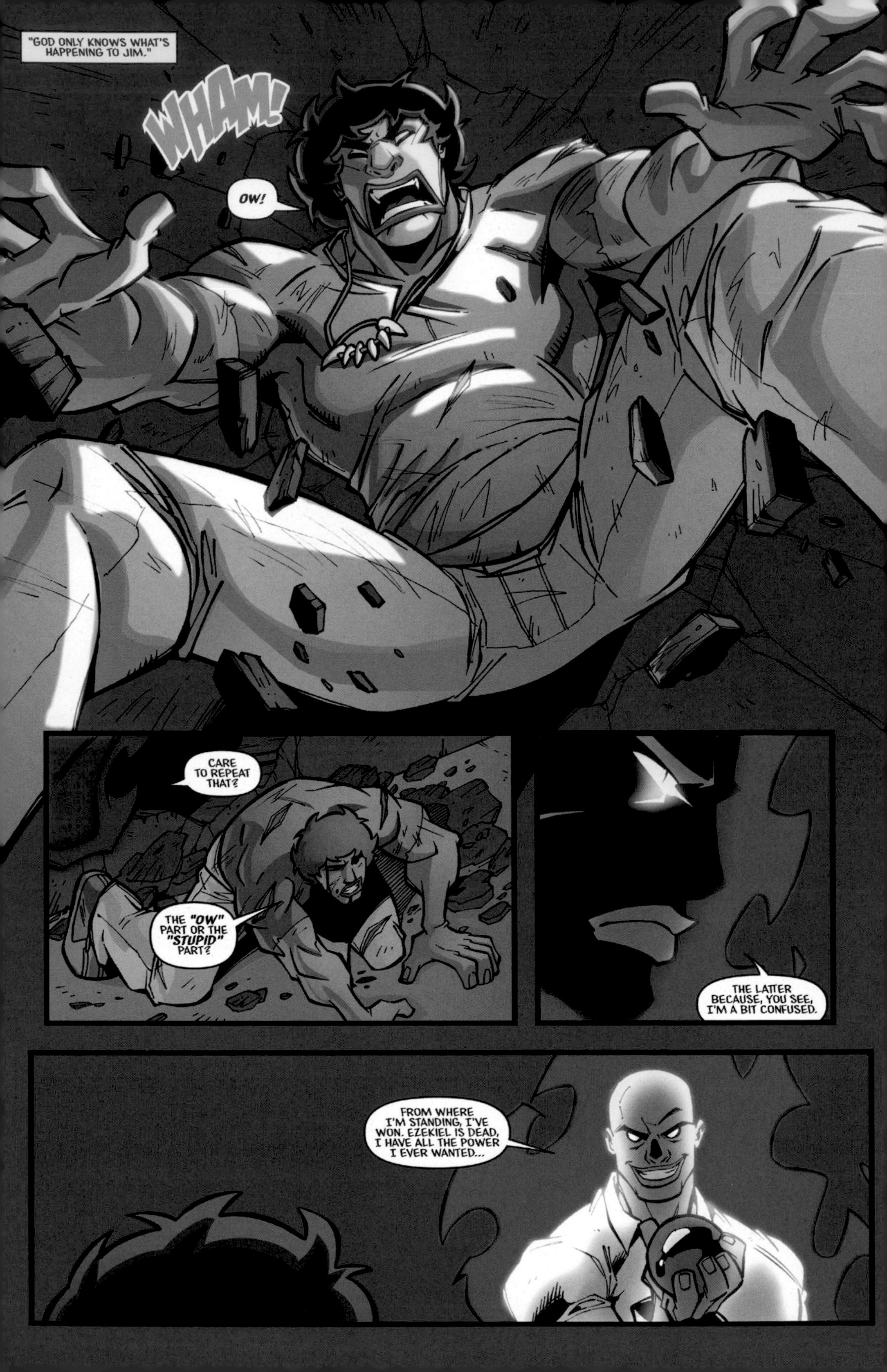
"GOD ONLY KNOWS WHAT'S HAPPENING TO JIM."
WHAM!
OW!
CARE TO REPEAT THAT?
THE "OW" PART OR THE "STUPID" PART?
THE LATTER BECAUSE, YOU SEE, I'M A BIT CONFUSED.
FROM WHERE I'M STANDING, I'VE WON. EZEKIEL IS DEAD, I HAVE ALL THE POWER I EVER WANTED...

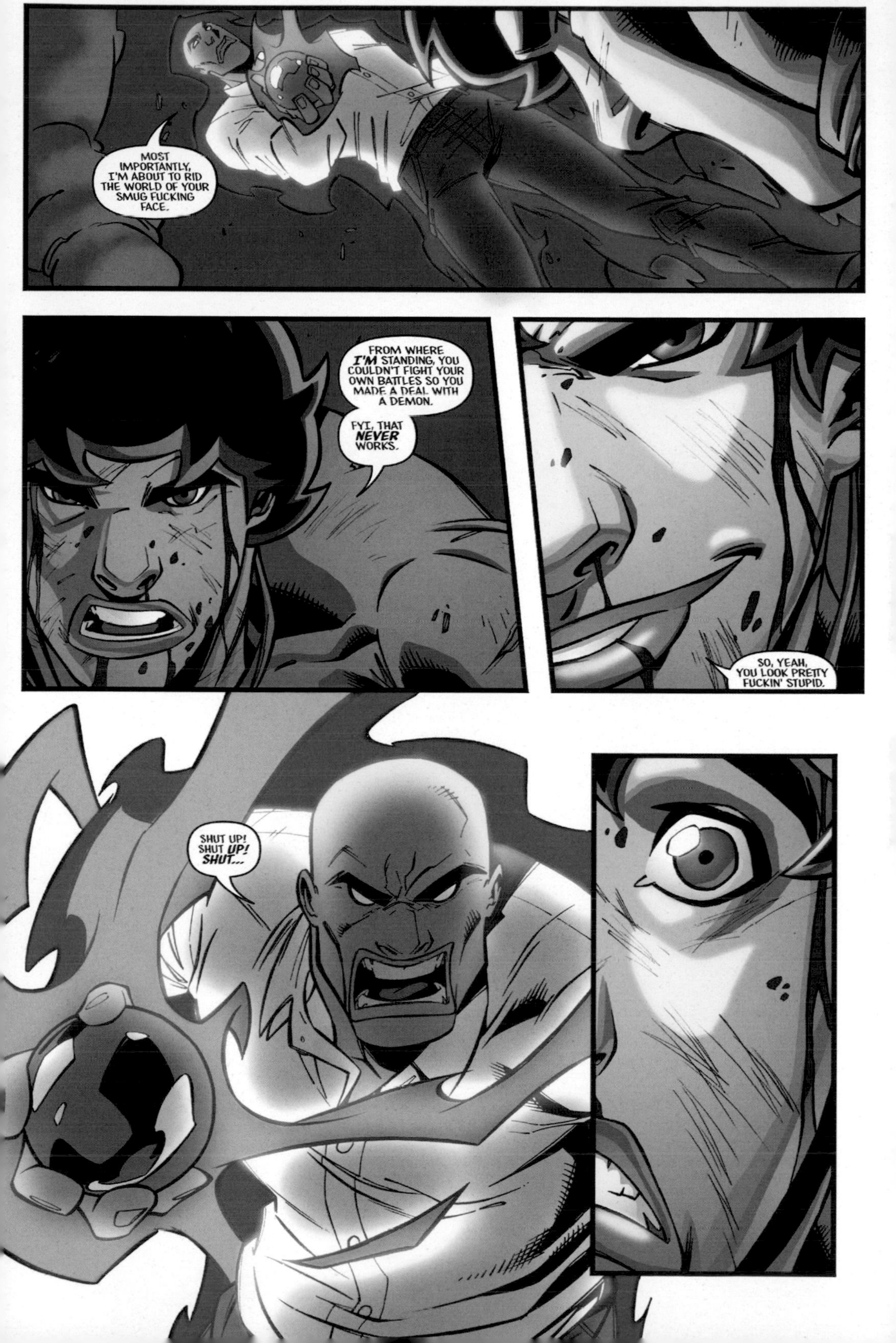
MOST IMPORTANTLY, I'M ABOUT TO RID THE WORLD OF YOUR SMUG FUCKING FACE.
FROM WHERE I'M STANDING, YOU COULDN'T FIGHT YOUR OWN BATTLES SO YOU MADE A DEAL WITH A DEMON.
FYI, THAT NEVER WORKS.
SO, YEAH, YOU LOOK PRETTY FUCKIN' STUPID.
SHUT UP! SHUT UP! SHUT...

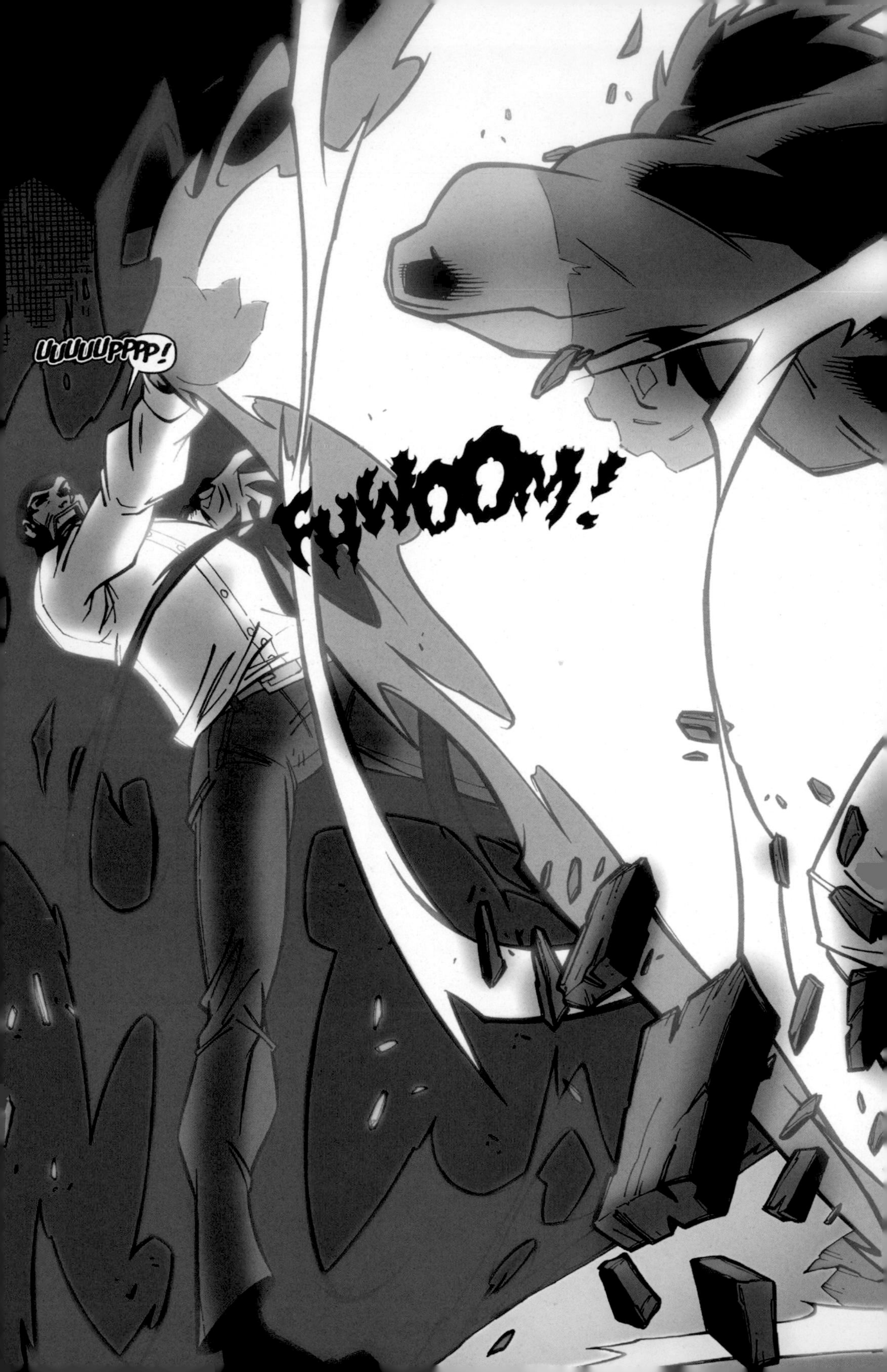
UUUUUPPPP!
FHWOOM!

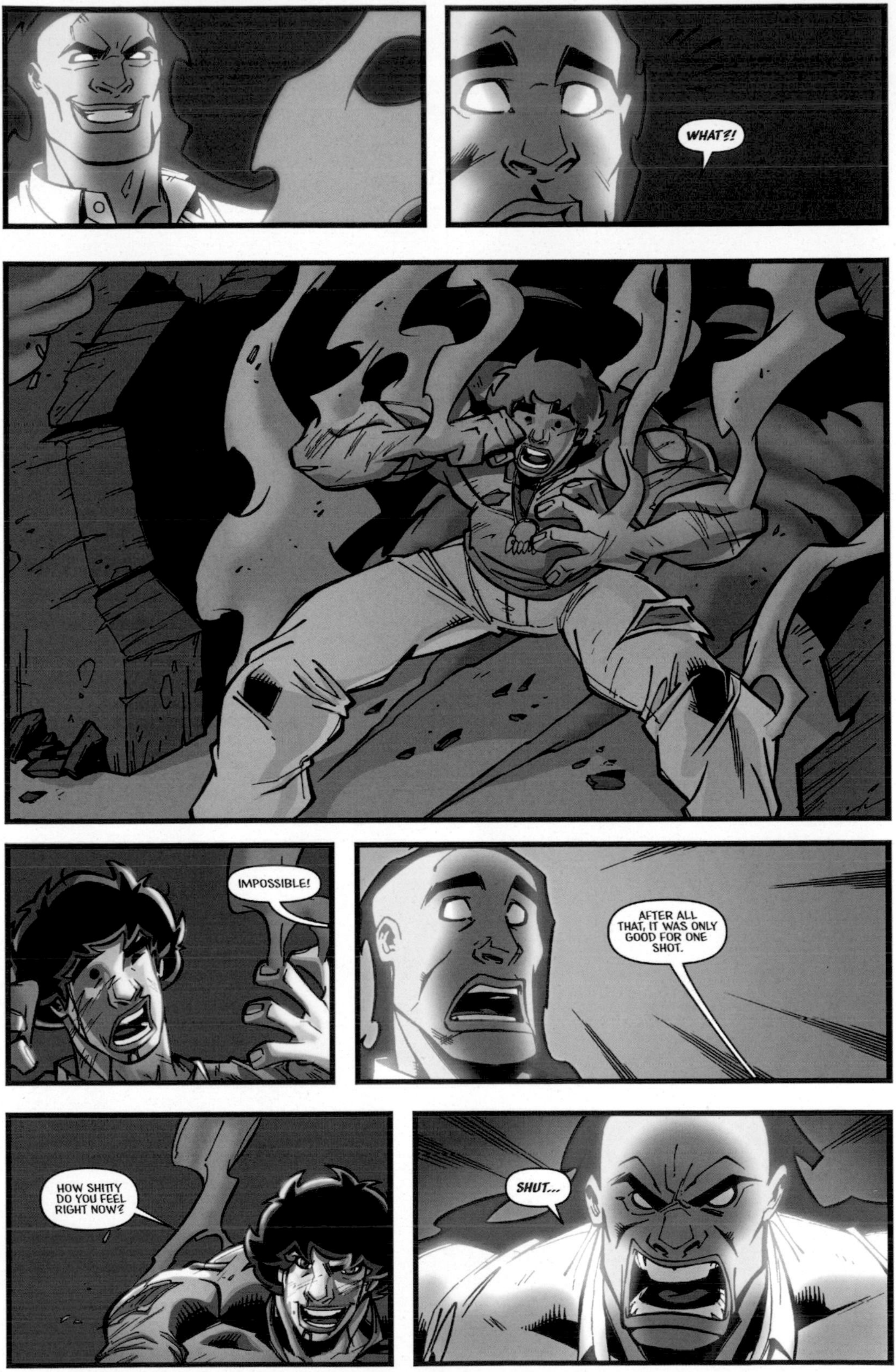
WHAT?!
IMPOSSIBLE!
AFTER ALL THAT, IT WAS ONLY GOOD FOR ONE SHOT.
HOW SHITTY DO YOU FEEL RIGHT NOW?
SHUT...

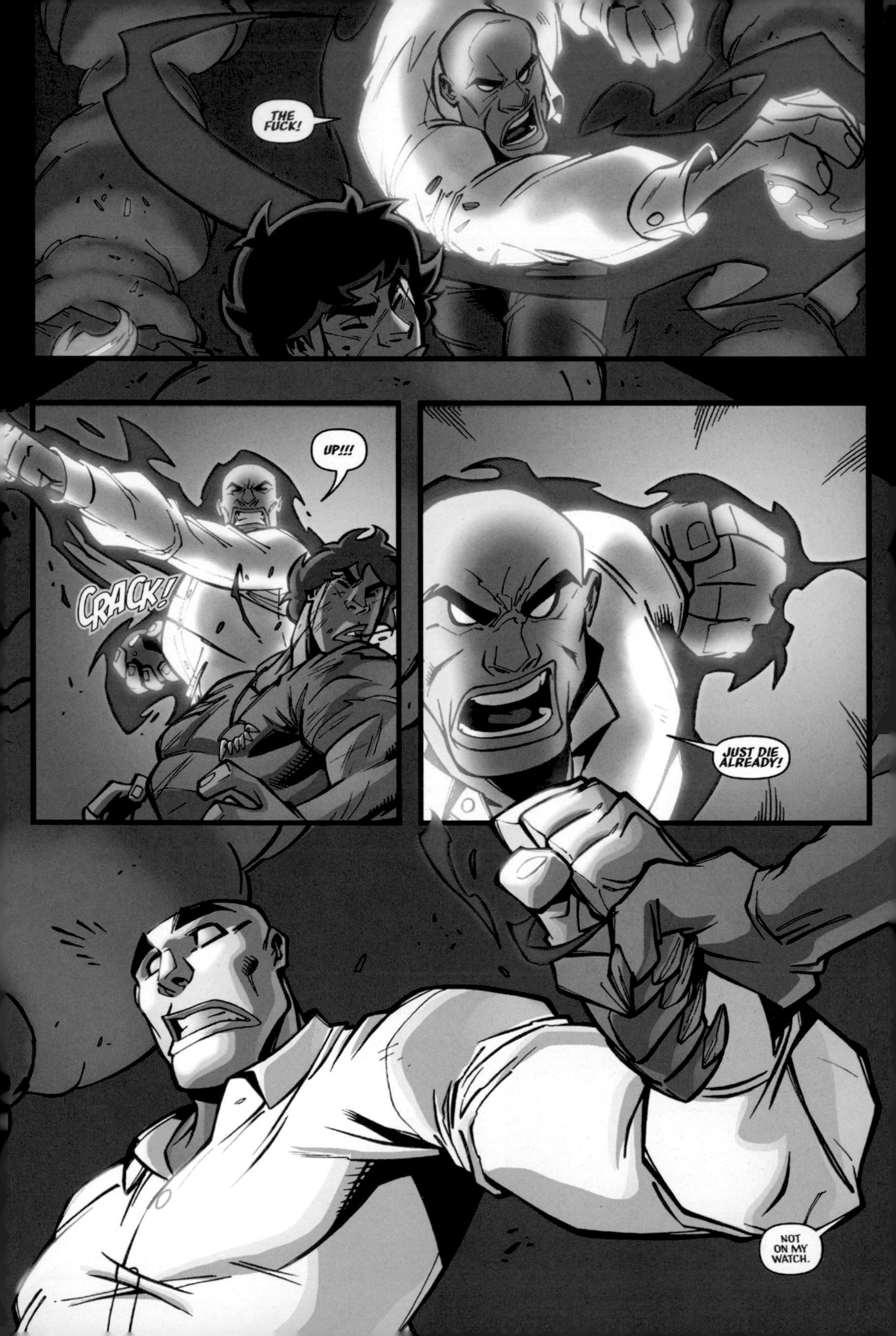
THE FUCK!
UP!!!
CRACK!
JUST DIE ALREADY!
NOT ON MY WATCH.

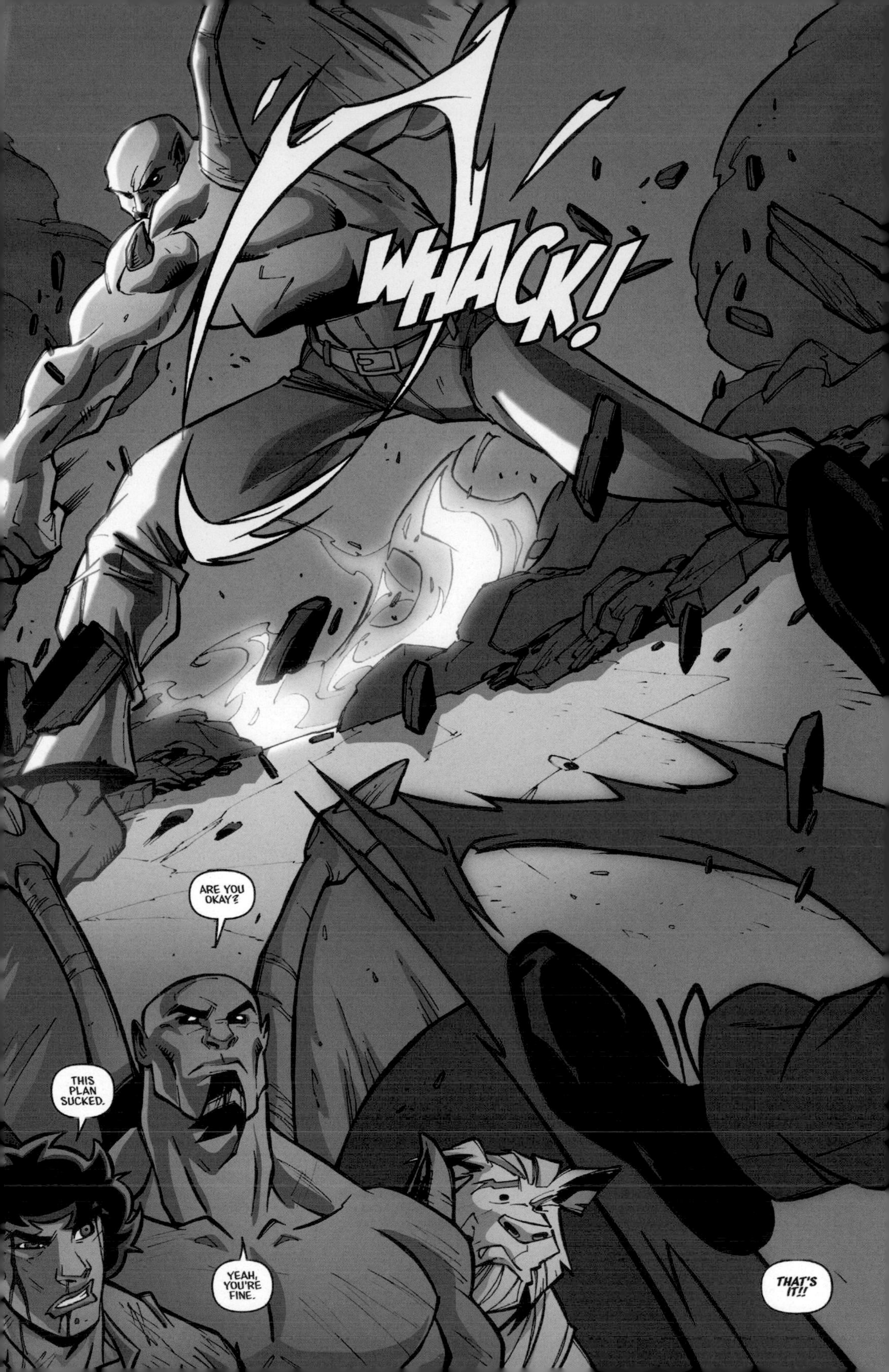
WHACK!
ARE YOU OKAY?
THIS PLAN SUCKED.
YEAH, YOU'RE FINE.
THAT'S IT!!

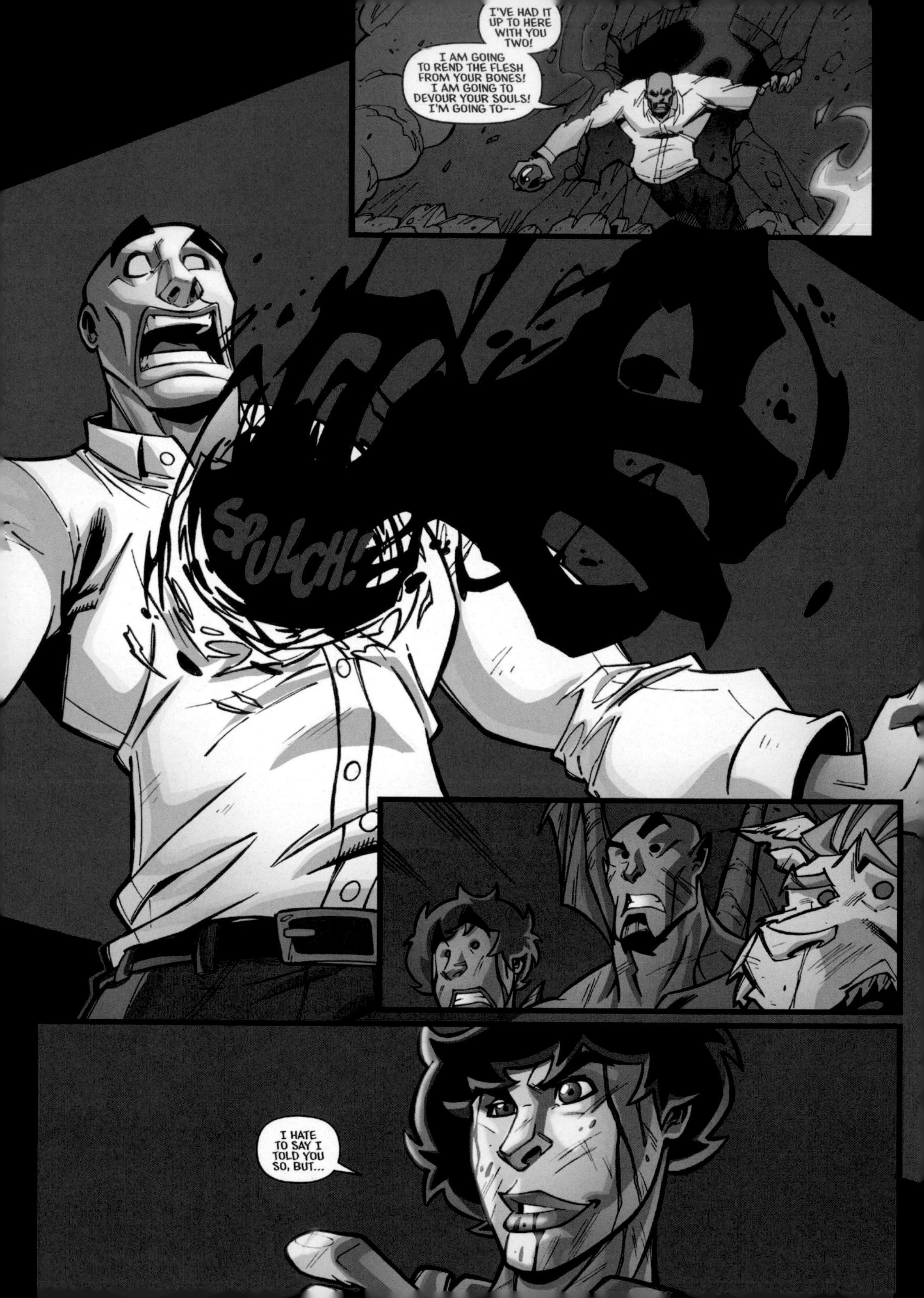
I'VE HAD IT UP TO HERE WITH YOU TWO!
I AM GOING TO REND THE FLESH FROM YOUR BONES! I AM GOING TO DEVOUR YOUR SOULS! I'M GOING TO--
SPULCH!
I HATE TO SAY I TOLD YOU SO, BUT...

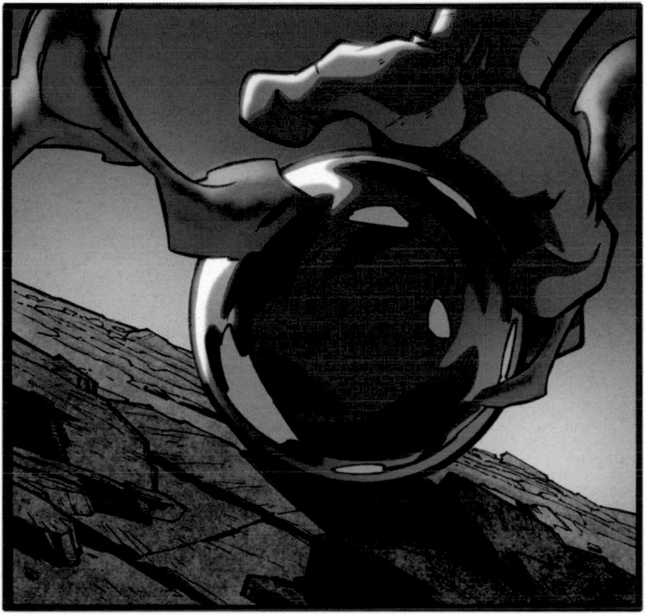

CHAPTER SIX

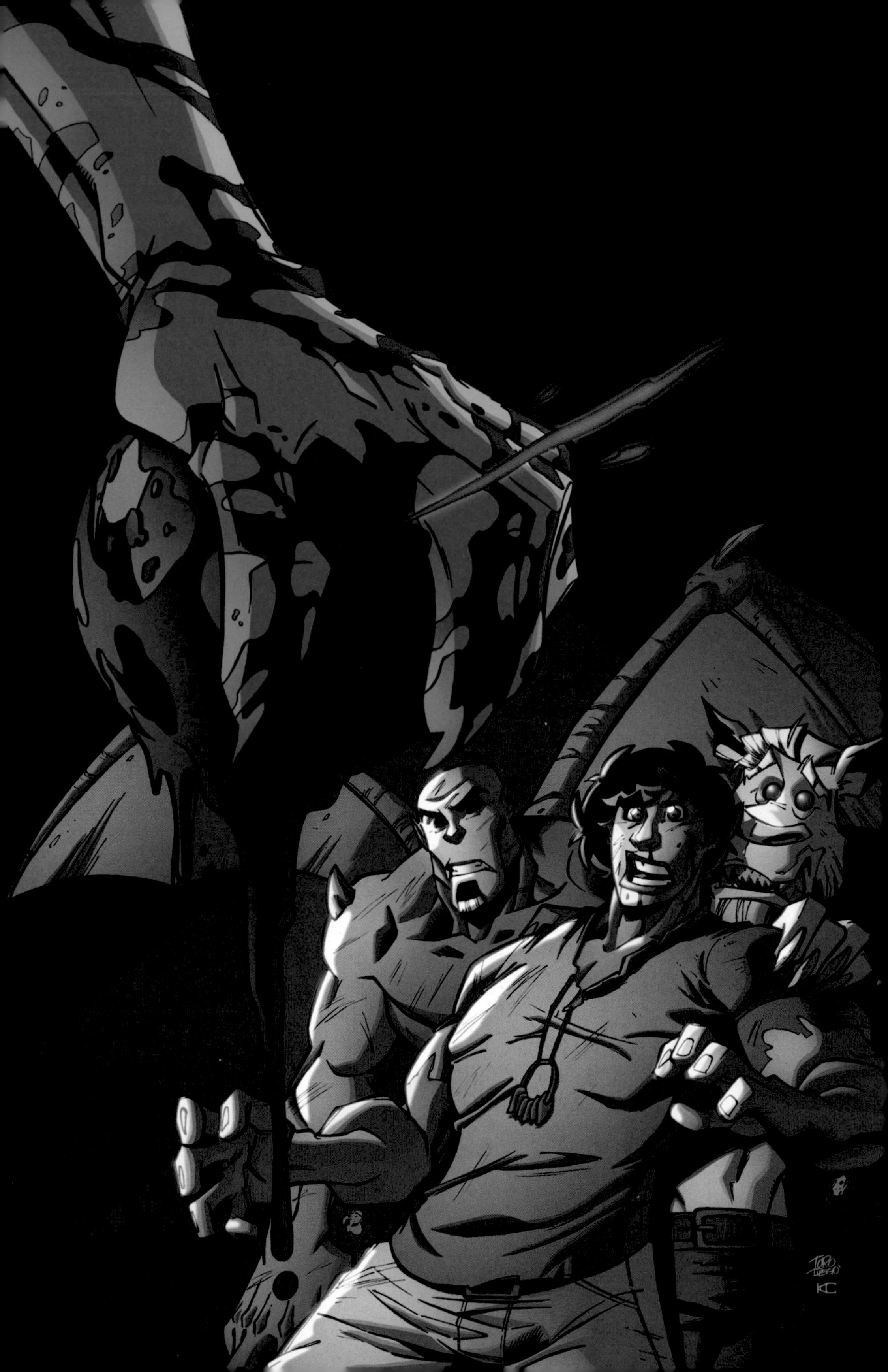

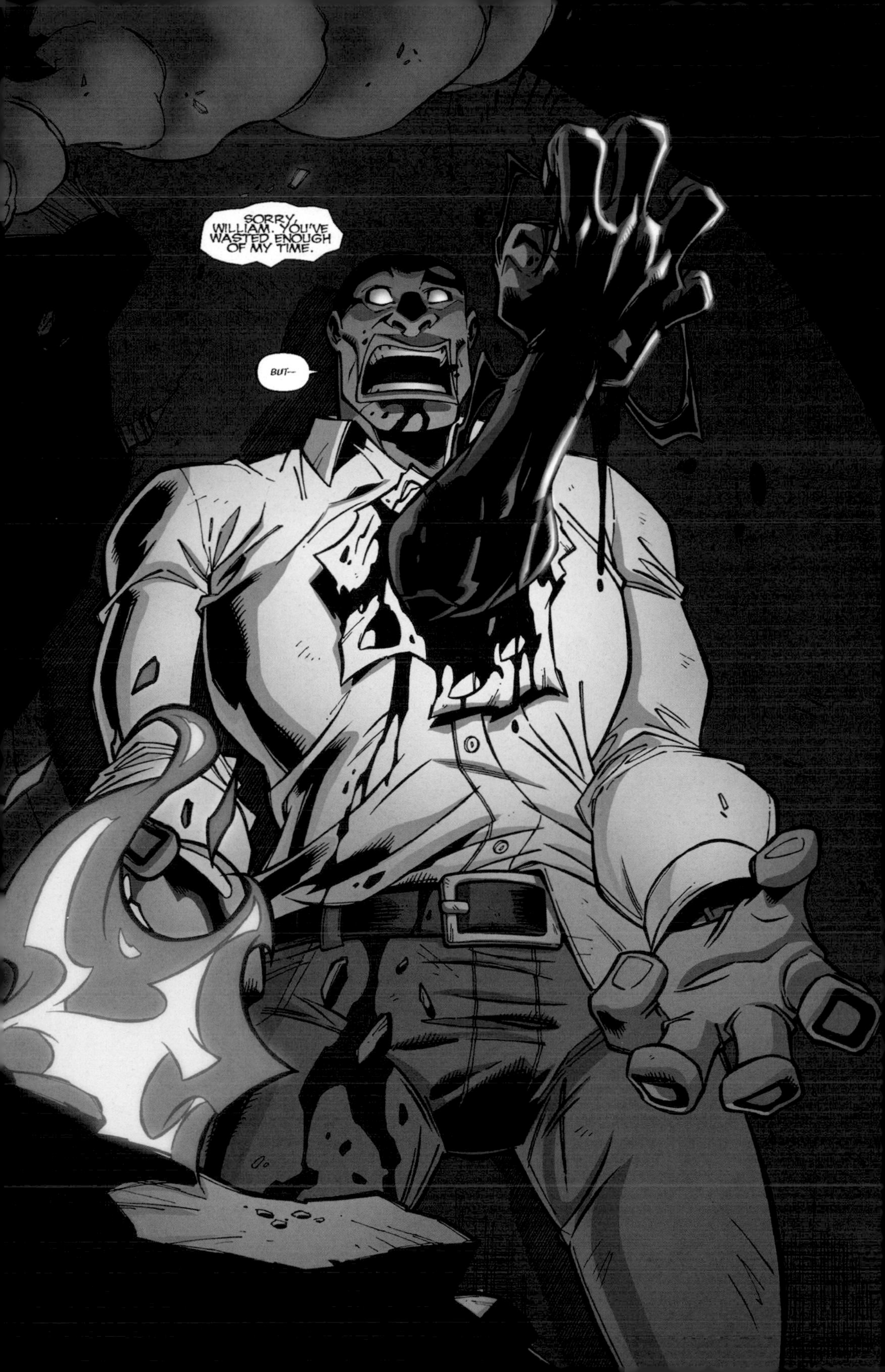
SORRY, WILLIAM. YOU'VE WASTED ENOUGH OF MY TIME.
BUT--

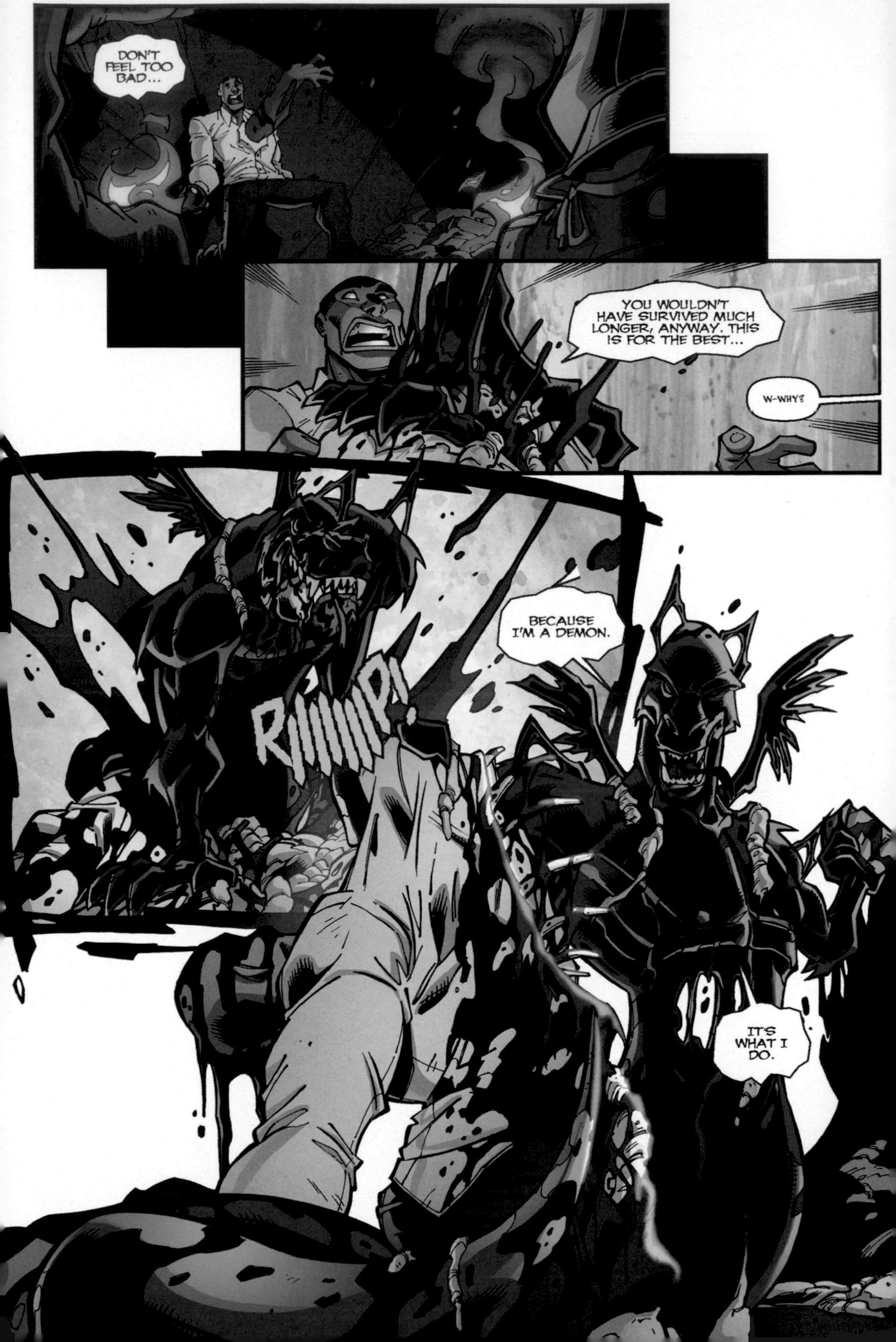
DON'T FEEL TOO BAD...
YOU WOULDN'T HAVE SURVIVED MUCH LONGER, ANYWAY. THIS IS FOR THE BEST...
W-WHY?
BECAUSE I'M A DEMON.
RIIIIIIP!
IT'S WHAT I DO.

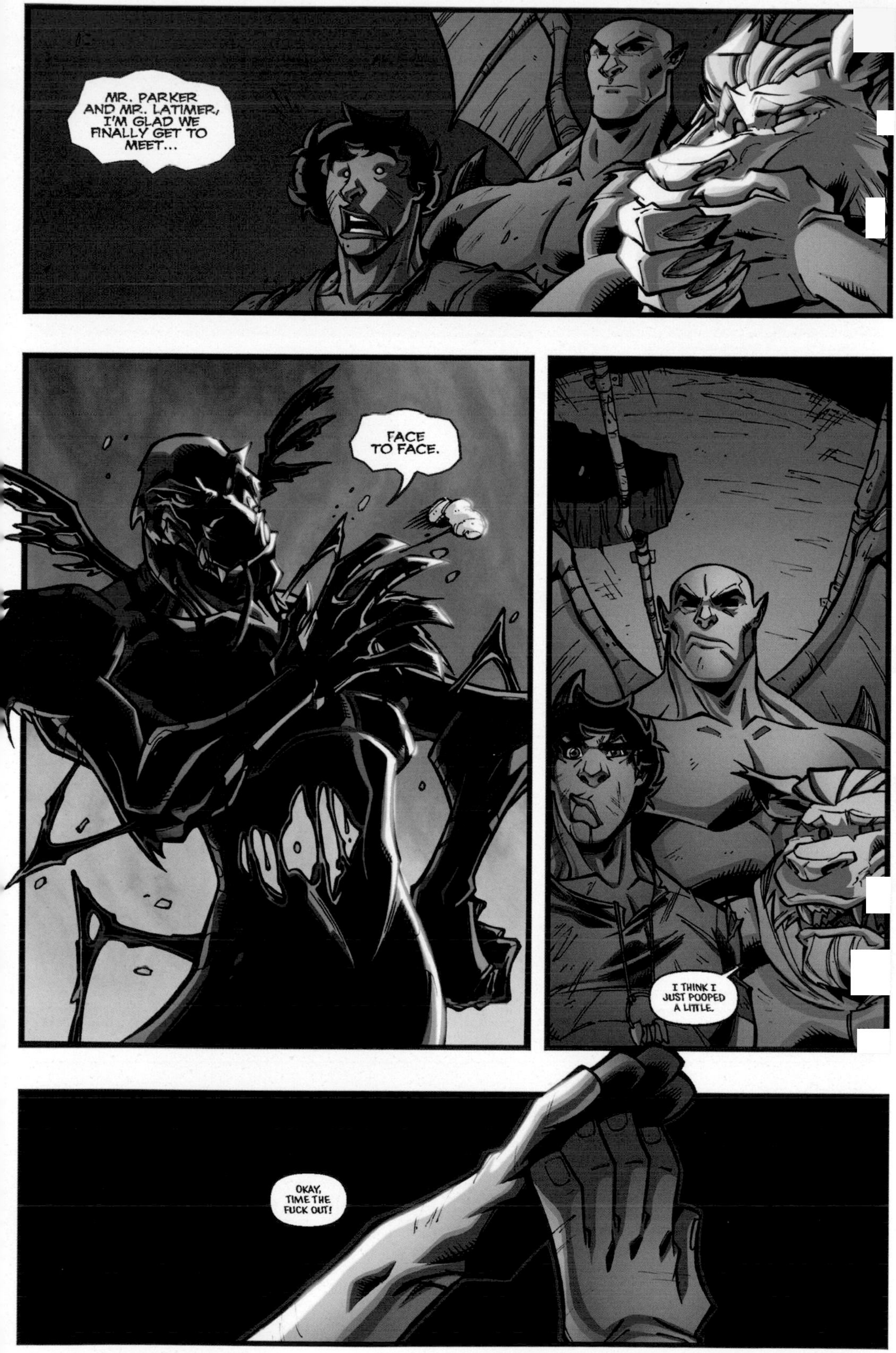
MR. PARKER AND MR. LATIMER, I'M GLAD WE FINALLY GET TO MEET...
FACE TO FACE.
I THINK I JUST POOPED A LITTLE.
OKAY, TIME THE FUCK OUT!

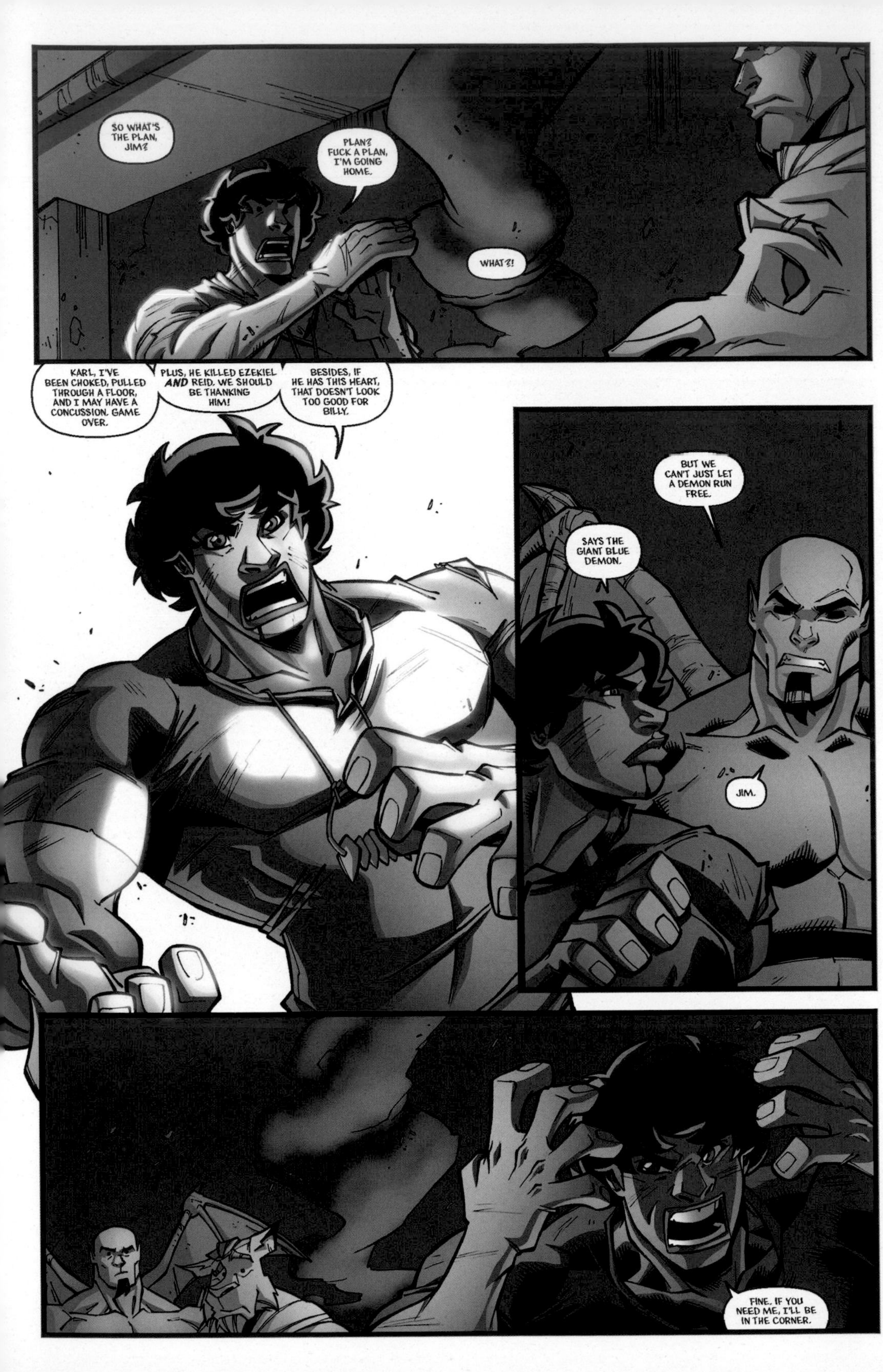
SO WHAT'S THE PLAN, JIM?
PLAN? FUCK A PLAN, I'M GOING HOME.
WHAT?!
KARL, I'VE BEEN CHOKED, PULLED THROUGH A FLOOR, AND I MAY HAVE A CONCUSSION. GAME OVER.
PLUS, HE KILLED EZEKIEL *AND* REID. WE SHOULD BE THANKING HIM!
BESIDES, IF HE HAS THIS HEART, THAT DOESN'T LOOK TOO GOOD FOR BILLY.
BUT WE CAN'T JUST LET A DEMON RUN FREE.
SAYS THE GIANT BLUE DEMON.
JIM.
FINE. IF YOU NEED ME, I'LL BE IN THE CORNER.

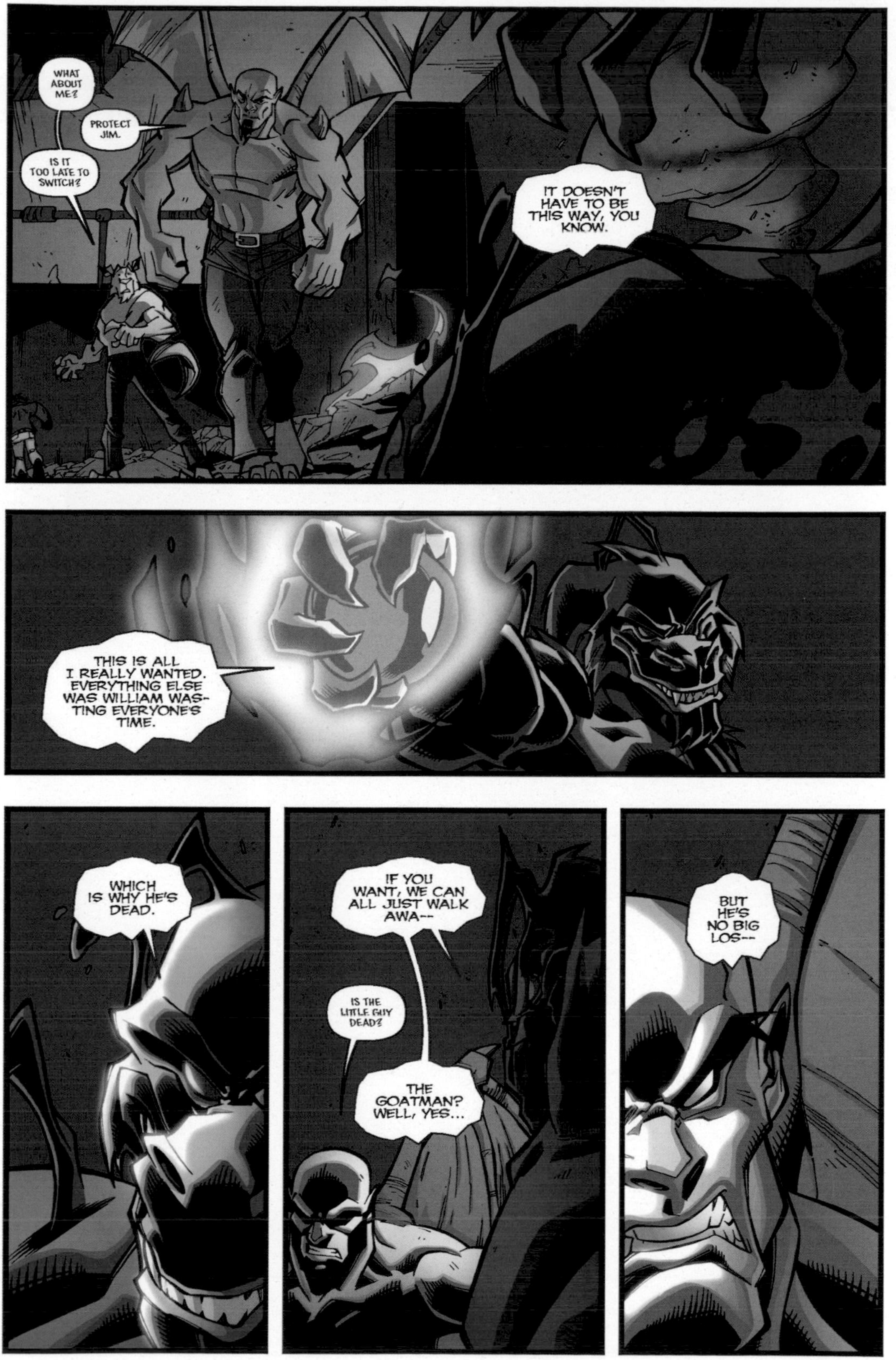
WHAT ABOUT ME?
PROTECT JIM.
IS IT TOO LATE TO SWITCH?
IT DOESN'T HAVE TO BE THIS WAY, YOU KNOW.
THIS IS ALL I REALLY WANTED. EVERYTHING ELSE WAS WILLIAM WASTING EVERYONE'S TIME.
WHICH IS WHY HE'S DEAD.
IF YOU WANT, WE CAN ALL JUST WALK AWA--
IS THE LITTLE GUY DEAD?
THE GOATMAN? WELL, YES...
BUT HE'S NO BIG LOS--

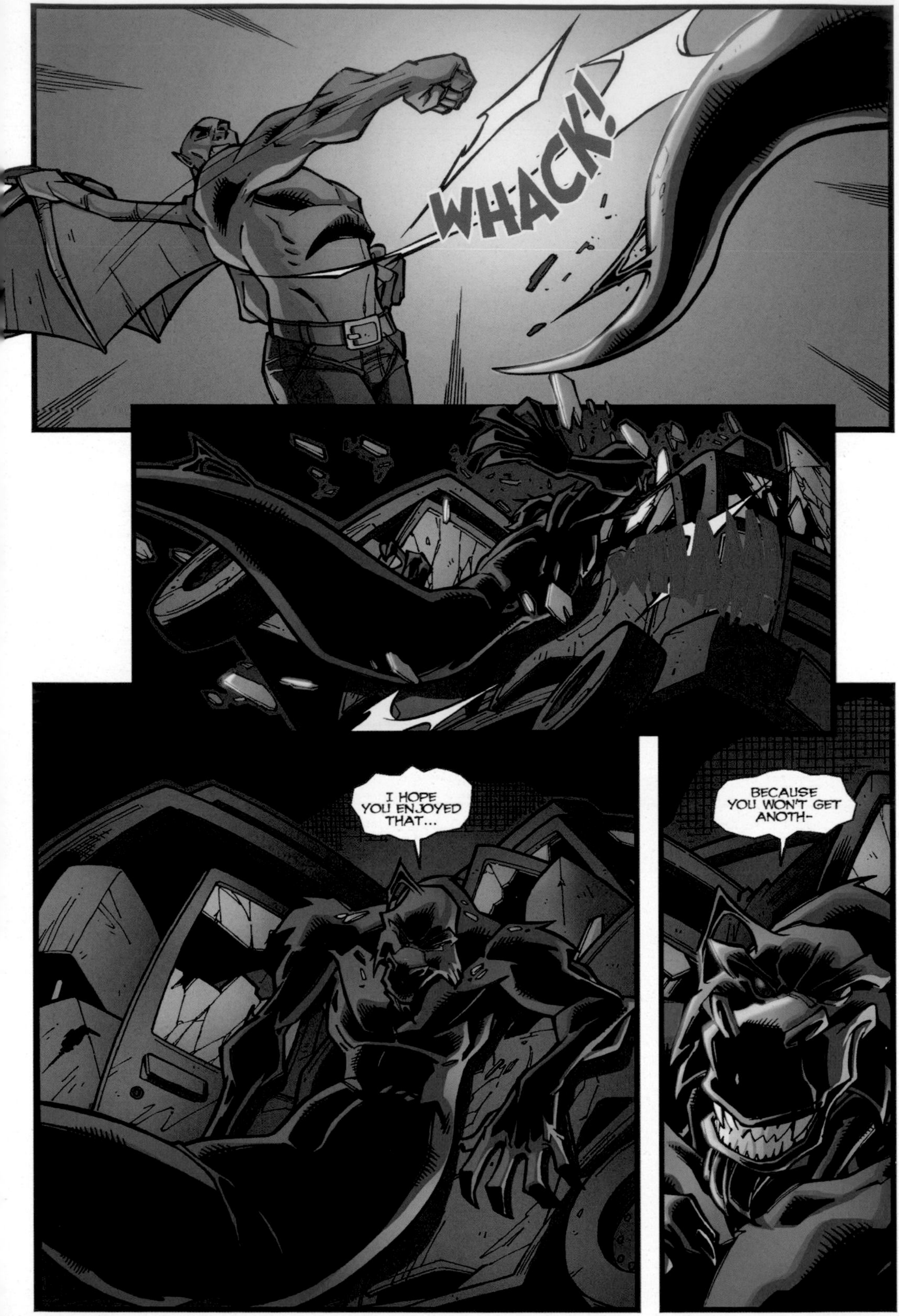
WHACK!
I HOPE YOU ENJOYED THAT...
BECAUSE YOU WON'T GET ANOTH-

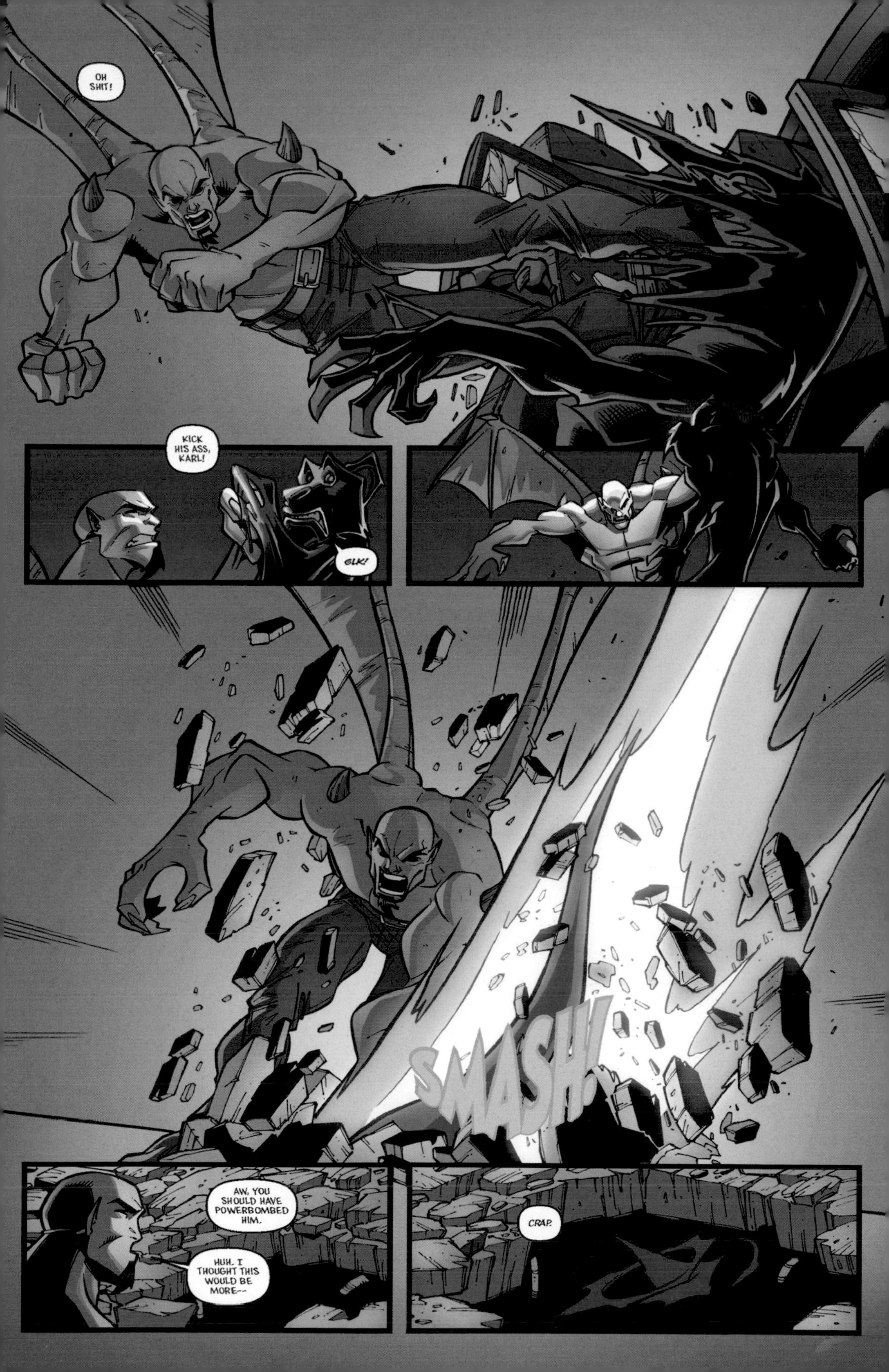
OH SHIT!
KICK HIS ASS, KARL!
GLK!
SMASH!
AW, YOU SHOULD HAVE POWERBOMBED HIM.
HUH. I THOUGHT THIS WOULD BE MORE--
CRAP.

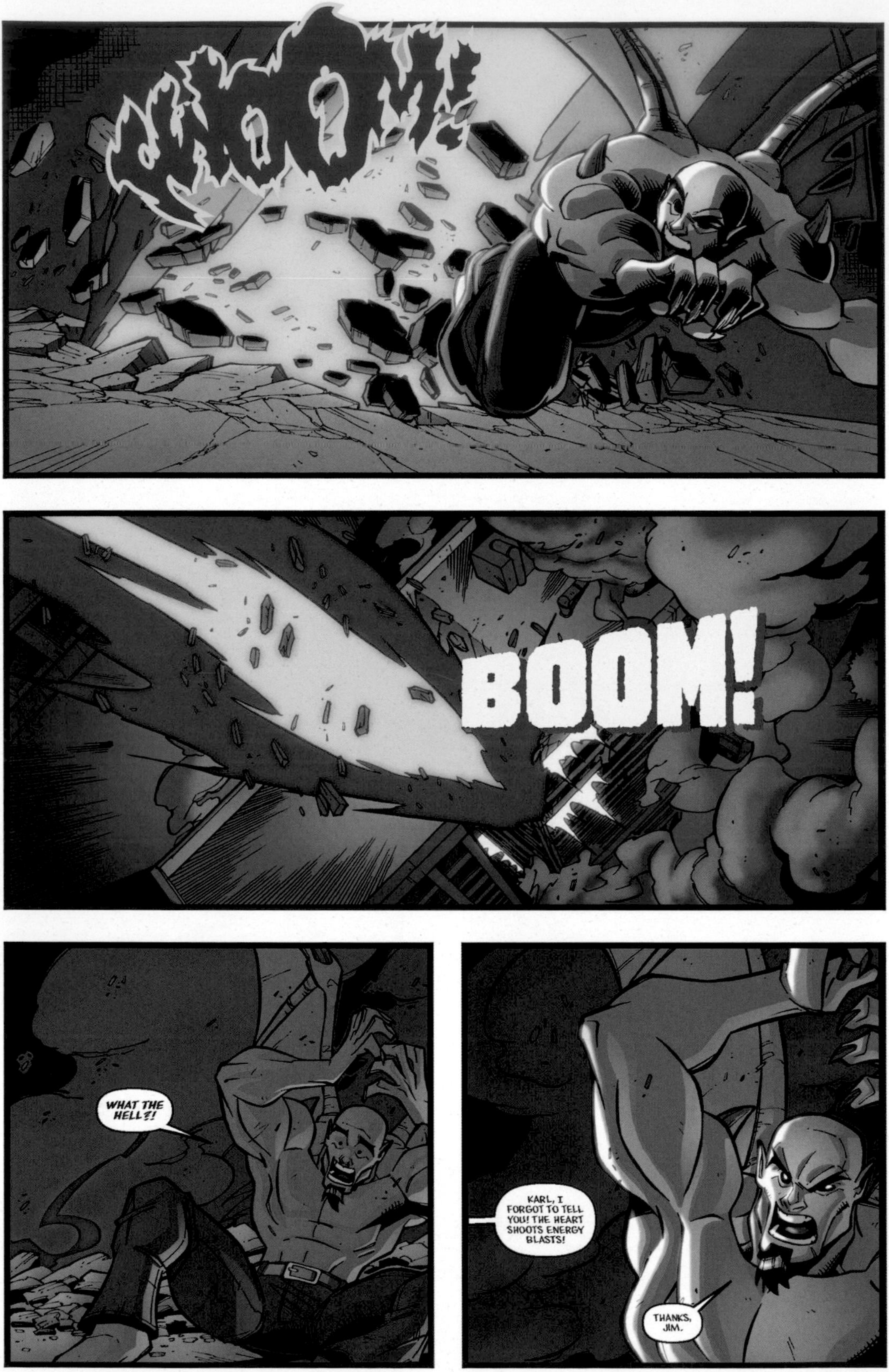
BOOM!
WHAT THE HELL?!
KARL, I FORGOT TO TELL YOU! THE HEART SHOOTS ENERGY BLASTS!
THANKS, JIM.

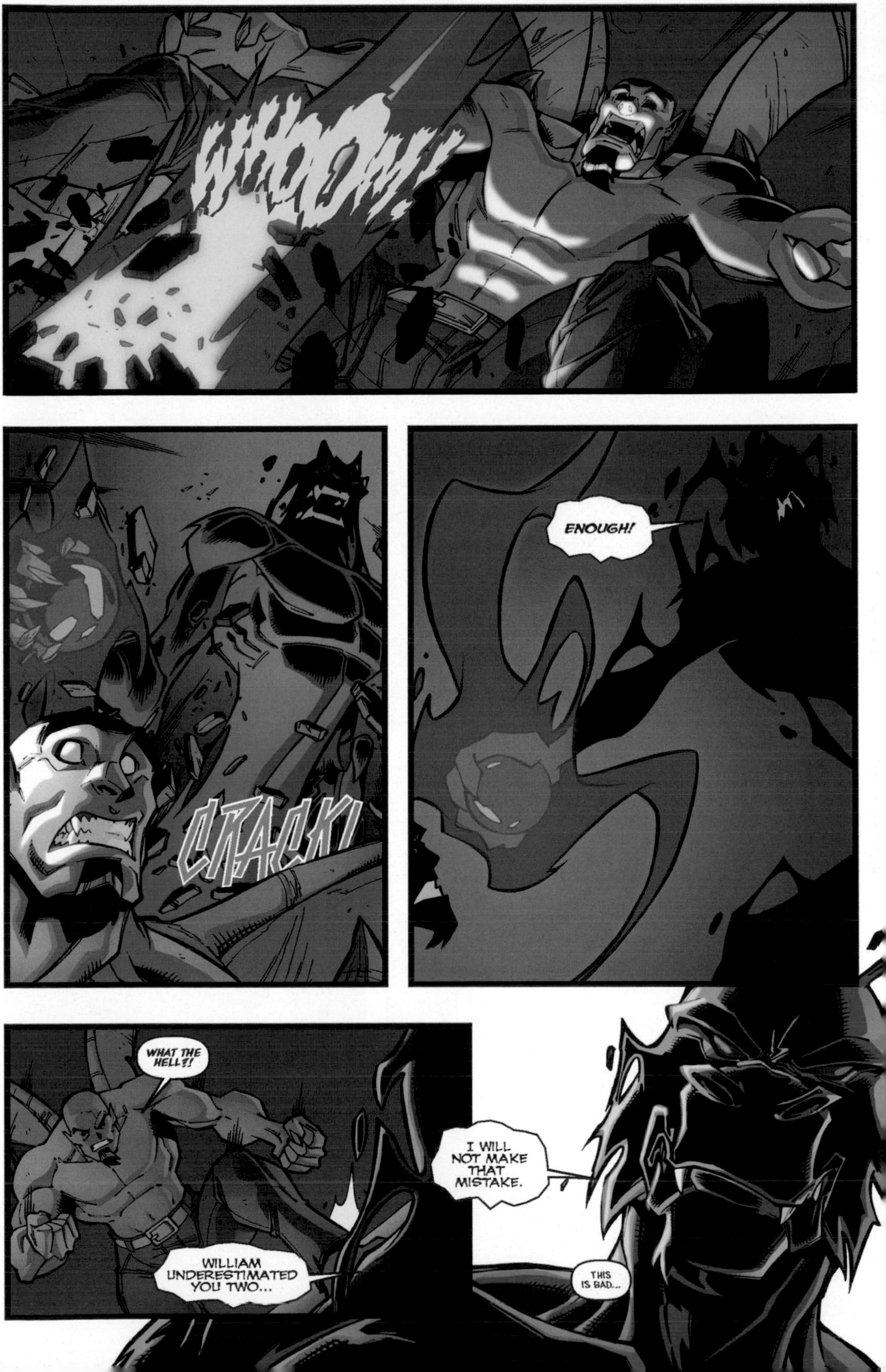
WHOOM!!
CRACK!
ENOUGH!
WHAT THE HELL?!
WILLIAM UNDERESTIMATED YOU TWO...
I WILL NOT MAKE THAT MISTAKE.
THIS IS BAD...

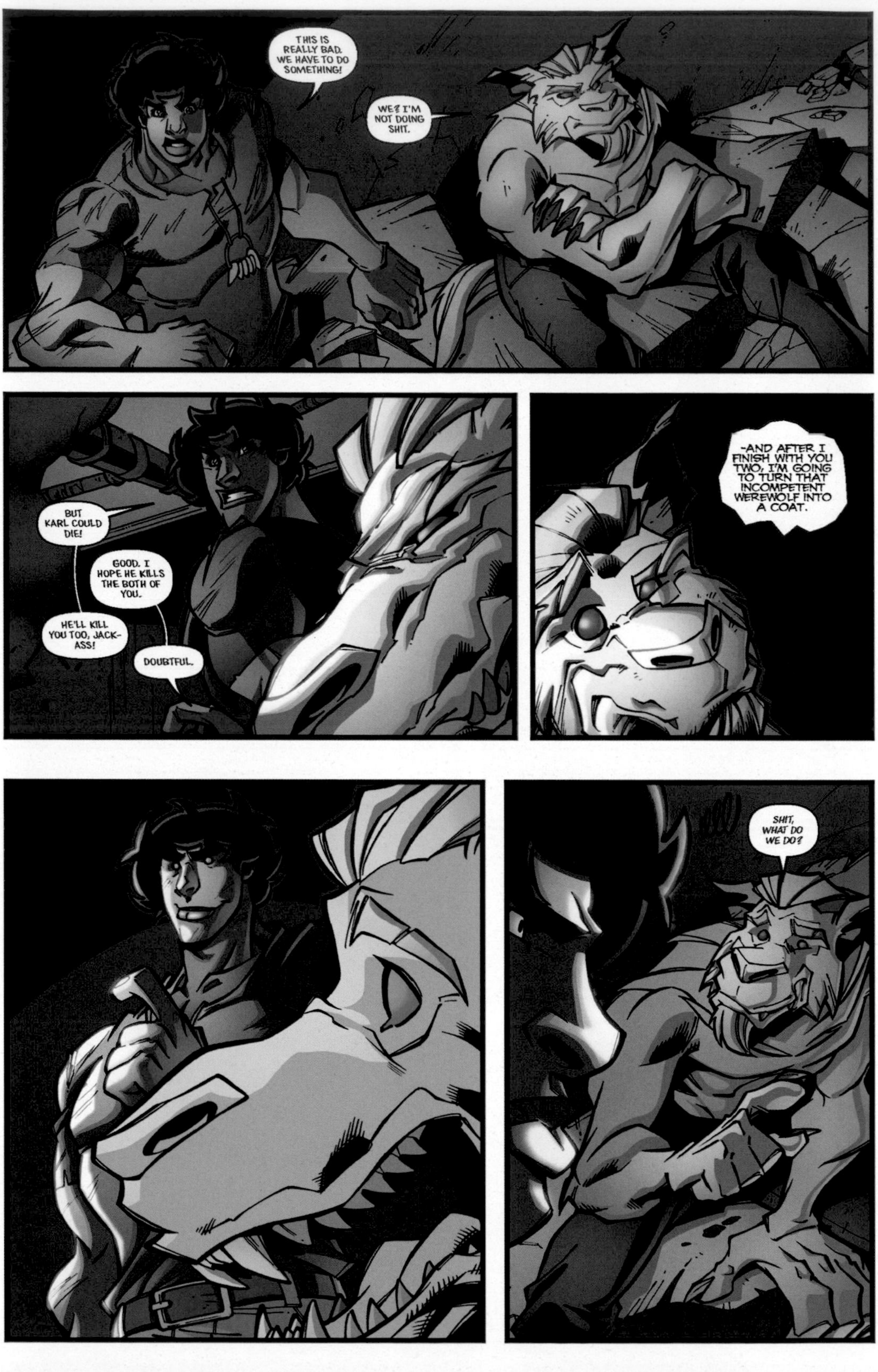
THIS IS REALLY BAD. WE HAVE TO DO SOMETHING!
WE? I'M NOT DOING SHIT.
BUT KARL COULD DIE!
GOOD. I HOPE HE KILLS THE BOTH OF YOU.
HE'LL KILL YOU TOO, JACK-ASS!
DOUBTFUL.
-AND AFTER I FINISH WITH YOU TWO, I'M GOING TO TURN THAT INCOMPETENT WEREWOLF INTO A COAT.
SHIT, WHAT DO WE DO?

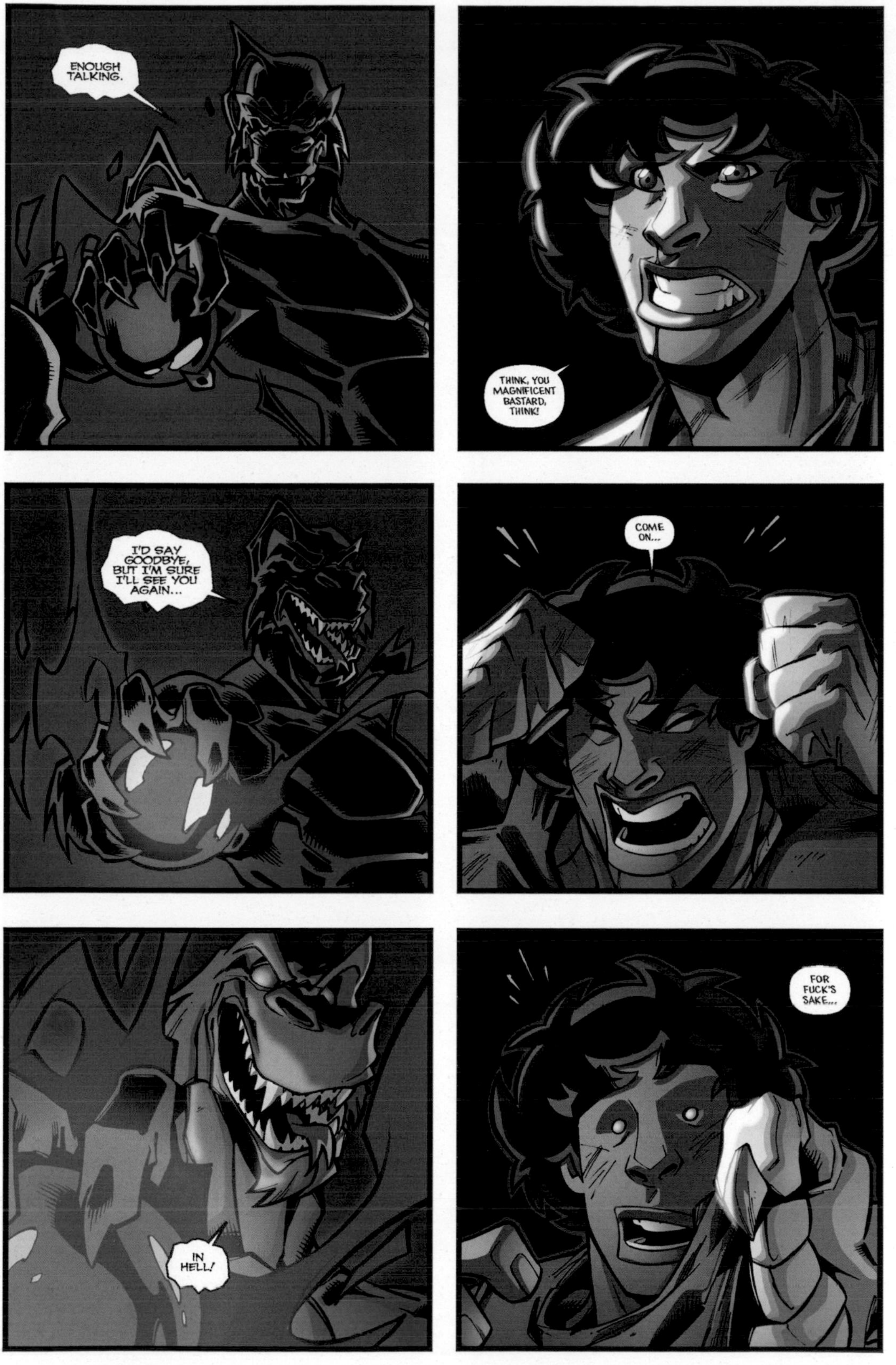
ENOUGH TALKING.
THINK, YOU MAGNIFICENT BASTARD, THINK!
I'D SAY GOODBYE, BUT I'M SURE I'LL SEE YOU AGAIN...
COME ON...
IN HELL!
FOR FUCK'S SAKE...

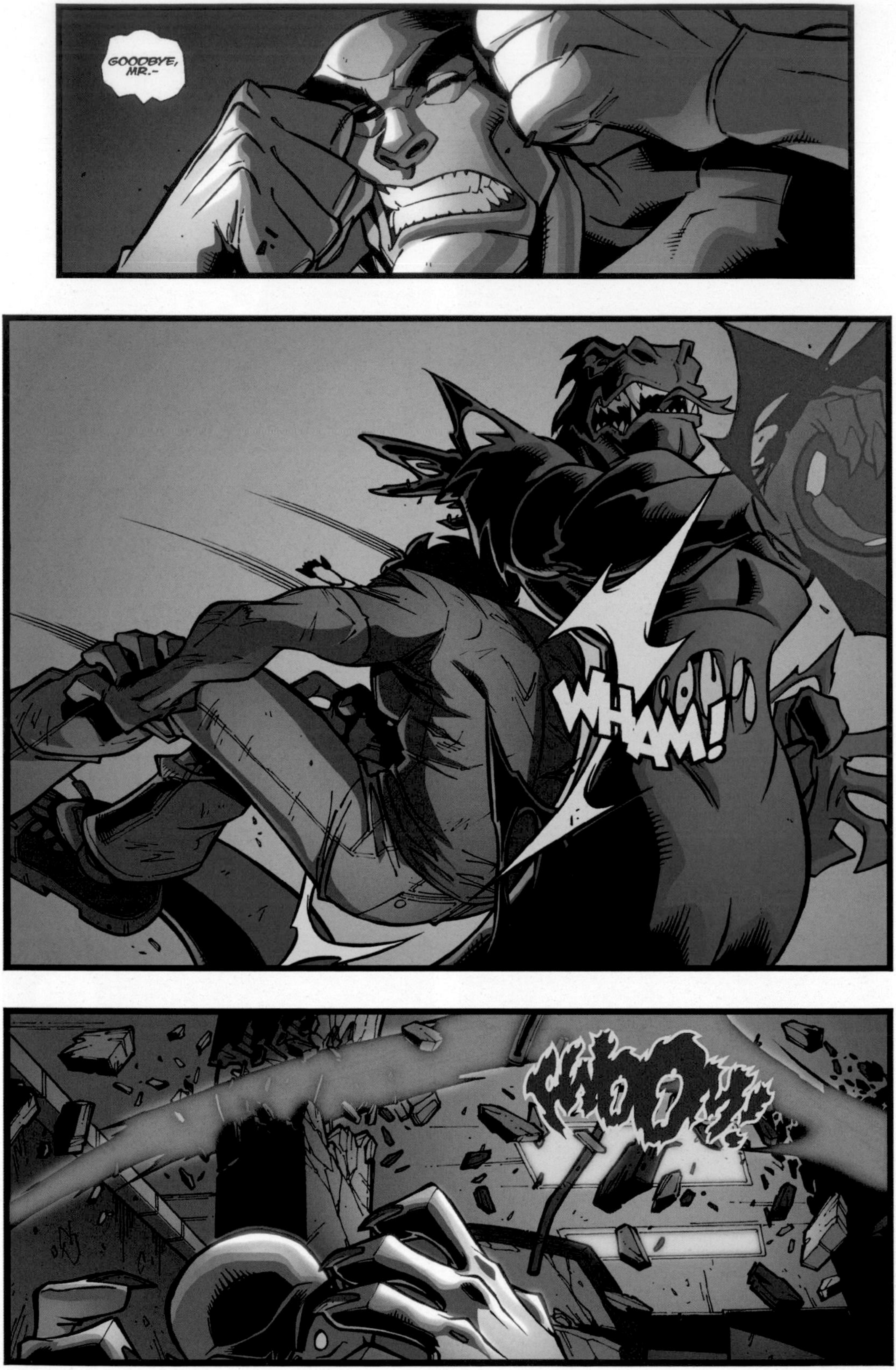
GOODBYE, MR.-
WHAM!

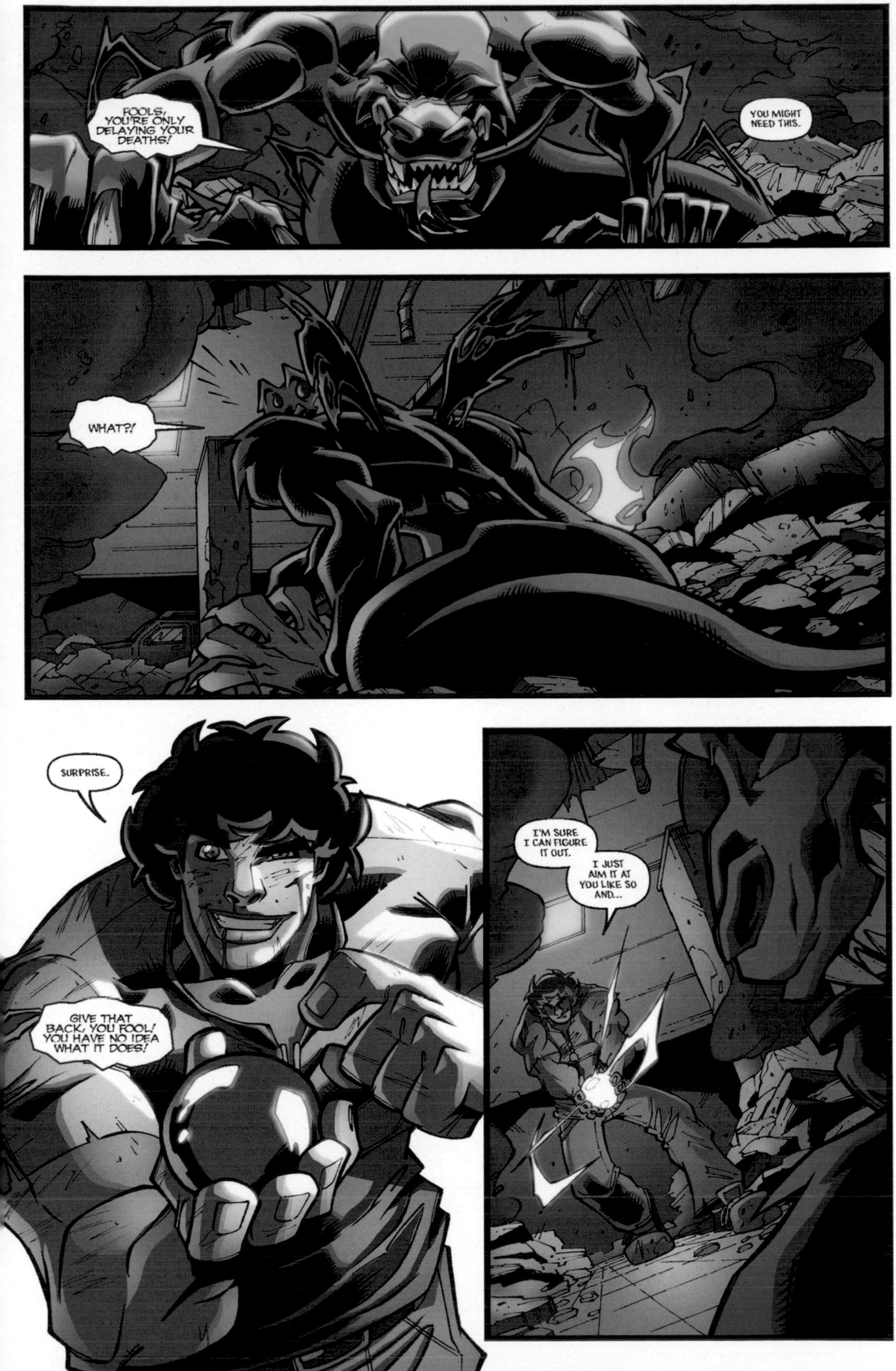
FOOLS, YOU'RE ONLY DELAYING YOUR DEATHS!
YOU MIGHT NEED THIS.
WHAT?!
SURPRISE.
GIVE THAT BACK, YOU FOOL! YOU HAVE NO IDEA WHAT IT DOES!
I'M SURE I CAN FIGURE IT OUT.
I JUST AIM IT AT YOU LIKE SO AND...

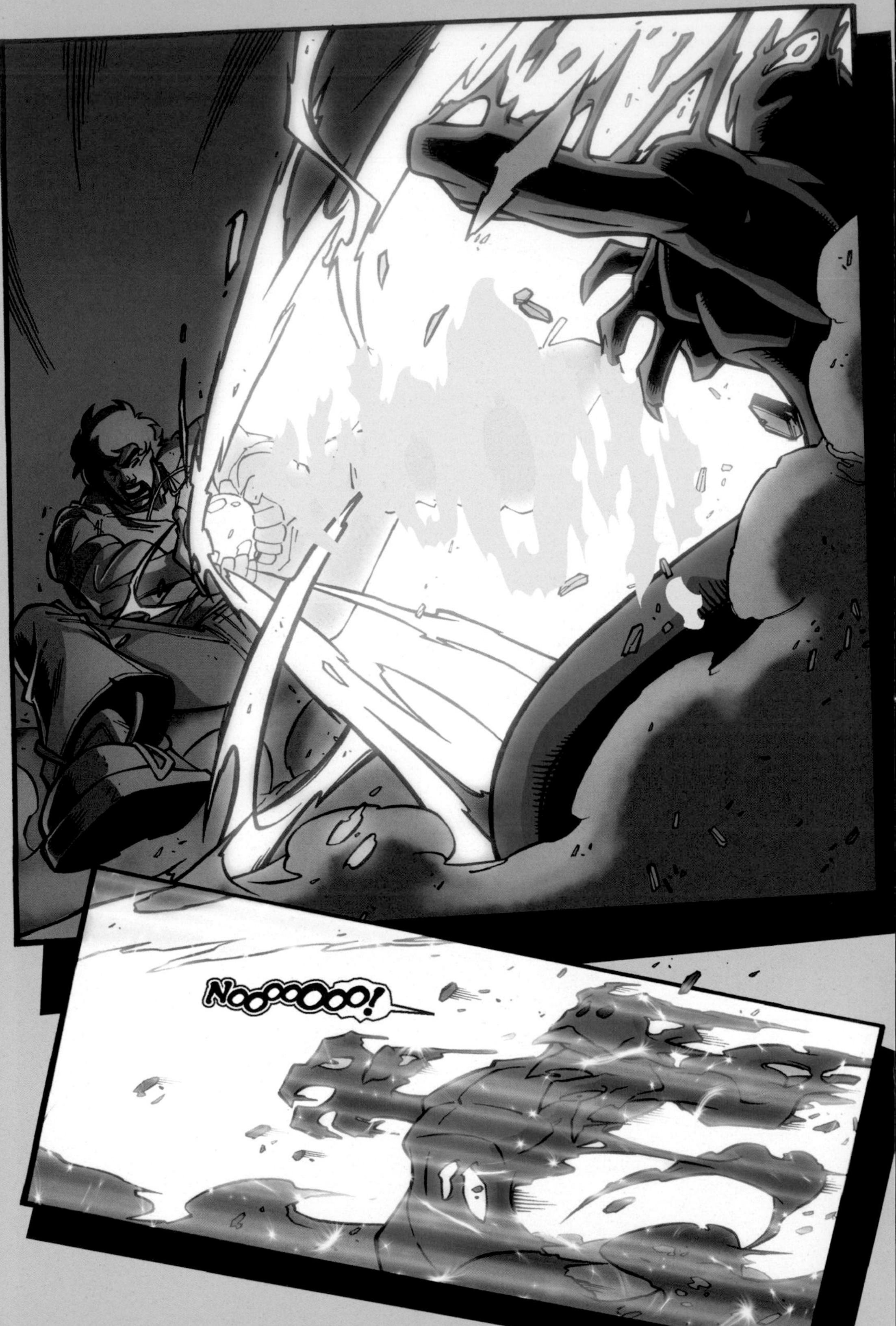
NOOOOOOO!

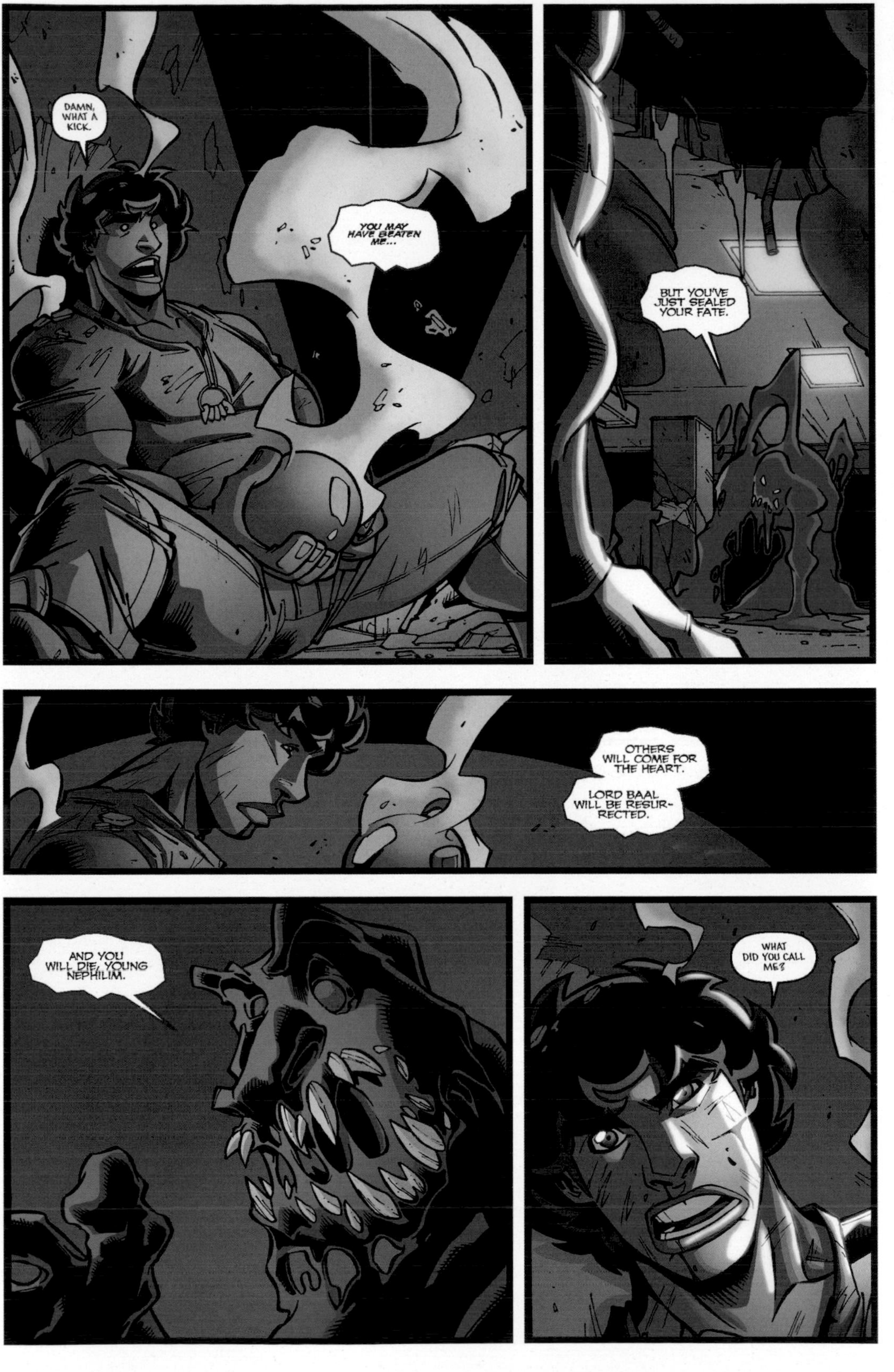

DAMN, WHAT A KICK.
YOU MAY HAVE BEATEN ME...
BUT YOU'VE JUST SEALED YOUR FATE.
OTHERS WILL COME FOR THE HEART.
LORD BAAL WILL BE RESUR-RECTED.
AND YOU WILL DIE, YOUNG NEPHILIM.
WHAT DID YOU CALL ME?

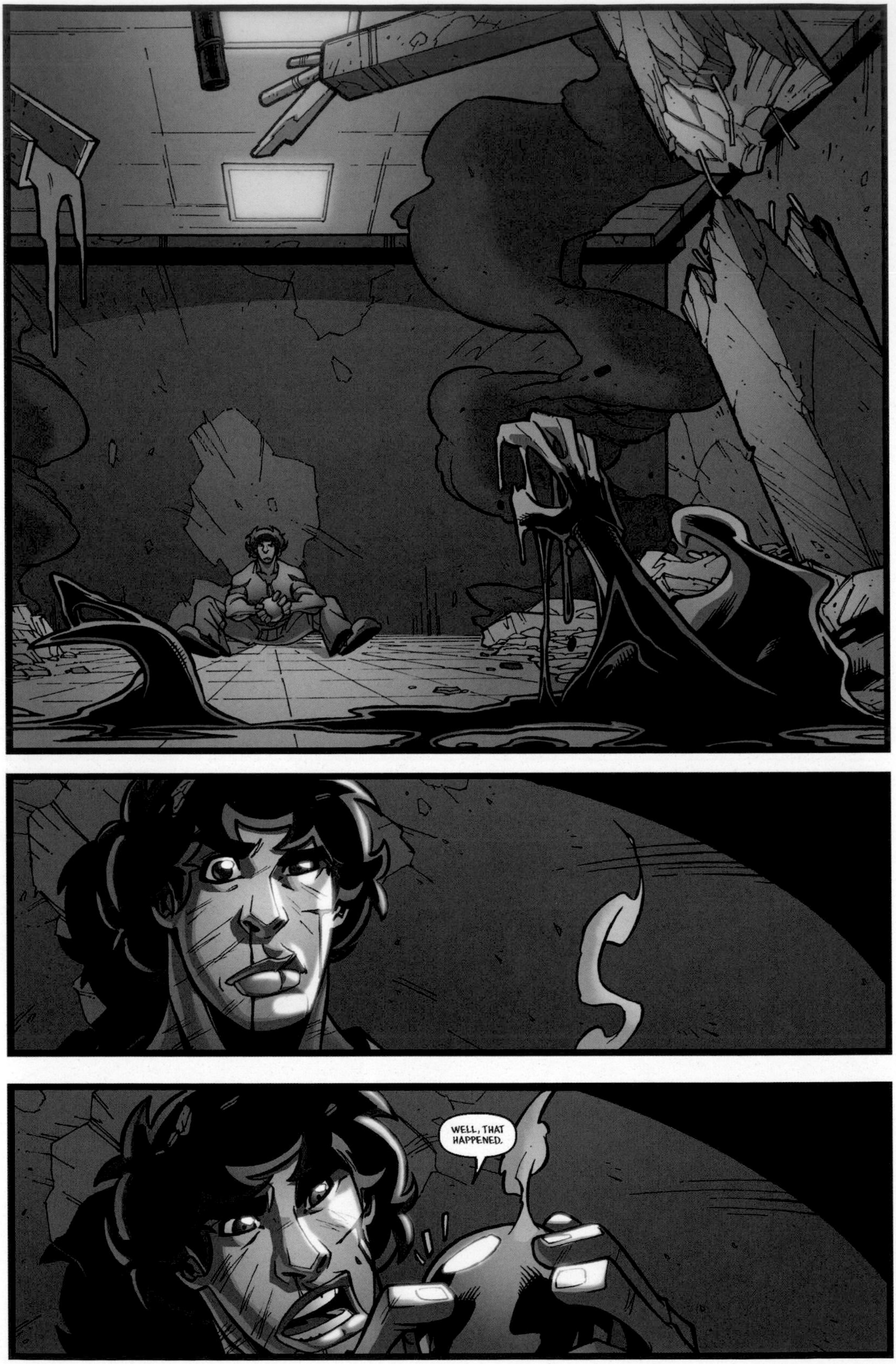
WELL, THAT HAPPENED.

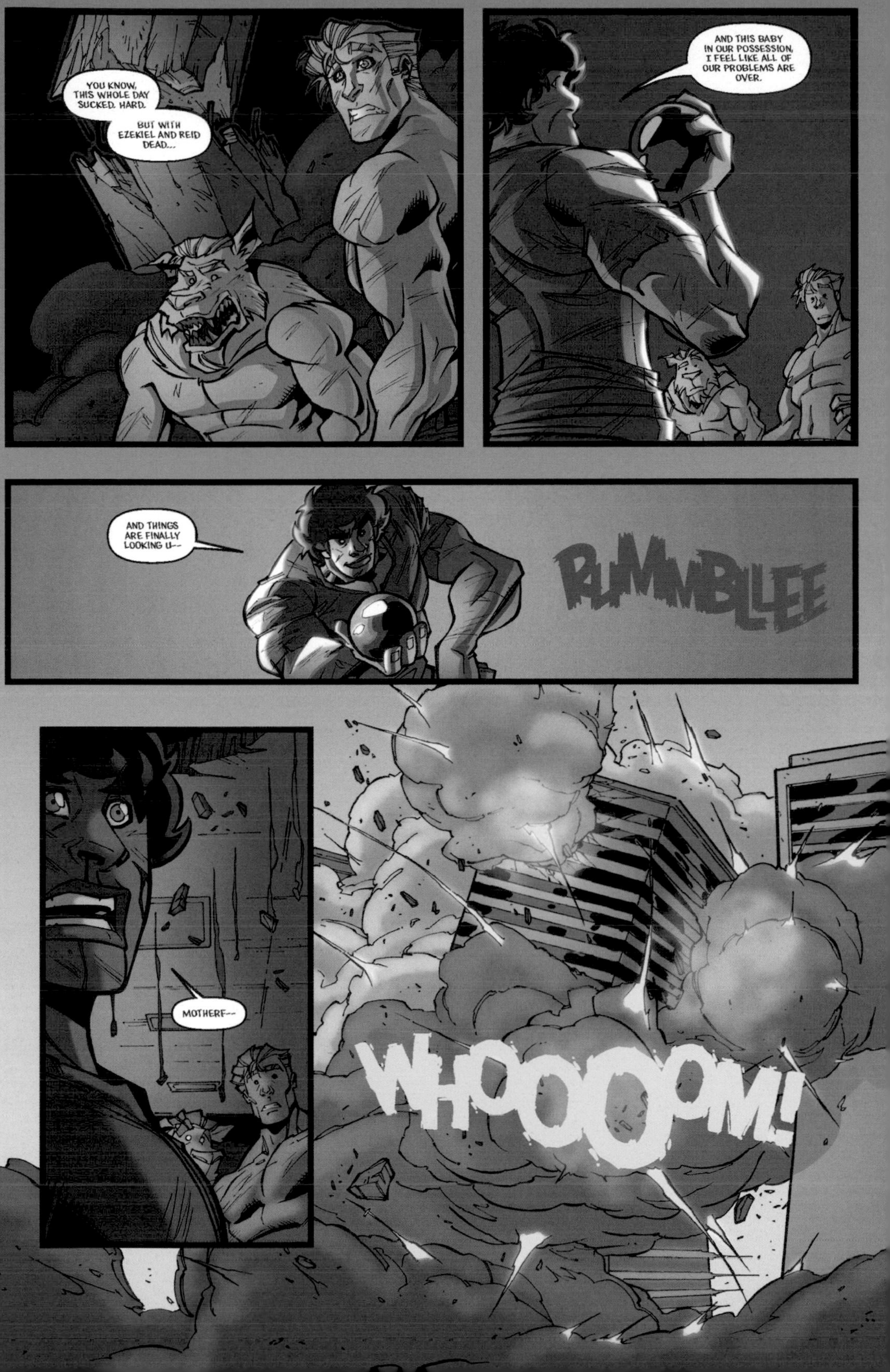
YOU KNOW, THIS WHOLE DAY SUCKED. HARD.
BUT WITH EZEKIEL AND REID DEAD...
AND THIS BABY IN OUR POSSESSION, I FEEL LIKE ALL OF OUR PROBLEMS ARE OVER.
AND THINGS ARE FINALLY LOOKING U--
RUMMBLLEE
MOTHERF--
WHOOOOM!

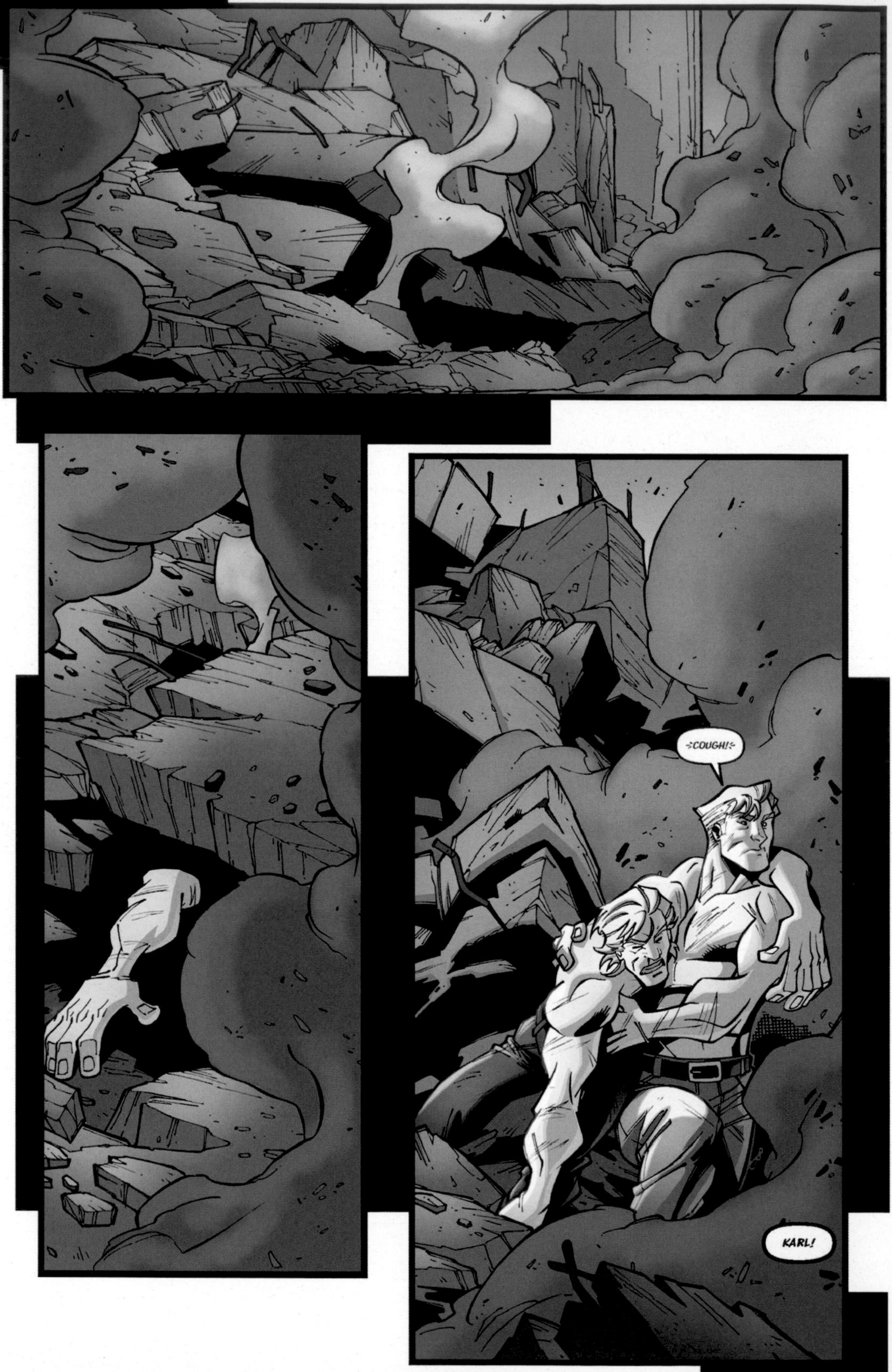
COUGH!
KARL!

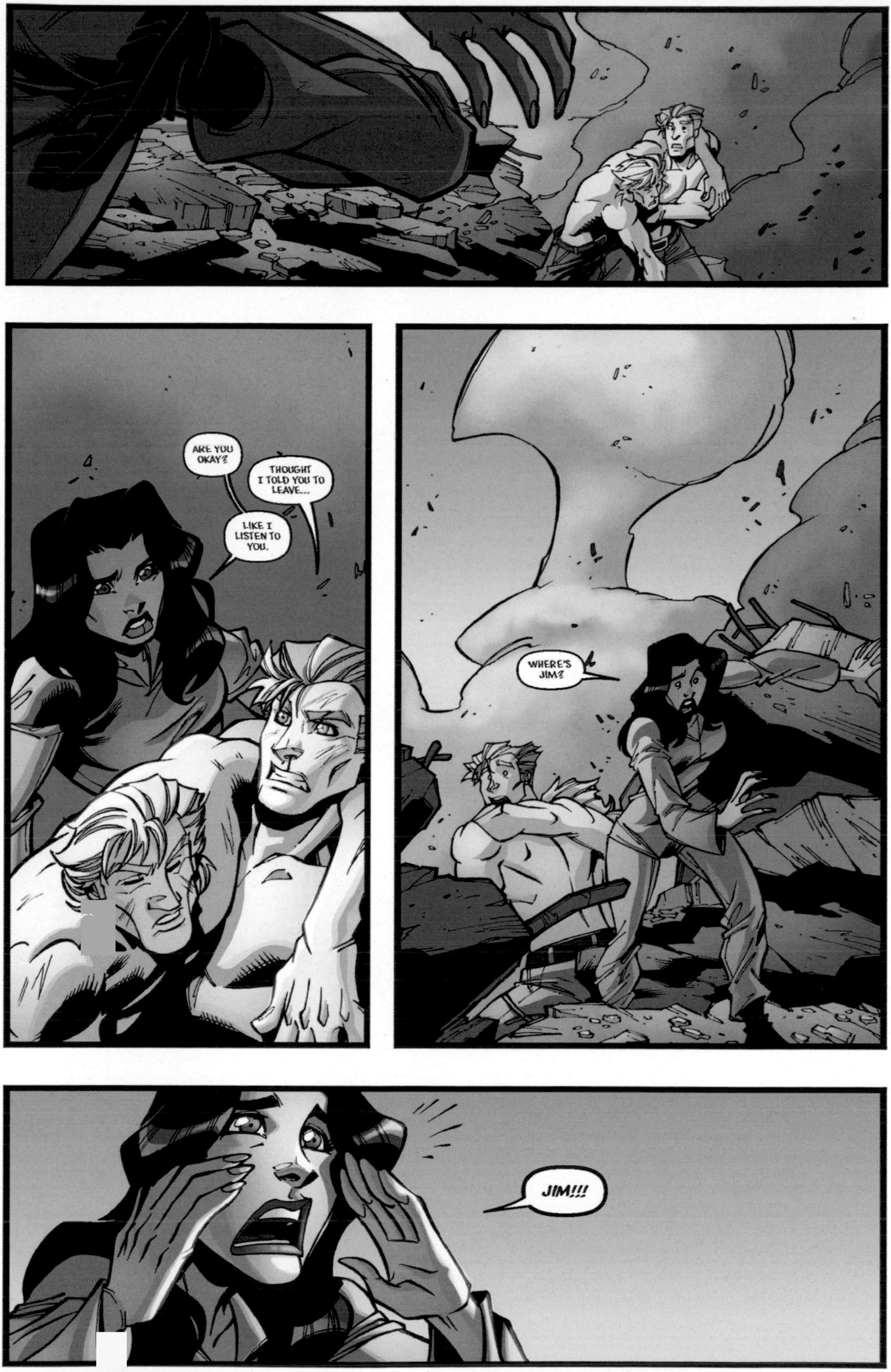
ARE YOU OKAY?
THOUGHT I TOLD YOU TO LEAVE...
LIKE I LISTEN TO YOU.
WHERE'S JIM?
JIM!!!

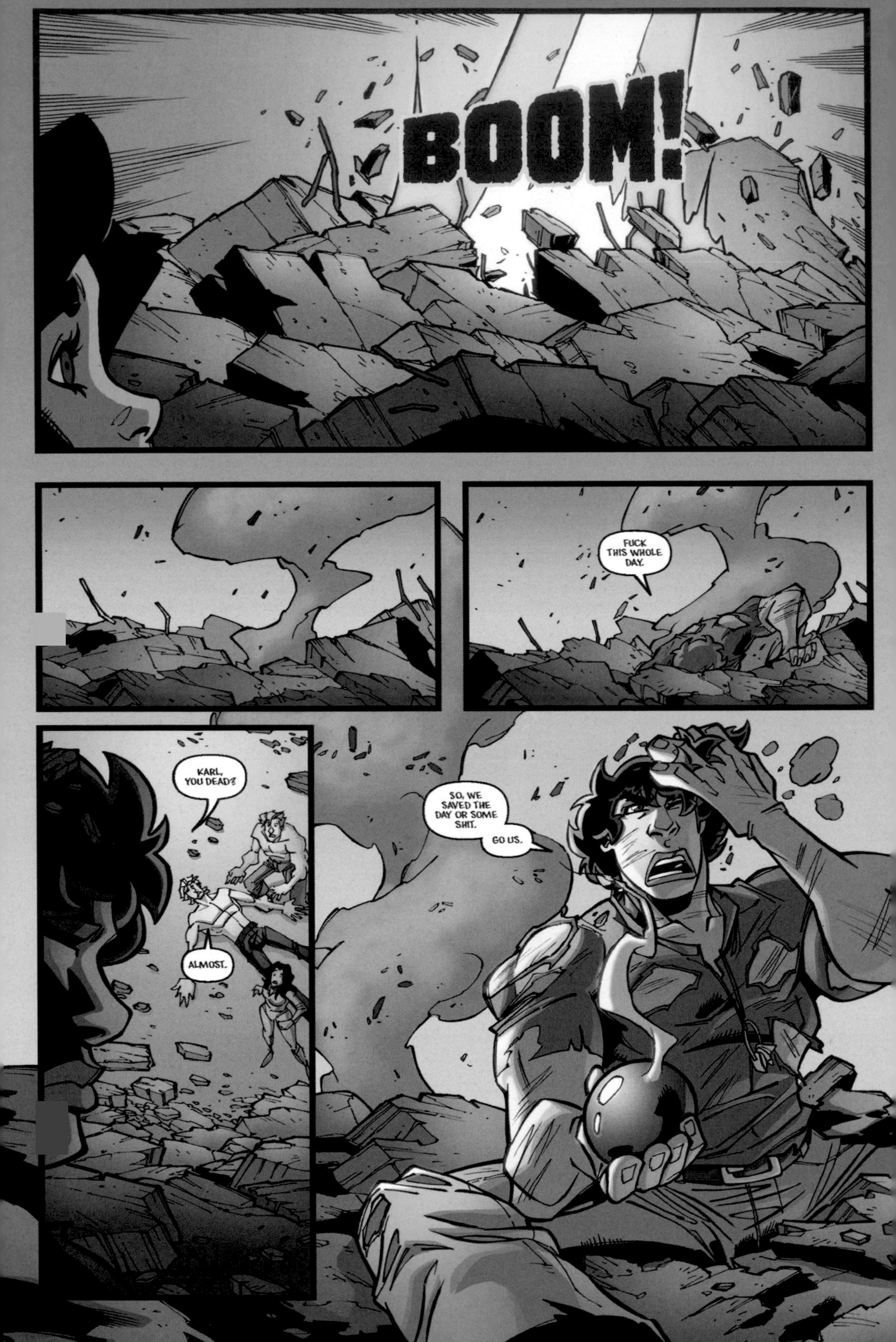
BOOM!
FUCK THIS WHOLE DAY.
KARL, YOU DEAD?
ALMOST.
SO, WE SAVED THE DAY OR SOME SHIT.
GO US.

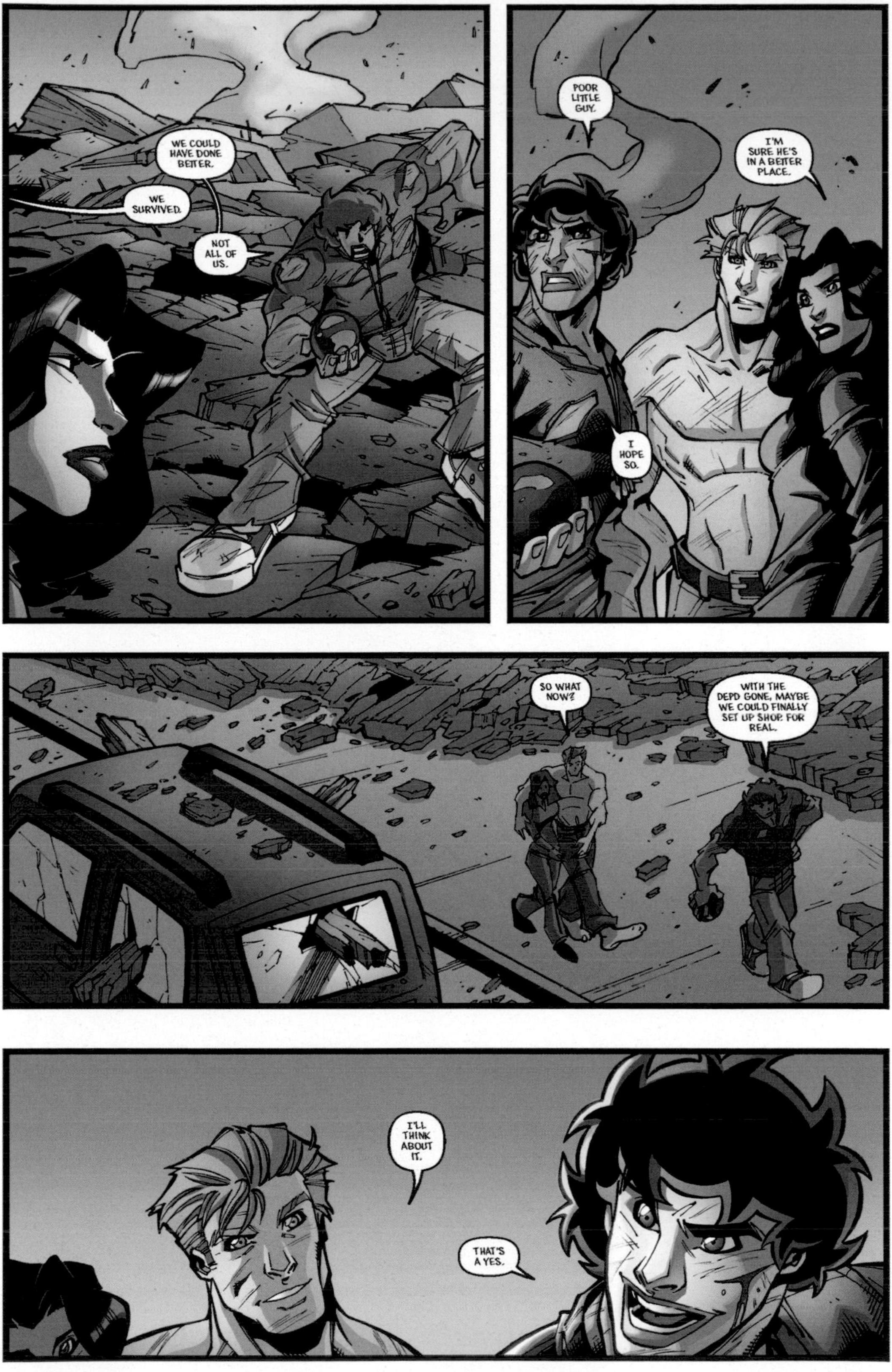
WE COULD HAVE DONE BETTER.
WE SURVIVED.
NOT ALL OF US.
POOR LITTLE GUY.
I'M SURE HE'S IN A BETTER PLACE.
I HOPE SO.
SO WHAT NOW?
WITH THE DEPD GONE, MAYBE WE COULD FINALLY SET UP SHOP FOR REAL.
I'LL THINK ABOUT IT.
THAT'S A YES.

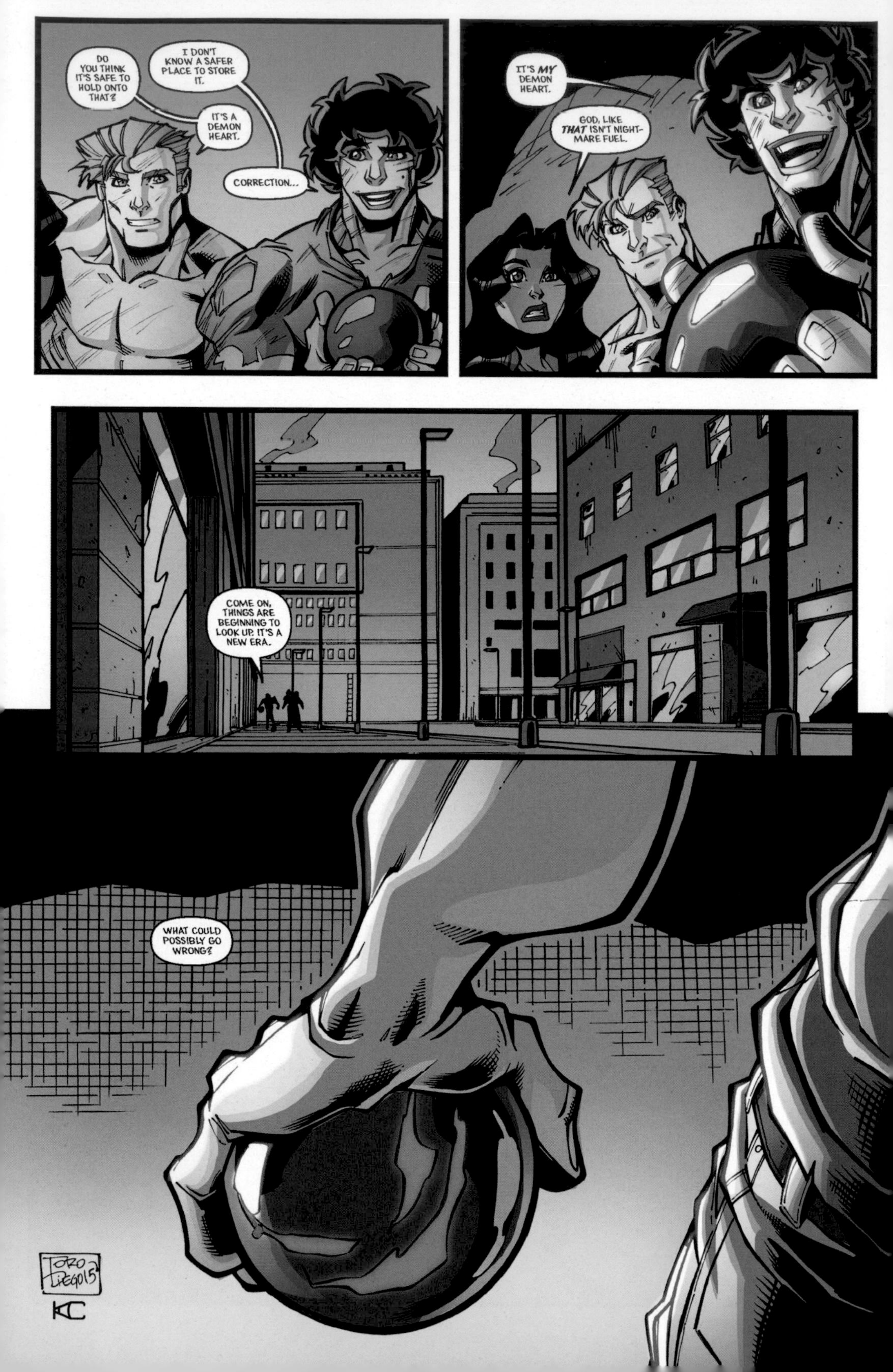
DO YOU THINK IT'S SAFE TO HOLD ONTO THAT?
I DON'T KNOW A SAFER PLACE TO STORE IT.
IT'S A DEMON HEART.
CORRECTION...
IT'S *MY* DEMON HEART.
GOD, LIKE ***THAT*** ISN'T NIGHT-MARE FUEL.
COME ON, THINGS ARE BEGINNING TO LOOK UP. IT'S A NEW ERA.
WHAT COULD POSSIBLY GO WRONG?
TORO DIEGO 15
KC

Pin-Ups
Eduardo Jiminez
Juan Romera
Daniel Franco
Dexter Wee
Character Sketches
Diego Toro

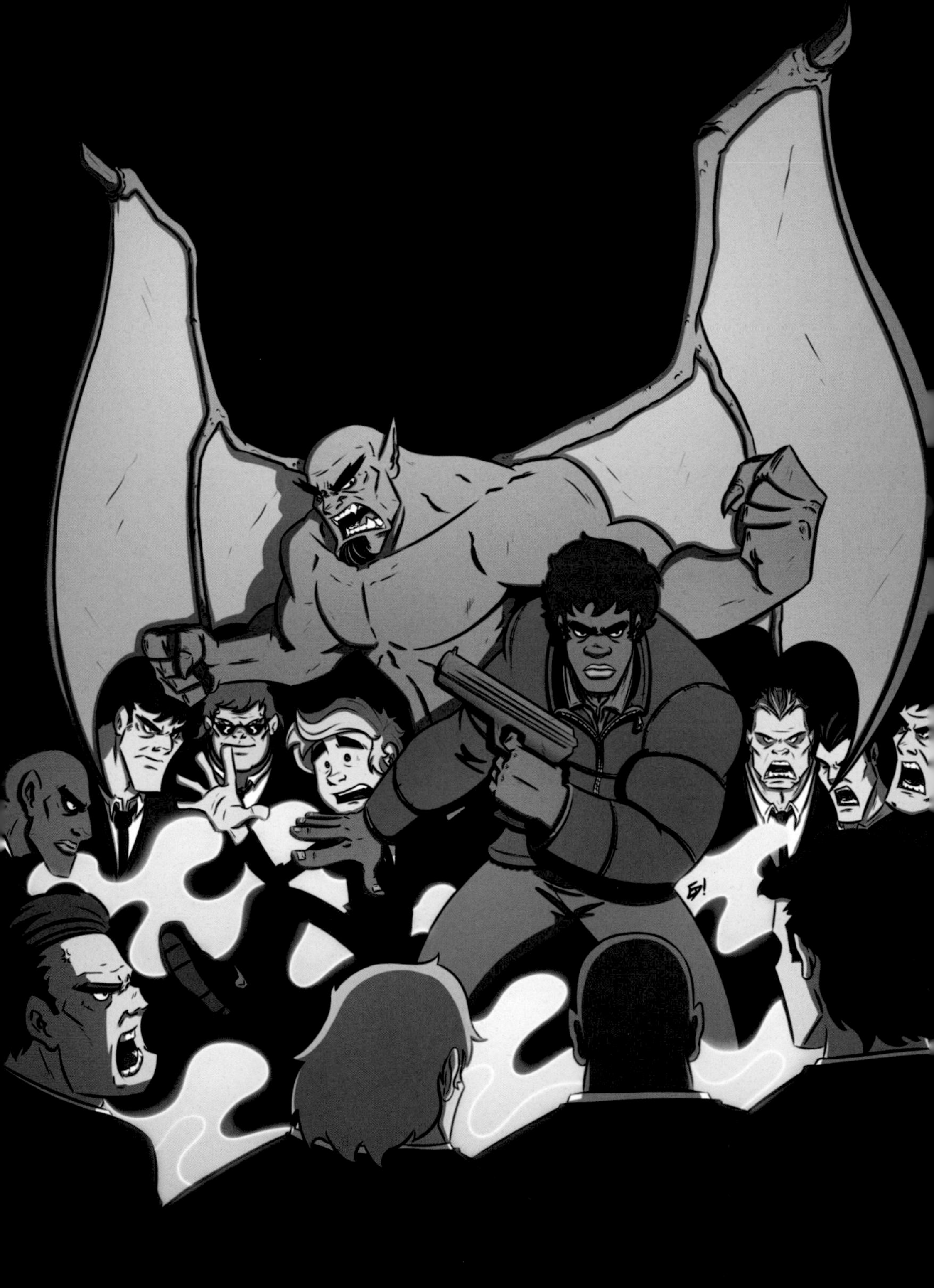

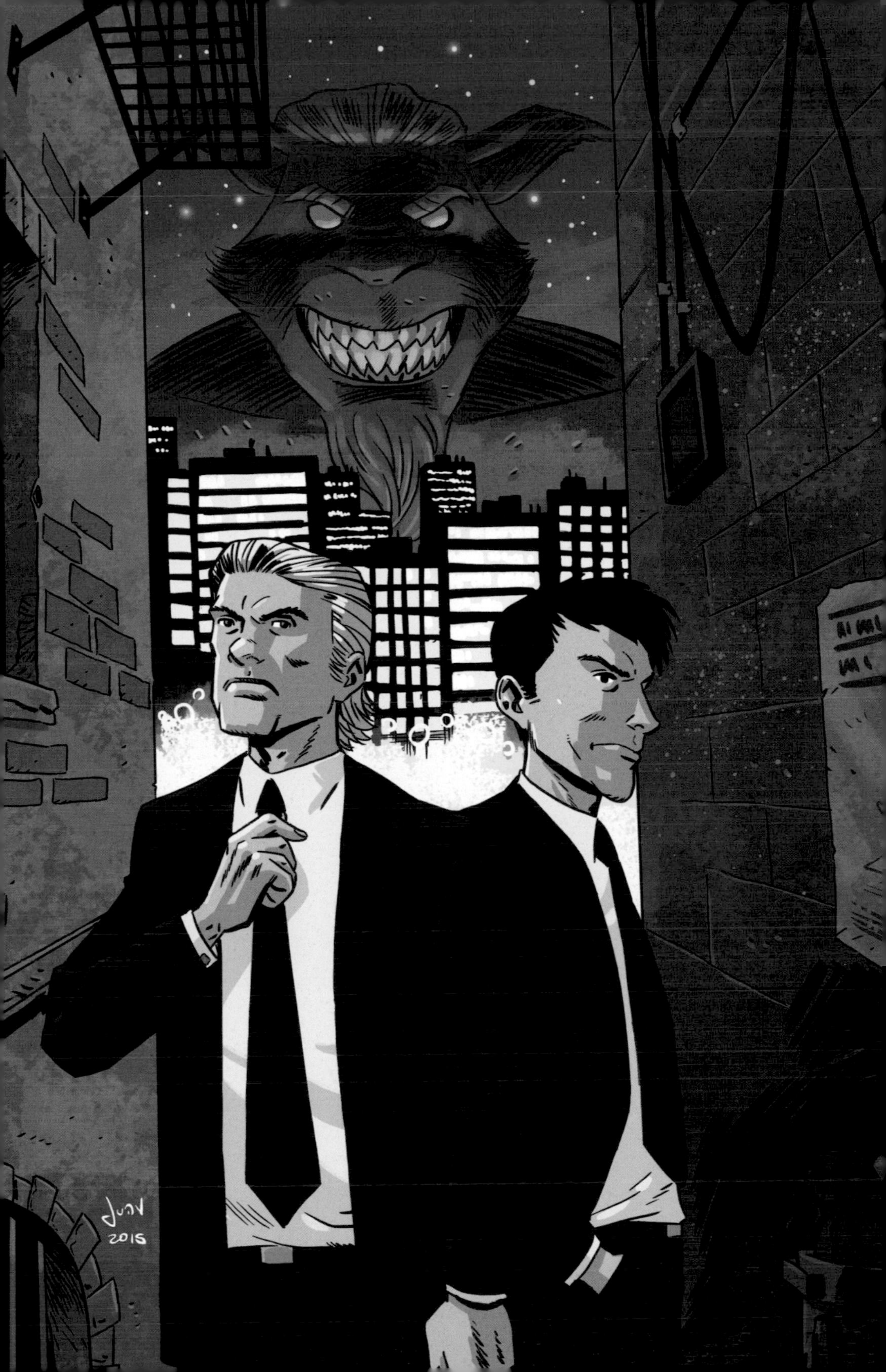
2015

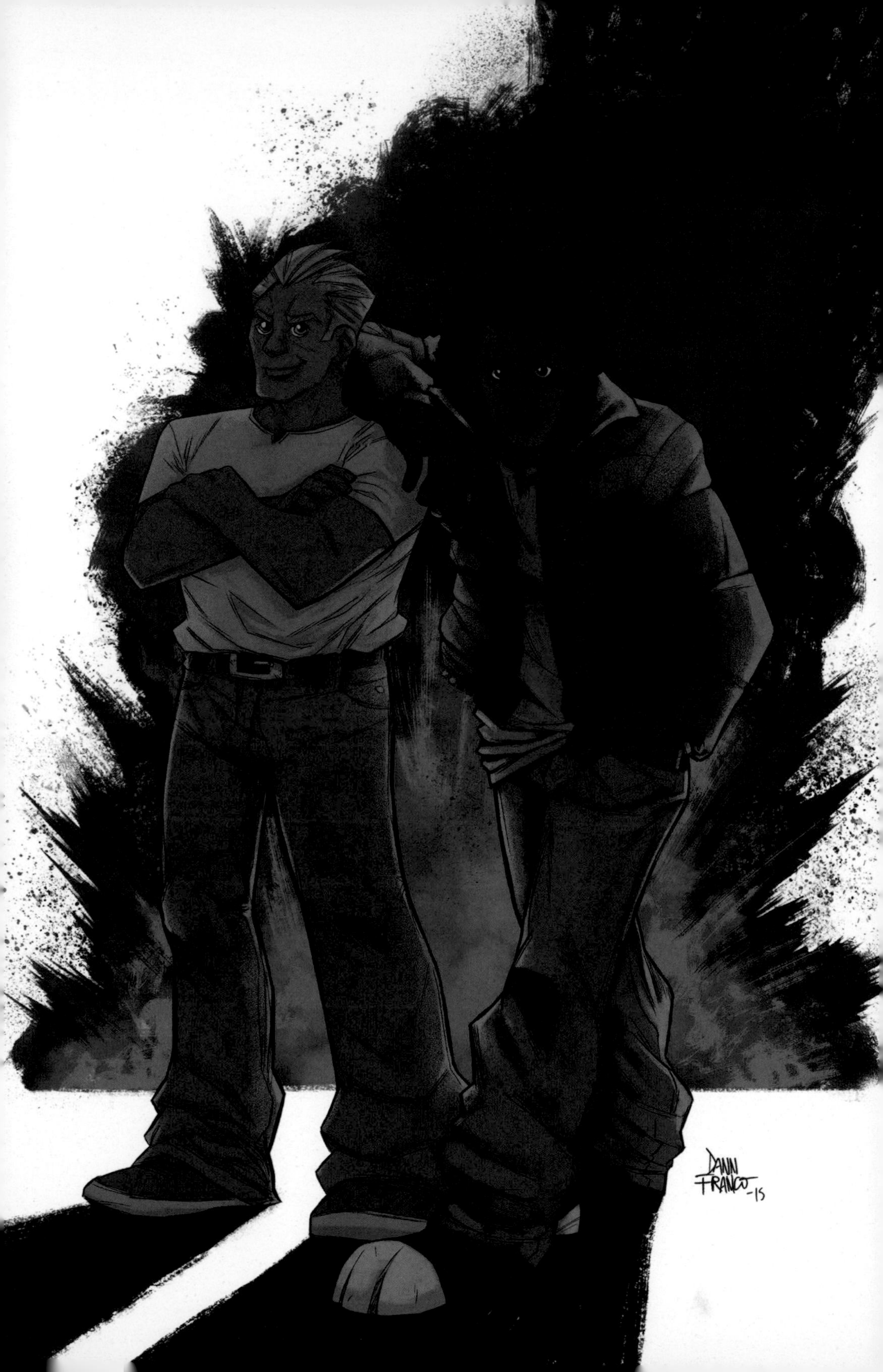
DANN FRANCO -15

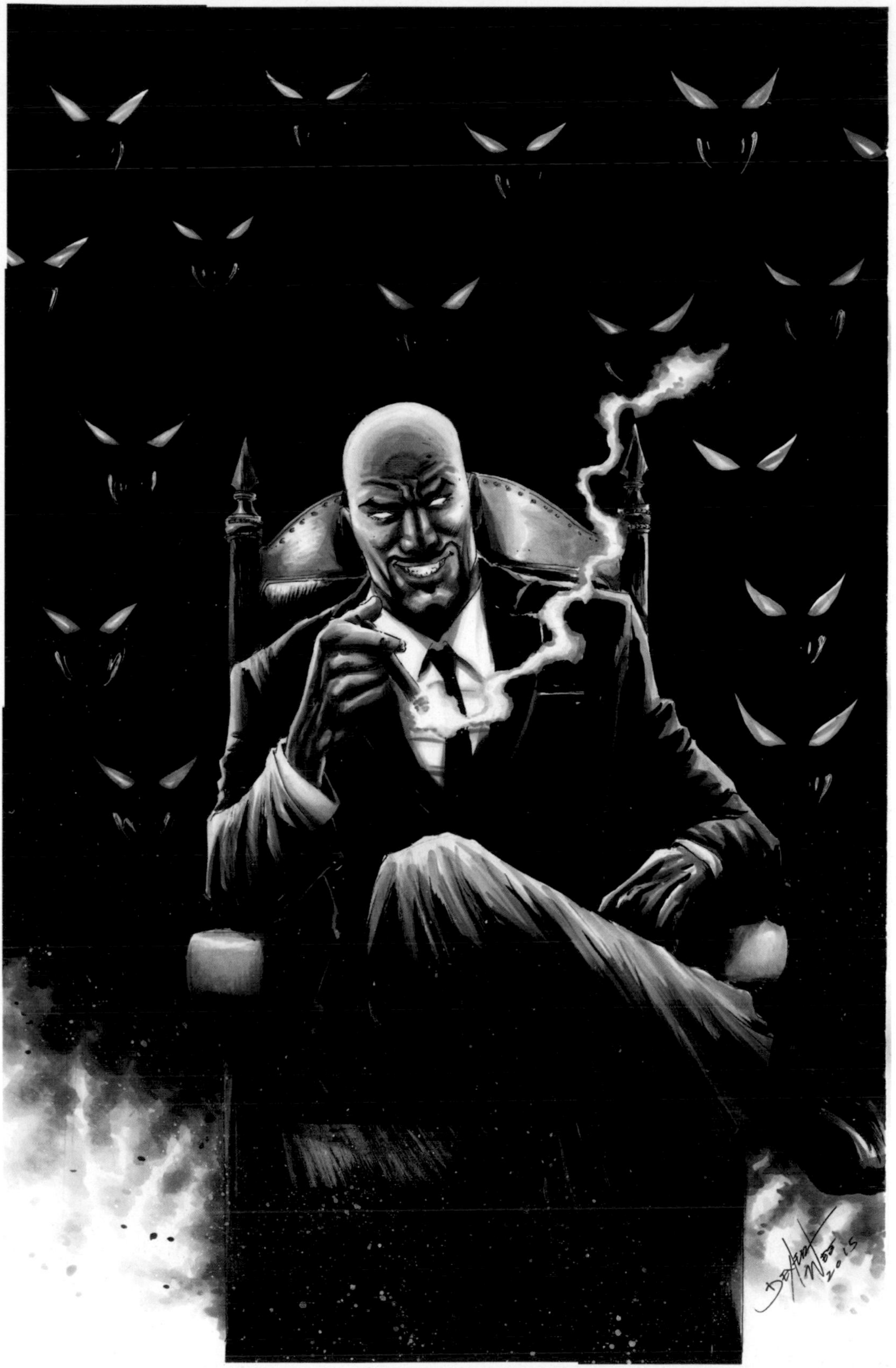

TORO DIEGO NAME: DATE: BOOK: ISSUE: PAGE#:

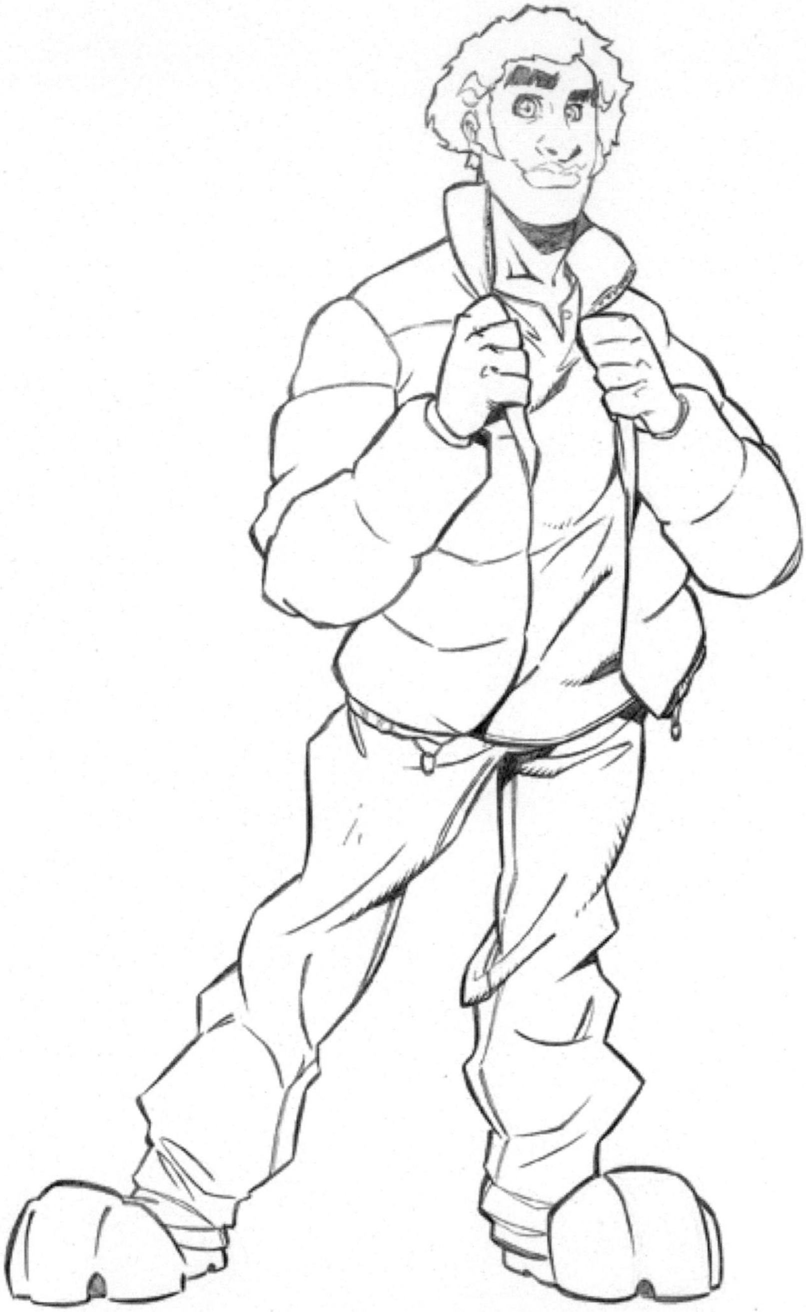

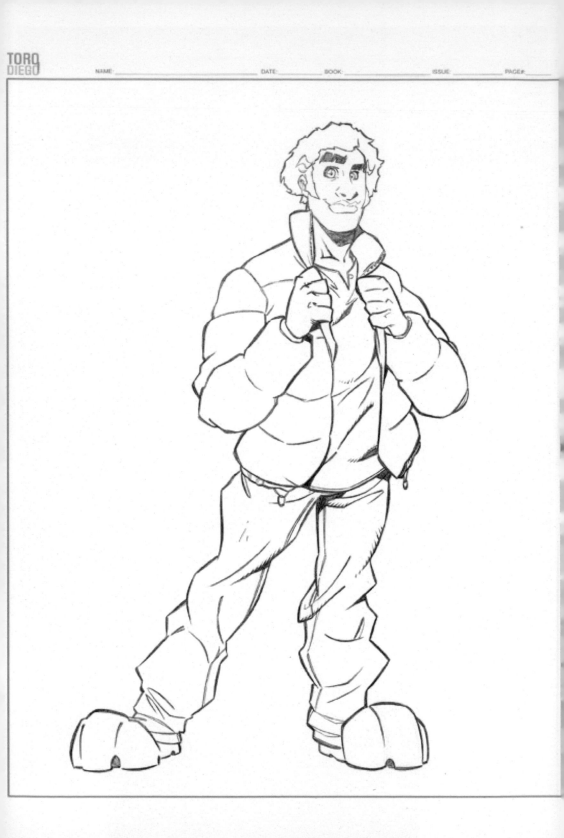

TORO DIEGO NAME: DATE: BOOK: ISSUE: PAGE#:

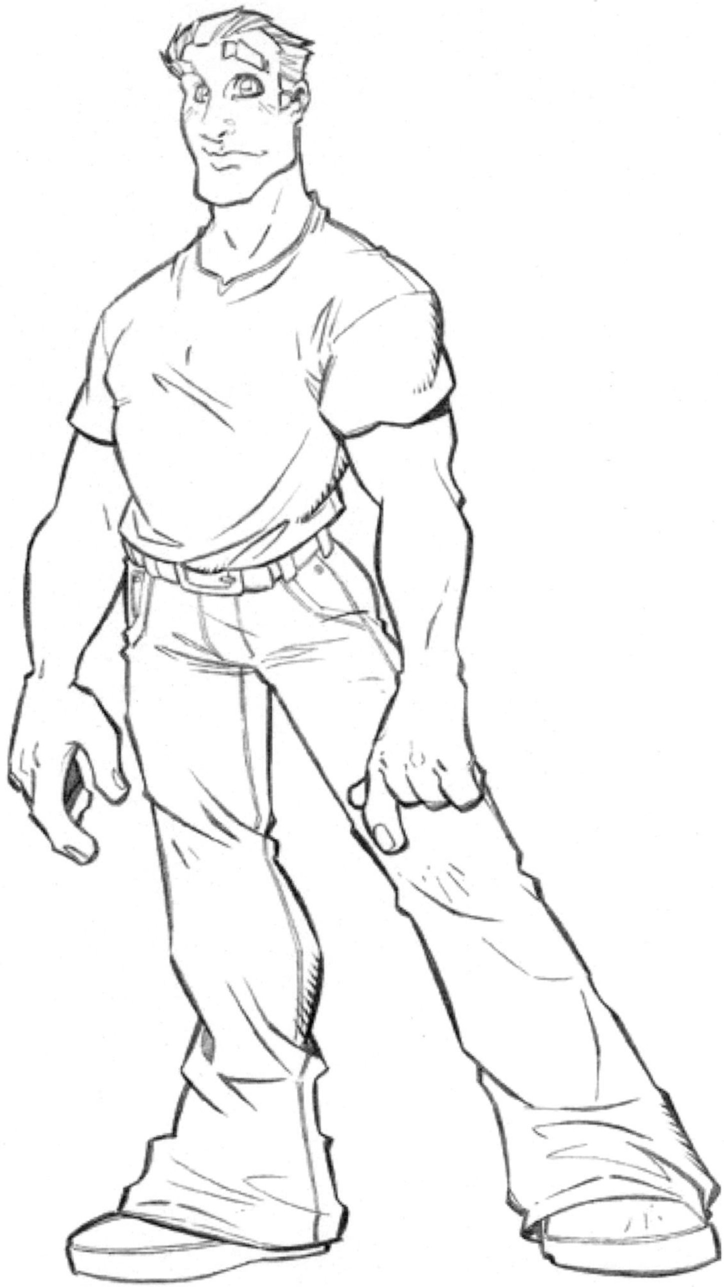

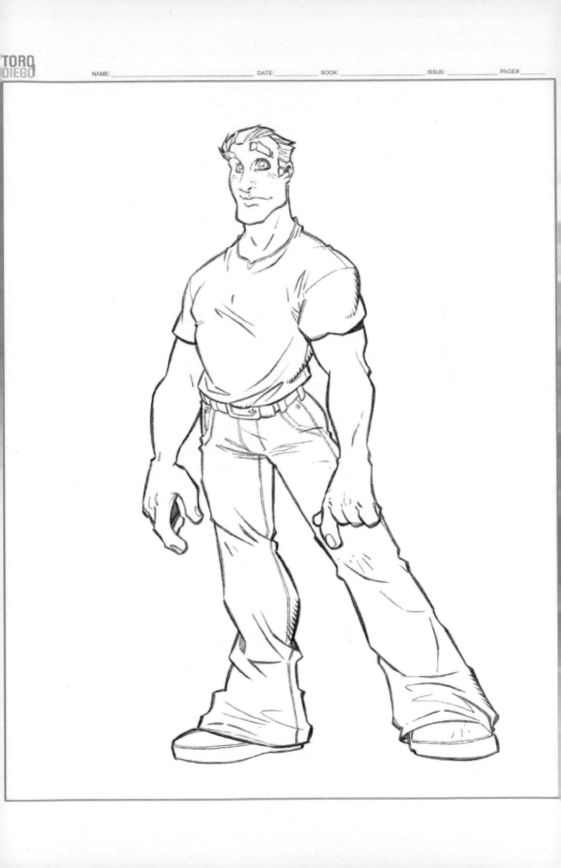

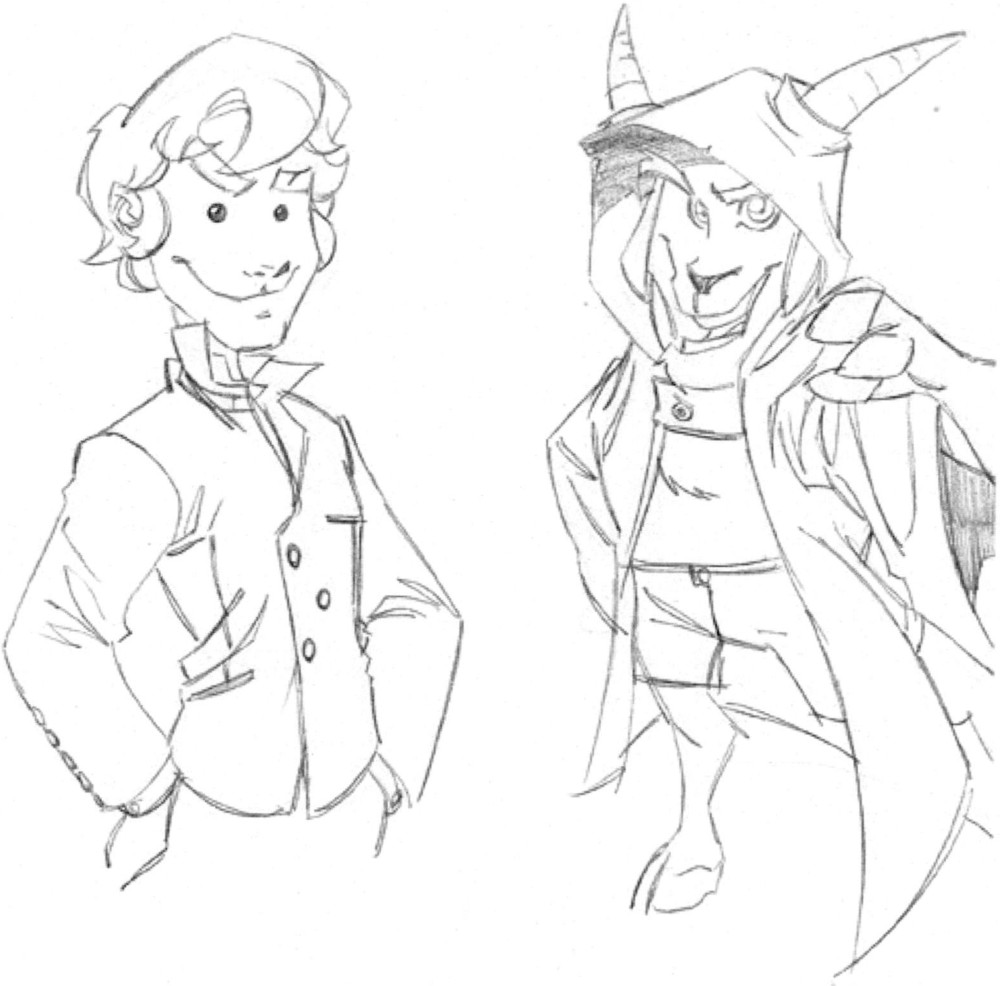

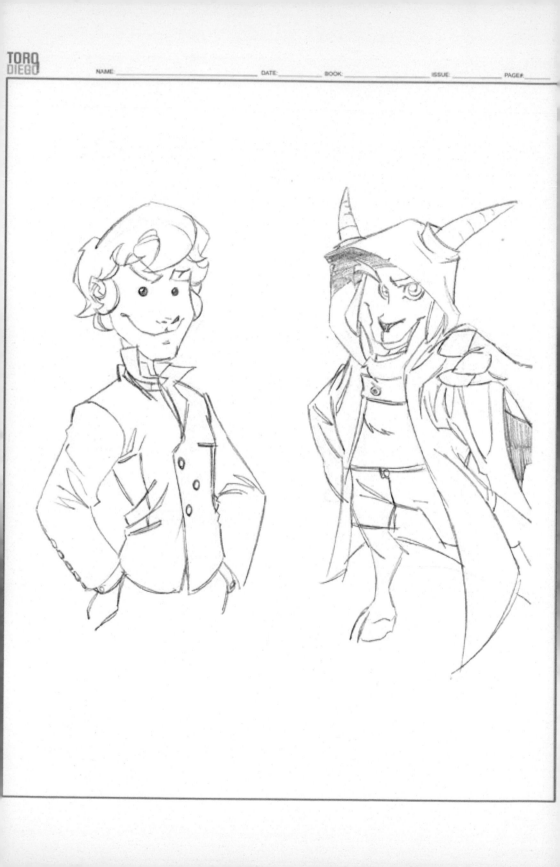

TORO DIEGO NAME: DATE: BOOK: ISSUE: PAGE#:

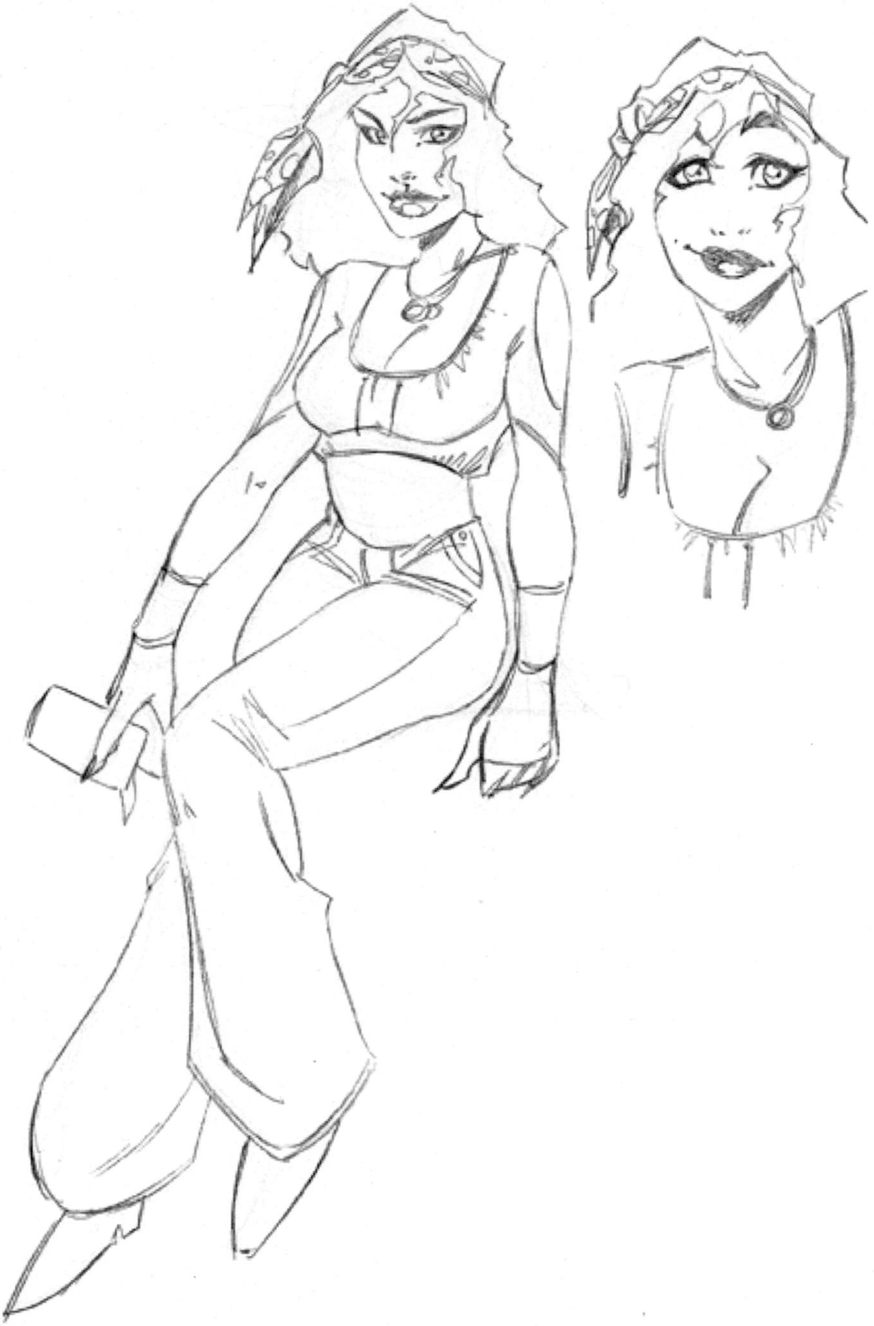

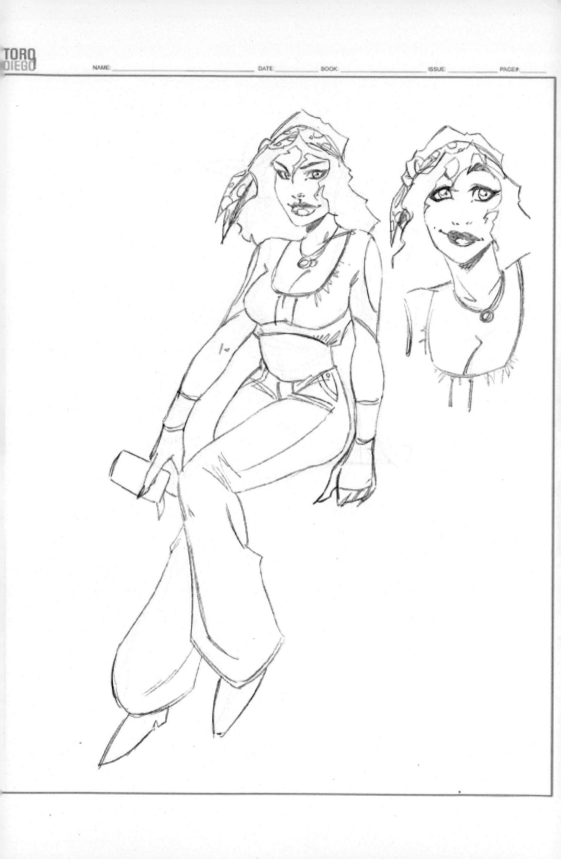

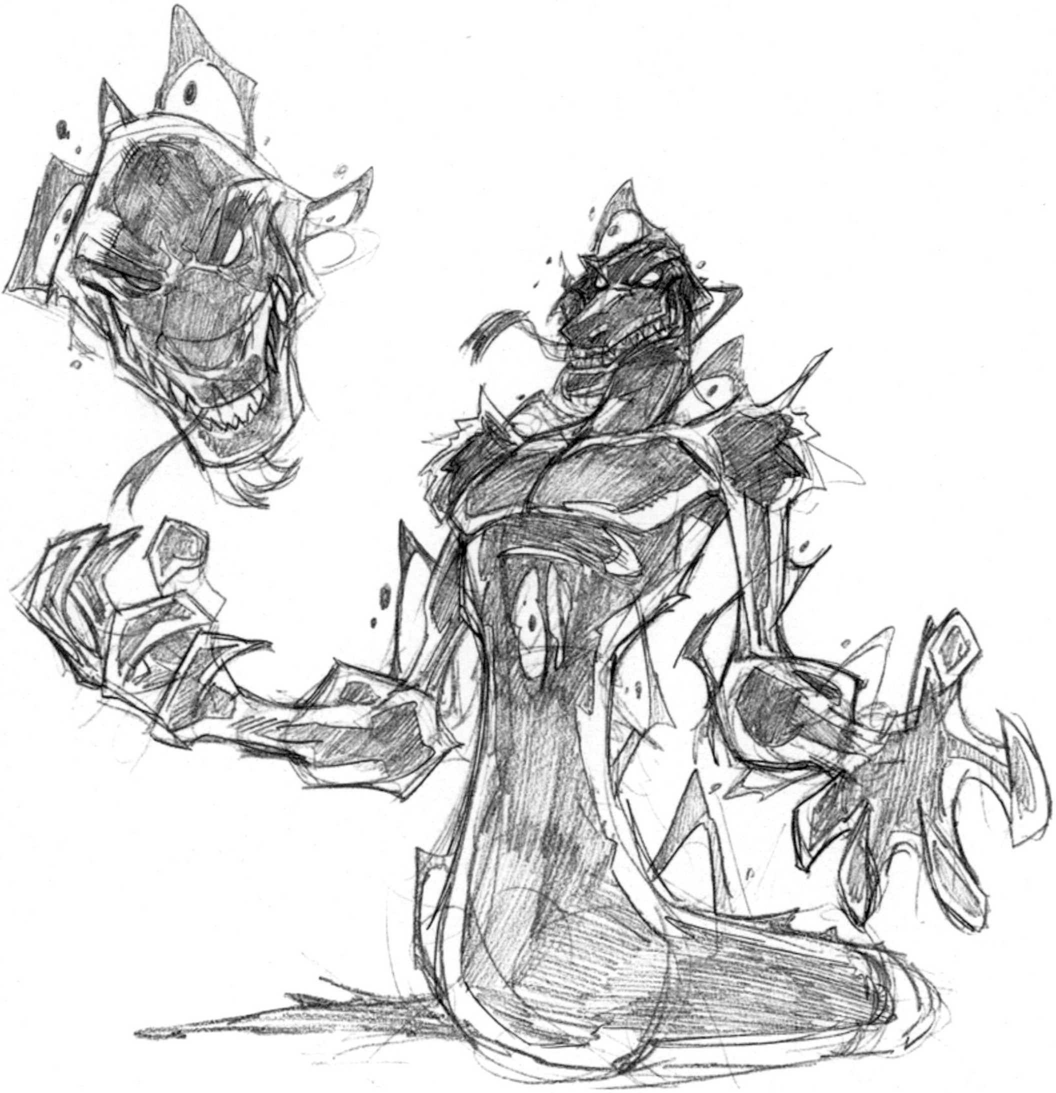

Special Thanks to Everyone Who Backed This Project:

Andy Hartshorn
Mike & Jen Vance
Rob Ryan
Thoms Werner
Thomas Zilling
J. Cebron Cook
Lee
Nate Sexton
Loreto Varela
Dominic Quach
Molly Harmon
Kay Hace
Nathan Seabolt
Chris Stewart
Georgieanna
K. N.
Isaac 'Will It Work' Dansicker
SwordFire
Thomas Skulan
Andrea Speed
www.realityhappens.com
Master Plot Comics
Stratum Comics
Rik Favino
Caleb Plamquist
David Lara
Splendidgeek
Yasmine Pirouz
Tim Cecil
Jon Dickson
Joshua Langhorne
Mark Bertolini
Peter Simeti
Wade Harrison III
Edward Wellman

Thomas Fluty
Ian Yarington
@anthonybachman
Bond, Ryan Bond
Lily Cleveland
Brad Burdick
C. Neil Milton
Dino Buffetta Jr.
Erica Ward
Will Nelson
Aaron Walther
Ryan and Laura Demarest
John MacLeod
Paul y cod asyn Jarman
Nathanael Errol Lynn Quashie
Auntie Crystal
Christine
Steven Hoveke
Edna Random
Abram Deyo
Erin Cataldi
Steve Johnson
James Edward Reed
Shawn Demumbrum
Rayfield Johnson Jr.
Jerome Williams
Penny Phillips
Blakdar
James Roche
Will Rincon
Ambush Vin
David Heidorn
Sean Tonelli

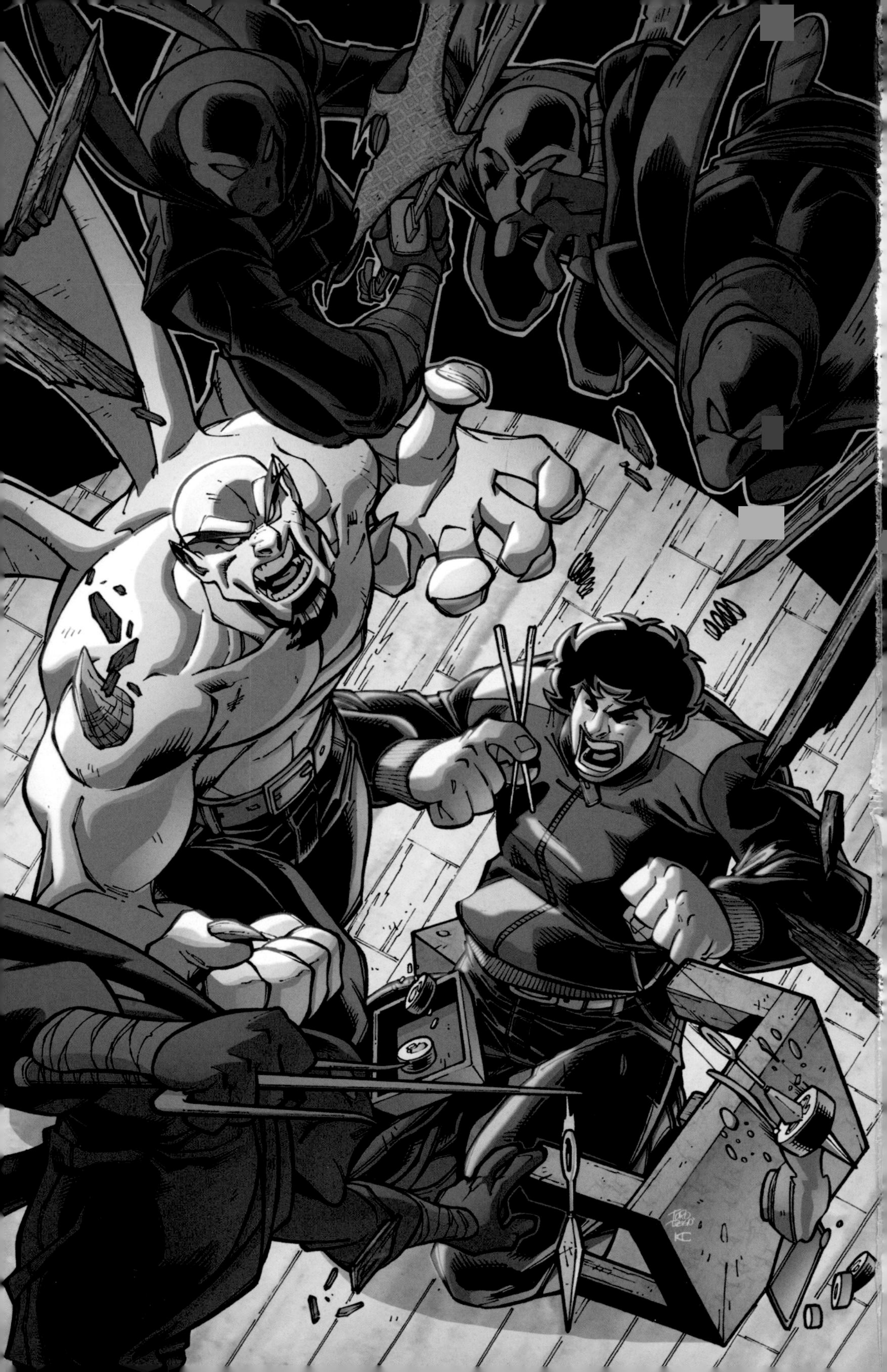